Identity, Capabilities, a
Changing Economics

C000094945

Mainstream economics assumes economic agents act and make decisions to maximize their utility. This model of economic behavior, based on rational choice theory, has come under increasing attack in economics because it does not accurately reflect the way people behave and reason. The shift toward a more realistic account of economic agents has been mostly associated with the rise of behavioral economics, which views individuals through the lens of bounded rationality. *Identity, Capabilities, and Changing Economics* goes further and uses identity analysis to build on this critique of the utility conception of individuals, arguing it should be replaced by a conception of economic agents in an uncertain world as socially embedded and identified with their capabilities. Written by one of the world's leading philosophers of economics, this book develops a new approach to economics' theory of the individual, explaining individuals as adaptive and reflexive rather than utility maximizing.

JOHN B. DAVIS is Professor Emeritus of Economics at both Marquette University and University of Amsterdam. He is the author of *Keynes's Philosophical Development* (1994), *The Theory of the Individual in Economics* (2003), and *Individuals and Identity in Economics* (Cambridge University Press, 2010) and a former co-editor of the *Journal of Economic Methodology* and former editor of the *Review of Social Economy*.

Identity, Capabilities, and Changing Economics

Reflexive, Adaptive, Socially Embedded Individuals

JOHN B. DAVIS

Marquette University and University of Amsterdam

CAMBRIDGE
UNIVERSITY PRESS

CAMBRIDGE
UNIVERSITY PRESS

Shaftesbury Road, Cambridge CB2 8EA, United Kingdom

One Liberty Plaza, 20th Floor, New York, NY 10006, USA

477 Williamstown Road, Port Melbourne, VIC 3207, Australia

314–321, 3rd Floor, Plot 3, Splendor Forum, Jasola District Centre,
New Delhi – 110025, India

103 Penang Road, #05–06/07, Visioncrest Commercial, Singapore 238467

Cambridge University Press is part of Cambridge University Press & Assessment,
a department of the University of Cambridge.

We share the University's mission to contribute to society through the pursuit of
education, learning and research at the highest international levels of excellence.

www.cambridge.org
Information on this title: www.cambridge.org/9781009438230

DOI: 10.1017/9781009438247

© John B. Davis 2024

First published 2024

A catalogue record for this publication is available from the British Library

Library of Congress Cataloging-in-Publication Data
Names: Davis, John B., author.
Title: Identity, capabilities, and changing economics : reflexive, adaptive,
socially embedded individuals / John B. Davis, Marquette University,
Wisconsin and University of Amsterdam.
Description: Cambridge, United Kingdom ; New York, NY : Cambridge
University Press, 2024. | Includes bibliographical references and index.
Identifiers: LCCN 2023051145 | ISBN 9781009438230 (hardback) |
ISBN 9781009438247 (ebook)
Subjects: LCSH: Economics – Sociological aspects. |
Group identity – Economic aspects. | Equality – Economic aspects.
Classification: LCC HM548 .D376 2024 | DDC 305–dc23/eng/20231102
LC record available at https://lccn.loc.gov/2023051145

ISBN 978-1-009-43823-0 Hardback
ISBN 978-1-009-43825-4 Paperback

For Zohreh

Contents

List of Tables		*page* viii
List of Boxes		ix
Preface		xi
Acknowledgments		xiii
Part I The Failed Pathway and Exit Strategies		**1**
1	Objectivity in Economics and the Problem of the Individual	3
2	The Untenability of the Unembedded *Homo economicus*	27
3	From the "Reconciliation Problem" to an Individuality Reconstruction Problem	53
Part II Building a Socially Embedded Individual Conception		**79**
4	Adaptive Reflexive Individuals: A Capability Conception of the Person	83
5	A General Theory of Social Economic Stratification: Stigmatization, Exclusion, and Capability Shortfalls	109
6	Roads Not Taken Yet to Be Taken: Enhanced Capabilities	135
Part III Value and Subjectivity		**161**
7	Economics as a Normative Discipline: Value Disentanglement in an "Objective" Economics	165
8	Individual Realization? Rethinking Subjectivity in Economics	192
9	Change in and Changing Economics	219
References		246
Index		279

Tables

1.1 Characteristics of open and closed science   *page* 15
1.2 Open and closed science practices   15
4.1 Limitations of small world and large world strategies   99
4.2 Counterfactual thinking and capability adjustment   104
5.1 Two types of social identity   116
5.2 Standard taxonomy of goods   126
7.1 Disciplinary relationships and economics and ethics   188
7.2 Two possible conceptions of an ethics in economics   190

Boxes

2.1 A fallacious inference   *page* 35
2.2 Coase's inference   37
2.3 Sen's inference   42
4.1 A continuous reflexive feedback loop pattern of
    behavioral adjustment   94
4.2 An ability/stock$_x$ – action/flow$_{xy}$ – ability/stock$_y$ pattern
    of reflexive adjustment   95
4.3 A capability–action–capability pattern of reflexive
    adjustment   97
5.1 A "microeconomics" of selective stigmatization   120
5.2 Simon's complex systems model   130
7.1 The mainstream normative economic framework   173
7.2 The capability approach normative economic framework   179
9.1 Change in economics   222
9.2 External forces influencing change in economics   224
9.3 Emancipative values in the shift from survival to
    self-expression values   240

Preface

The dominant economic paradigm is facing a crisis of legitimacy. There are numerous dimensions to this fall from grace – rising inequality and economic insecurity; raw memories of the global financial crisis and the impunity enjoyed by those who provoked it; and a pattern of globalization perceived to privilege large corporations and the financial elite. Looming over it all is the specter of climate change. These fault lines are undermining trust in institutions, both national and global, and sometimes even provoking a backlash in the form of insularity and a tilt toward extremism. [...] This shift in turn requires a serious rethink about the ethical foundations of modern economics.

Annet (2018)

This book looks backward in order to look forward, or rather it sees economics' recent past from the point of view of its possible future. Edward Bellamy did this in his highly successful *Looking Backward: 2000–1887* (Bellamy, 1889; Davis, 1988), a book that soon after publication sold over 400,000 copies, a vast number only exceeded at the time in copies sold by Harriet Beecher Stowe's searing condemnation of slavery in *Uncle Tom's Cabin* (Stowe, 1852). Bellamy in 1887 imagined life in future Boston in 2000 and saw that future as a product of its past and one explaining it. The past, he believed, could only be understood in terms of its possible future, and its meaning in itself was empty which by itself only asked one to search even further backward for its dim antecedents. In the years I taught History of Recent Economics at University of Amsterdam, I began by arguing that the present is a history that is open-ended with its future lying ahead depending on choices made today and that we needed to read the present and the past as history in the same way. The mistake often made in much reading of the past is to see it as it appears at its time, done and closed to the future as if people never thought about where things were going. Studying the history of the economics of the present with an undetermined future thus serves as a corrective to much backward-looking thinking in the economics today. It gives us a lens through which we can examine today's economics. The issue is not where have we come from but where are we going.

This book about the nature and identity of the individual in economics builds upon my two previous books on the individual in economics (Davis, 2003b, 2011) but goes well beyond them in advancing a specific conception of individuals as adaptive – a reflexive capability conception – alternative to the standard *Homo economicus* utility maximization atomistic individual conception. By reflexive, as I have argued previously, I mean an essential part of what individuals are is that they operate with working self-concepts and a continually developing sense of themselves. A subject only of interest to a relatively small number of scholars? That depends on whether you see people today as simply instrumental calculators without self-awareness or as concerned with who they are.

Mainstream economics' individual conception is highly idealized and reflects the nature of human individuality in at best a limited way that serves the goal of explaining the social world as a market process. But what it means to be and survive as an individual in an our increasingly complex social world matters to people. It thus seems incumbent upon economics, with its tremendous influence in the world, to do more to explain individual life than it has and seeks to do.

I worry that economics is not only not up to the job of dealing with the future but seems oriented in a backward-looking way on ignoring what the future may bring given its uses in the world. Thus this book aims to make one contribution to reorienting the field in connection with what has long seemed to me to be its most important subject, what individuals are in economic life. My belief is that individual conceptions in economics not systematically grounded in identity analysis are unlikely to provide secure foundations for good causal explanations in economics, and likely to be ideological in promoting policies and normative views more reflective of dominant political thinking. For individuals, identity is paramount. But my more long-range concern is that individuality is at risk, a fragile achievement of our recent history, threatened by many emerging forces. This book will hardly address everything this agenda calls for, but it is an effort in the direction of making thinking about what individuals are in economics a needed focus.

Acknowledgments

Though I began writing this book when the pandemic began, I have been working on its ideas for many years, and so there are many people with whom I've interacted during that time who have contributed to and influenced my thinking to whom I am indebted and grateful. Many have commented on what I've written and stimulated my thinking in different ways including in sharing their own ideas and research. I list them as best I can recall and apologize to any I have not included.

Morris Altman, Carolina Alves, Angela Ambrosino, Erik Angner, Richard Arena, Fikret Adaman, Brian Arthur, Emrah Aydinonat, Sina Badiei, Antoinette Baujard, Jeff Biddle, Mark Blaug, Dieter Bögenhold, Mauro Boianovsky, Marcel Boumans, Gabriel Brida, Nicolas Brisset, Dan Bromley, Merve Burnazoglu, Gilles Campagnolo, Anna Carabelli, Scott Carter, Mario Cedrini, Alessandra Cenci, Shu-Heng Chen, Emanuele Citera, Asimina Christoforou, Dave Colander, Annie Cot, Ricardo Crespo, Victor Cruz-e-Silva, Muriel Dal Pont, Joe Daniels, Sandy Darity, Leila Davis, George DeMartino, Tyler DesRoches, Malte Dold, Sheila Dow, Amitava Dutt, Wilfrid Dolfsma, Wolfram Elsner, Valentina Erasmo, Deb Figart, Ben Fine, Stefano Fiori, Steve Fleetwood, Evelyn Forget, Chris Fuller, Cesar Garcia-Diaz, Des Gasper, Muriel Gilardone, Nils Goldschmidt, James Grayot, Geoff Harcourt, Glenn Harrison, Cyril Hedoin, Carsten Hermann-Pillath, Floris Heukelom, Geoff Hodgson, Cars Hommes, Franck Jovanovic, Dorian Jullien, Rouslan Koumakhov, Alan Kirman, Harry Konstantinidis, Theodore Koutsobinas, Dave Krause, Mike Lawlor, Tony Lawson, Guilhem Lecouteux, Robert Leonard, Ortrud Leßmann, Harro Maas, Ramzi Mabsout, Uskali Mäki, Magdalena Małecka, Roberto Marchionatti, Soroush Marouzi, Cristina Marcuzzo, Tiago Mata, Roger McCain, Steve Medema, Ivan Mitrouchev, Philippe Mongin, Ellen Mutari, Nuno Martins, Solange Marin, Bob McMaster, Jamie Morgan, Mary Morgan, Ivan Moscati, Vitor Neves, Eddie Nik-Khah, Franklin Obeng-Odoom, Edward O'Boyle, Jeff Pagel, Enrico Petracca, Steve Pressman, Dave Primrose, Paolo Ramazotti, Constantinos Repapis, Geert Reuten, Agustín Reyes, Andres Rius, Don Ross, Barkley Rosser, Jochen Runde, Malcolm Rutherford, Warren Samuels, Ana Santos,

Stephanie Seguino, Amartya Sen, Esther-Mirjam Sent, Paolo Silvestri, Heath Spong, Irene van Staveren, Luca Storti, Leigh Tesfatsion, Raimo Tuomela, Vela Vellipulai, Philippe Verreault-Julien, Andrea Vigorito, Jack Vromen, Mark White, and Carlo Zappia.

I owe special thanks to Wade Hands who read a previous version of the entire book and commented upon it extensively section by section. Our collaboration as editors of the *Journal of Economic Methodology* has been a highlight of my professional life. Thank you Wade.

I also owe special thanks to Zohreh Emami with whom virtually every idea and argument in this book has been discussed and examined. She has constantly reminded me of what I may have overlooked and provided continual encouragement to expand my thinking, especially regarding the complex nature of social identity. I am also very grateful for her support and patience over the time given over to working on this book, as well as to my earlier work. Thank you Zohreh.

I am grateful to Marquette University and the University of Amsterdam for their support – from both my colleagues and particularly my many students over the years at Amsterdam my Mastersvak History of Recent Economics seminar – and for support from the Institute for New Economic Thinking.

I am also grateful for opportunities to give lectures and talks at Reims, Nice, Turin, Siegen, Paris, Coimbra, Montevideo, and at many conferences.

I thank Phil Good at Cambridge University Press for his kind support, development of an economics and philosophy list, and expert editorship at the Press. I am very grateful for indexing to Victoria George.

Earlier versions of some chapters and parts of chapters appeared as papers elsewhere:

"Introduction: The Status of the Concept of Identity in Economics," *Forum for Social Economics* 50:1(2020):1–9.

"A General Theory of Social Economic Stratification: Stigmatization, Exclusion, and Capability Shortfalls," *Review of Evolutionary Political Economy* 3: 3 (2022): 493–513.

"Economics as a Normative Discipline: Value Disentanglement in an 'Objective' Economics," in eds. Sina Badiei and Agnès Grivaux, *The Positive and the Normative in Economic Thought*, London: Routledge (2022): 87–107.

"Objectivity in Economics and the Problem of the Individual," *Journal of Economic Methodology* (2023) DOI: 10.1080/1350178X.2023.2181374

PART I

The Failed Pathway
and Exit Strategies

Chapters 1, 2, and 3 in this first part of the book make the case for replacement of the *Homo economicus* individual conception. I argue that explaining what individuals are requires explaining their identity. Once an identity analysis is adopted, we see that the mainstream socially *un*embedded atomistic individual conception fails to explain what individuals are, and begin to see what an alternative socially embedded individual conception involves. Chapters 4–9 of the book develop that alternative conception and its normative implications.

Chapter 1 discusses the issue of scientific objectivity in economics. It criticizes a closed science "view from nowhere" conception of economics and defends an open science "view from somewhere" conception of economics as an objective science. The first conception is ascribed to current mainstream economics, is associated with its principle practices – reductionist modeling, formalization, limited interdisciplinarity, and value neutrality – and has as its foundation the abstract *Homo economicus* conception. Two problematic consequences of these practices are:

(i) value blindness regarding the range and complexity of human values;
(ii) fatalism regarding human behavior in employing a tenseless rather than tensed representation of time.

In contrast, the principle practices of an open science "view from somewhere" conception of economics as a science – complexity modeling, mixed methods, strong relationships to other disciplines, and value diversity – provide the foundations of a socially and historically embedded individual conception. Chapter 1 closes with discussion of the question: Might mainstream economics be a science bubble?

Chapter 2 introduces identity analysis and uses it to examine whether the *Homo economicus* conception can identify real-world individuals. It describes the self-referential, circular character of that conception and shows that the belief that *Homo economicus* identifies

1

real-world individuals rests on a fallacious inference known as affirming the consequent. Chapter 2 reviews how the identity concept came into economics by making a person's individual identity their utility function. This is compared with how social identity theory understands individual identity, and economics and social identity's view of representative agents is then distinguished. Sen's multiple selves view of individual identity is contrasted with both in light of its ontological basis. Section 3 of Chapter 2 critically evaluates rationality theory's two independence axioms regarding preferences, the logical basis for saying choice is context-independent and for the unembedded *Homo economicus* individual conception. It argues neither can be defended and that not only must choice be seen to be context-dependent, but that individuals need to be seen as socially and historically embedded.

Chapter 3 links context-dependent choice with what has recently been called in economics the "reconciliation problem" between positive and normative economics, and argues that efforts to solve that problem have led to a number of different strategies for reconstructing economics' individual conception. It first reviews the mainstream's "inner rational agent" attempt to preserve *Homo economicus* and then contrasts two broad strategies for reconstructing economics' individual conception based on opposing views of individual autonomy: an "internalist" view that makes it depend on private subjectivity and an "externalist" view that makes it depend on economic and social institutions. Chapter 3 reviews four, recent strategies in the literature which take the "externalist" view and move toward a socially embedded individual conception. All four make ability to adjust part of what people are, but all four remain attached to the idea that individuals are only made up of preferences. Thus, I argue they fail to explain how people are autonomous individuals able to choose and act freely.

1 | *Objectivity in Economics and the Problem of the Individual*

Scientific knowledge is social both in the ways it is created and in the uses it serves.

Longino (1990, p. 180)

In its excessive quest for generality, utility-maximising rational choice theory fails to focus on the historically and geographically specific features of socio-economic systems. As long as such theory is confined to ahistorical generalities, then it will remain highly limited in dealing with the real world.

Hodgson (2012, p. 94)

And one might almost say that these foundation walls are carried by the whole house.

Wittgenstein (1974, sect. 248)

1 Objectivity in Economics: The Mainstream View from Nowhere Science Conception

Might mainstream economics be a science bubble? The long history of science is filled with examples of dominant, influential approaches that were later shown to be based on mistaken conceptual foundations, and a case can be made that this is so of mainstream economics. Sciences, like other world views, historically evolve, change, and get superseded. In the history of science, worries often first emerge when significant evidence cannot be readily accommodated within an approach or must be strenuously interpreted to fit preexisting conceptual commitments. The emergence of behavioral economics might signal the beginnings of such worries regarding mainstream rational choice theory. Yet in the long run, the issue is whether a science approach somehow produces objective science. This raises the question: What does objectivity in science involve and what basis is it thought to have in mainstream economics? Most of this chapter addresses this issue, and at the end, I return to the science bubble question.

The first influential use of the term "mainstream economics" was in seventeenth edition of Paul Samuelson and William Nordhaus' *Economics* textbook (Samuelson and Nordhaus, 2001). Since then, there has been considerable discussion regarding what "mainstream" means. Some have emphasized the differences between neoclassical or orthodox and heterodox economics (Lawson, 2003, 2006; Dequech, 2007–2008; Lee, 2009; Mearman, 2011; Jo et al., 2017; Dow, 2021). Others have emphasized how new approaches in economics have shifted economics in varying ways and degrees away from an exclusively neoclassical economics toward a more multisided economics that draws on both traditional heterodoxy and increasingly other social science disciplines, and how these new research strategies contest many fundamental neoclassical principles and assumptions (Colander, Holt, and Rosser, 2004, 2006; Rodrik, 2015; Angner, 2019; Crespo, 2020b; Bögenhold, 2021; De Vroey and Pensieroso, 2021; Primrose et al., 2022; Ross, 2022; Truc, 2022).

I share many of the ideas in these two approaches but differentiate mainstream and non-mainstream approaches according to whether they employ closed or open conceptions of science. This distinction – originated by Ludwig von Bertalanffy (1968) – has been used in a number different ways in history and philosophy of science and more recently used effectively in economics to characterize different schools of thought (Dow, 2004; Chick and Dow, 2005; see Davis, 2023a) and in Critical realist philosophy of economics (Lawson, 1997, 2003, 2023). I add to this the distinction between a "view from nowhere" conception of science and a "view from somewhere" conception of science. I then associate these two conceptions and views with two alternative ways of looking at research practices in economics.

Objectivity in science is far from being an issue that concerns most mainstream economists, but if called upon to address it they might rest their defense of economics' objectivity as a science on what are often regarded as the mainstream's principle research practices:

reductionist modeling;
mathematical formalization;
limited relations to other disciplines;
value neutrality.

If then asked to explain why these practices make economics an objective science, they might say that they make economics like the physical and natural sciences that secure objectivity by enabling scientists to, as it were, "stand outside" their subject matter in a disinterested way.

This is the famous "view from nowhere" idea in science (Nagel, 1986; Sugden, 2018; Reiss and Sprenger, 2020). The rationale behind it is that objectivity in science depends on scientists being independent of their subject matter. Economics' principle practices, then, would presumably produce this independence. It would follow, were this stance indeed to produce objective science, that the contents of mainstream economics, including the *Homo economicus* doctrine and the full range of analysis dependent upon it, would provide an objective representation of economic life – just as if economists saw the nature of world as it is in itself clearly through a glass window.

Yet this is not the view of science that many physical and natural scientists hold. Their idea is that objectivity in science involves a "view from somewhere" and scientists instead "standing inside" their subject matters in an interested way. For example, astronomers, preeminently physical, natural scientists, are able to investigate a wide range of the electromagnetic spectrum not visible to the human eye because they have developed a number of specialized "viewing" technologies designed to allow them to also "see" the infrared, ultraviolet, radio, gamma, microwaves, and X-ray bands of the spectrum. That is, *what* science sees in the world depends on *how* scientists see, where this depends on their understanding of how their investigation influences what they see. Scientists always stand inside their subject matters, and the idea that they could stand outside them is a fiction that distorts their representation of the world and impedes their investigation.

In mainstream economics, I argue, this creates two false impressions about the economy: first, that what mainstream economists say exists in the economy is all that there is to be seen; second, that the economy appears to be a relatively deterministic system independently there to be discovered. The two corresponding effects of this misconception are: The first blinds us to the full range and complexity of human values and the different roles they play in economic life and society; the second, contrary to human freedom, imposes fatalism on economics regarding how people direct their lives and how economies can be constructed to promote human well-being and social goals. I argue, then, that both effects derive from the *Homo economicus* doctrine that I have argued is foundational to mainstream economics and the lynchpin of its view from nowhere understanding of economics as a science (Davis, 2003b, 2011).

a Mainstream Economics' Value Blindness

The mainstream *Homo economicus* doctrine narrows people down to being self-regarding or essentially self-interested, isolated individuals, who only interact at a distance from each other through markets, and for whom direct interaction is an "externality" that can make markets inefficient. The means by which it does this narrowing down is its commitment to value blindness. Central to this, and the foundation of its utility maximization understanding of individual behavior, is the concept of subjective preference. Preference is of course a value concept, but though there exists extensive thinking about of the nature of value and valuing in science, literature, philosophy, and human thought generally, the only value the mainstream sees is subjective preference. This, it defines quite rigorously via rational theory's standard axioms that reduce value to a single, abstract relation. Only then does it makes sense to say people maximize utility, since were we to acknowledge the many different ways and things people value, it would make little sense to say people maximize just one thing.[1]

Thus, all one is permitted to say/see when we speak of the many ways people value things is captured by the ordinal preference relation. All different motivations people might have for why they prefer one thing to another, how much so, how any one set of preferences relates to other sets of preferences, and how preferences are related to different kinds of values (ethical, prudential, personal, aesthetic, attitudinal, etc.) are all set aside with the claim that because preferences are subjective, nothing else can be said about their content.

This commitment to an abstract, logical representation of the preference concept is rarely explained or justified. Most rational choice

---

[1] There are a variety of recent views in economics and philosophy of economics about what preferences are, ranging from simply choices without psychological characteristics (Gul and Pesendorfer, 2008) to "total comparative evaluations" more like judgments than desires (Hausman, 2012, p. x). Economists, however, generally seem to take preferences to essentially be desires (Angner, 2018) without much consideration of what their nature is and how as values they relate to other kinds of values.

theory practitioners do not recognize that it involves a philosophically controversial epistemological stance. Nor is there much methodological or historical discussion in economics regarding what gets assumed in this logical turn.[2] Why, we should ask, does rational choice theory need to be "rational" in this specifically logical way? What, moreover, are the grounds for this narrowing of the concept of value?

In twentieth-century philosophy, the idea that concepts and theories need logical formulation is associated with logicism, a Platonist philosophical view resurrected in the early twentieth century and associated with Gottlob Frege and Bertrand Russell's effort to reduce mathematics to logic and Ludwig Wittgenstein's early logical approach to philosophy. Though Kurt Gödel overturned their larger ambitions, the conviction that philosophy and science required logical foundations was influential, and a succession of individuals now seen as the founders of modern economics – Ragnar Frisch, John von Neumann and Oskar Morgenstern, Jacob Marschak, Kenneth Arrow, Gerard Debreu, Paul Samuelson, and others – subsequently transferred this vision to the interpretation of neoclassical economic theory in developing the axiomatic foundations of what became rational choice theory. In contrast to earlier neoclassical thinking dating back to the late nineteenth century that treated preference as a broad, heuristic concept, preference became a concept that depended upon very specific logical formulation. People's rational behavior then reflected that they possessed "stable, well-ordered preferences."[3]

Rational choice theory has this history at its foundation. Though now it is commonly thought the theory implies people are rational in terms of their reasoning capacity, what "rational" really means is that their behavior can be explained in term of a set of logical axioms that allows us to say they have stable, well-ordered preferences. Not questioned is whether there are scientific reasons to think this, what philosophical commitments this involves, what their possible epistemological limitations might be, and whether there are conceptual and theoretical consequences of this commitment for economics as

---

[2] There are important exceptions (see especially Weintraub, 2002; Giocoli, 2003; Moscati, 2018). See Hands (2001) for the early and later twentieth-century history of methodology and philosophy of economics.

[3] See Hansson and Grüne-Yanoff (2022) for the history of development of the preference concept in economics.

a science – all despite the evident narrowing of the concept of value that this produced.

For proponents of the theory, then, rather than engage these questions and enter into discussion over what kind of concepts economics should rest on, particularly regarding one of the most human of all concepts, better to say that economics is simply about people's preferences rigorously understood, distance the preference concept from the broader idea of value, and say values in the broader sense are "non-scientific" and do not belong in economics. Value concepts, then, are "non-scientific" specifically because they lack precise logical foundations. Given this, one is then left to devote oneself to mathematically modeling behavior in rational choice terms. This ties "progress" in economics to "[t]he development and use of mathematical models [that now] is indeed representative of what large parts of economics does as a modelling science," and means that "theoretical progress is no longer what economists primarily aim to achieve" (Boumans and Herfeld, 2023, 224, 225). In terms of recent behavioral economics reasoning, this is a kind of confirmation bias in which the theory can never be falsified or overturned.[4]

A basic principle of science this move violates is to close off the development of a science to new information. Scientific theory constantly undergoes change and development as it accommodates new kinds of information, as occurred when astronomers and physicists changed their theory of what we can see when they developed new technologies that replaced seeing by human vision alone with what can be seen in the electromagnetic spectrum. It is ironic, then, that until quite recently mainstream economics barred experiments as a technology of investigation, claiming that they offered nothing new to be seen that rational choice theory did not already explain. Now of course experimentation is widely practiced in economics, and how choice is "rational" has become an issue. Why, then, should most economists continue to defend the theory?

One possible rationale is that were preference relationships allowed to be more complicated incorporating many kinds of values, the whole

---

[4] As Mary Morgan has put it in her "world in the model" examination of economics' postwar modeling practice: "As models replaced more general principles and laws, so economists came to interpret the behavior and phenomena they saw in the economic world directly in terms of those models" (Morgan, 2012, p. 3).

apparatus of predictable equilibrium, supply-and-demand relationships could break down, taking much of mainstream thinking with it. Then what would economics have to offer as a presumably objective science? I return to this issue in the following section in connection with the mainstream's fatalism problem. But ultimately, I believe, the deep rationale for the mainstream's narrow conception of preference/value rests on its narrowing the ontological conception of the person to what fits the idea that people are essentially self-regarding or self-interested, isolated individuals who interact mostly at a distance from one another through markets. I comment briefly on the Platonist philosophical instincts that undergird this view.

We can characterize the mainstream's narrow conception of preference/value, embodied in rational choice theory and the practice of reductionist modeling, as an abstract essentialism – the philosophical view that what science investigates can ultimately be reduced to sets of abstracts essences underlying the phenomena we observe. Plato elaborated this view long ago in his *Republic* (1941), arguing that society ought to be governed by "philosopher kings" who alone can see and fully apprehend these essences (or his transcendent Platonic forms). These "philosopher kings" tell us what we cannot see, and tell us what we ought to see, which only they can truly see. For the mainstream, this hidden underlying essence of value is the abstract preference relation (the basis of risk-free and risky choice analysis). As the essence of value, it secures economics' objectivity as a science, and thus the discipline's and economists' "philosopher king" role in producing a well-governed society explained in terms of the market mechanism – all as encapsulated in *Homo economicus* doctrine.

Plato's theory treated the everyday phenomena we observe as imperfect representations of the underlying essences on which they depend. What we ordinarily see is at best an approximation of those underlying essences. The error of the ordinary person for the abstract essentialist is to take the way the phenomena appear as meaningful and producing valuable information. What they should see were they able to grasp the hidden, underlying essential relationships is that empirical research in economics can ultimately only confirm rational choice theory. Experiments, should they contradict this, must be redone because they must somehow be mistaken. For example, if people sometimes appear to be altruistic, this somehow still needs to be shown to be really just utility maximizing behavior.

If people are believed to exhibit present bias and weakness of will rather than behave rationally, this can only be because their "true" inner preferences have not been correctly identified.

Consider now how mainstream value blindness goes hand-in-hand with a fatalism about economic life and ultimately a rejection of human freedom. I address this in connection with how the mainstream's view from nowhere imposes a particular conception of time upon economic life.

b Mainstream economics' fatalism and the problem of time

When we increase the number and kinds of values we say operate in economic and social life, human behavior becomes considerably more complex. In contrast to the mainstream reduction of value to one form that produces a single set of behavioral relationships, when different types of values interact in multiple, often in unexpected ways, human behavior becomes less predictable and equilibrium-like and more indeterminate. Indeterminacy is not same thing as human freedom, but it is a reason to suppose it exists whereas arguing that behavior is highly predictable and determinate puts human freedom in question. As Elizabeth Anscombe put it: "The truth of physical indeterminism is thus indispensable if we are to make anything of the claim to freedom" ([1971] 1981: 146).[5]

Indeed, if people are generally predictable, which a reduction of human values to preferences and the logic of preferences allows one to say, then there is no need to even use a freedom concept or say people behave "freely" other than to appeal to popular sentiments. Given that most people believe freedom exists in some form, it is not surprising that the concept is used informally in economics, as in the claim that economics is "choice" theory. Here, then, I argue that underlying the mainstream view is an understanding of time in which people really do not have choices.

The meaning and nature of time is a largely neglected subject in the methodology of economics, so we need to turn to philosophy to understand some of the main issues involved (see Gale, 1967; Emery, Markosian, and Sullivan, 2020). A key issue concerns the difference between the past–present–future temporal sequence and the

---

[5] She went on to add: "The physically undetermined is not thereby 'free.' For freedom at least involves the power of acting according to an idea..." (*Ibid.*). Drakopoulos in a pair of publications (2022, 2023) shows how the standard view's historically narrowing the preference concept to rule out interpersonal comparisons of utility serves its "conceptual resilience."

before-after temporal sequence.[6] The former involves tensed statements, where what is said to be true changes with the passage of time – known as a dynamic temporal idea. For example, one could say "Napoleon is alive" is true when he was, but can no longer say it is true after he was not. By contrast, the latter involves tenseless statements, where what is true is always true and not affected by the passage of time – known as a static temporal idea. For example, it will always be true that Napoleon died in 1821 and after the Battle of Waterloo.

Aristotle addressed one thing that mattered about the difference between these two ways of thinking in his famous future sea battle problem (known as the problem of future contingents), arguing that fatalism derives from trying to explain time in human affairs in tenseless, before-after terms (Aristotle, 1984). Imagine, he said in an early thought experiment, that at some date, it is true that a possible future sea battle can be avoided. If we think only in tenseless, before-after temporal terms, it would then also need be true in the future that it could be avoided. That is, when we say what is true is always true, this is not affected by the passage of time, and thus we must suppose a future sea battle will be avoided as predicted. But of course the passage of time overturns many predictions, and it can turn out that a predicted future sea battle ultimately cannot be avoided. The problem is that employing the before-after, tenseless, static time idea in connection with human affairs implies fatalism, or that it treats the future as predetermined and implies people lack the freedom to affect how it plays out. Aristotle concluded that in human affairs, we must think about time in tensed, dynamic past–present–future terms where something can be true at one time but cease to be true at a later time.[7]

Note that mainstream economics' *Homo economicus* maximization analysis employs a tenseless, before-after, static temporal thinking. If it is true that individuals maximize utility at any one time, since utility maximization in a risky choice world concerns what will happen in

---

[6] Called, respectively, the A-series and B-series (McTaggart, 1908; cf. Gale, 1967, pp. 65–85).

[7] Aristotle's critique of fatalism stood in opposition to a long tradition of belief in his time that the course of human events was divinely predetermined, as in the plays of Sophocles. That belief has periodically reoccurred in history and is associated with claims – sometimes by those in positions of power – that human affairs will proceed in some inevitable, even tragic, way.

the future, their expectations and beliefs about the future must also be true. If they were not, they would not maximize utility. Thus, the *Homo economicus* maximization view assumes what is true at one time is tenselessly always true, the future is predetermined, fatalism applies to human affairs, and choice never really occurs. Utility maximizing individuals must choose as they do.

However, if we instead think about time in tensed, dynamic past–present–future terms, where something can be true at one time but not at a later time, this would mean that what individuals expect and believe about the future could be true when they determine it to be so, but not be true after they act upon it. This is inconsistent with utility maximization, since it implies that maximizing utility today may not maximize utility. But it is not inconsistent with understanding individuals as constantly adjusting their behavior with the passage of time, doing as well as they can in the present, but acting on the assumption that things that are true might later not be, thus finding out they are often wrong about the future, thus needing to change what they think is true, and accordingly never really maximizing anything.

The mainstream, then, locks in its before-after, static temporal utility maximization thinking with its comparative static model of equilibrium adjustment. In that model, an equilibrium in which all individuals utility maximize can be upset by some unforeseeable exogenous shock. Individuals then adjust to shocks by determining what will again maximize utility. But that the world has changed does not imply it was not true they maximized utility before a shock. They did, but their expectations and beliefs about the future formed in the past are discontinuous with those they form after the shock. Thus, as if in an entirely new world, they can then again truly maximize utility based on their new expectations and beliefs about a new future, and it is not the case that what was true at an earlier time has ceased to be true at a later time. The world just unexplainably changed.

This comparative statics reasoning draws on the mainstream's abstract essentialism. The idea of an exogenous shock, a concept that really has no real temporal meaning, eliminates the passage of time, and makes the only temporal sequence possible the before–after static temporal understanding. In fact, this is really less a temporal idea and more a simple ordering idea. Like Plato's philosophy that defines reality in terms of timeless abstract essences, it tells us the passage of time is essentially unreal, and the phenomenon of time passing people say they experience is only an imperfect representation of the underlying nature of time as a simple ordering.[8]

Aristotle, who had a different understanding of science more like modern scientists' view from somewhere understanding, rejected Plato's transcendent forms or abstract essences view from nowhere conception, and instead sought to explain the phenomena as we observe them. He saw our predictions are often wrong, concluded fatalism was wrong, and argued that understanding human affairs required the past–present–future temporal sequence and the passage of time idea. This science thinking is also present in non-mainstream economic approaches that incorporate such phenomena as path dependency, hysteresis, irreversibility, and the idea that the economy is an institutionally rich, complex, evolving system. I add to this that employing the dynamic understanding of time also requires we give up *Homo economicus* conception for an understanding of individuals who are socially embedded with many kinds of values and historically embedded in continually adjusting their behavior in a changing economy – an adaptive individual conception.

This alternative understanding of the economy and individuals, taken up in more detail in Chapter 4 and the following chapters and implies a different view of what makes economics an objective science. I characterize it as an open science view from somewhere conception, and compare it in Section 2 to the mainstream's closed science view from nowhere conception.

2 Objectivity in Economics: A Non-mainstream View from Somewhere Science Conception

The open science idea is associated with the open science movement and the goals of reducing barriers to participation in scientific research and increasing worldwide access to its results to make scientific production more transparent, socially collaborative, and sustainable (OECD, 2015-10-15; UNESCO, 2021). Though the open science movement operates with a collection of different principles seen to generate open science, and though there are different competing theories of what

---

[8] McTaggart, who was also a proponent of thinking in terms of the before–after B-series, also claimed time was unreal, but instead argued for it on modern idealist grounds.

open science involves and how to foster it, I focus on one of the principles associated with open science – open methodology – and interpret open science from an epistemological or methodological perspective as a view from somewhere conception of science that relies on two main heuristic principles. Open sciences:

(i) employ provisional entry points subject to reevaluation in relation to the scientific frameworks they produce;
(ii) develop according to how the entry point–frameworks relationship evolves over time through an interplay of empirical and theoretical investigation.

These entry points are scientists' views from somewhere which reflect their understanding of the state of a science at any one time. As illustrated by the history and development of the evolution of the electromagnetic spectrum, the openness of a science can be interpreted as a matter of making it possible for *how* the different ways in which scientists see the world to influence and determine *what* they see, and then for *what* they see to drive scientific investigation of new ways for *how* they might see the world.

In that history of the evolution of the electromagnetic spectrum, early scientists had theories of the visible light spectrum, but having observed that white light breaks up into different colors when seen through glass prisms, it was inferred that the means or technology for how we see influences what we see, and this ultimately required that what the spectrum involves be redefined in ways that went beyond its human visibility understanding. In the nineteenth century, then, new technologies led to the discovery of infrared and ultraviolet radiation beyond the two ends and boundaries of the visible light spectrum. This initiated the redefining of what was "visible" that ultimately produced a theory of what became the electromagnetic radiation spectrum. This theory then led to the development of additional technologies that made possible the discovery of X-rays, gamma rays, radio waves, and microwave as further forms of radiation, which in turn allowed further refinements in the theory of the spectrum.

Objectivity in science, accordingly, is not a matter of applying and reapplying the same set of scientific principles, continually elaborating and redefining their existing meanings, with observation of the world organized around always confirming those same principles.

That type of view employs a closed view from nowhere science conception. Rather, it is a matter of how scientific principles evolve as they are put to use in the world, and how this may lead to discoveries of new phenomena that lead to the reconceptualization of those principles. That is, scientific ideas and technologies coevolve and at any one time presuppose an historical view from somewhere. I characterize this type of view as an open view from somewhere science conception.

Table 1.1 compares the two kinds of science conceptions in terms of their epistemological basis, their form of development, and their temporal nature.

How do these two science conceptions differ, then, in regard to their principle practices? Table 1.2 characterizes the practices that open and closed science approaches in economics employ with respect to types of modeling, methodological forms of analysis, relationships to other disciplines, and positions on values. Whereas the principle practices of mainstream economics are reductionist modeling, mathematical formalization, limited relations to other disciplines, and value neutrality, the principle practices of open science economics approaches are

Table 1.1 *Characteristics of open and closed science*

Science conception	Epistemological basis	Form of development	Temporal framework
Open	Reflexive	Two-way	Dynamic
Closed	Essentialist	One-way	Static

Table 1.2 *Open and closed science practices*

	Types of modeling	Methodological forms of analysis	Relationships to other disciplines	Positions on values
Open	Complexity	Mixed methods	Strong	Embraces value diversity
Closed	Reductionist	Mathematical formalization	Limited	Claims value neutrality

complexity modeling, mixed methods analysis, strong relationships to other disciplines, and emphasis on diverse values.[9]

The practices the mainstream closed science conception employs have the *Homo economicus* individual conception as their underlying basis. The practices that open science economic approaches employ have as their underlying basis a socially and historically embedded individual conception. I discuss the latter's practices from this vantage point.

a Complexity Modeling in Economics

Adopting a broader account of what motivates people's actions and choices in explanations of economic behavior takes us beyond the preference-based, deterministic accounts of how markets and economies work that the mainstream employs. While this means there is less predictability in economic explanations, it also creates a larger role for human freedom in descriptions of people's behavior and expands economics' policy space beyond the narrow scope of mainstream welfare efficiency analysis. Seen as an open science practice built around the two heuristic principles above, complexity modeling rejects the essentialist modeling of the mainstream, incorporates reflexivity in the form of feedback relationships, represents economics systems in a two-way and two-level manner, and explains the economy as dynamic and evolving.

The complexity literature in economics and science is now voluminous.[10] Here, I simply draw on Herbert Simon's early paradigmatic model of a complex system that succinctly illustrates its basic properties (Simon, 1962). Using the idea of what he called a "nearly decomposable system" (474), he showed how such a system operates using as an example how a building's temperature system works as a complex system. First, individual rooms in the building have independent

---

[9] I have chosen types of modeling, methodological forms of analysis, relationships to other disciplines, and positions on values as the basis for my comparison of open and closed science conceptions in economics to reflect the dominant influence of mainstream economic thinking on what constitute research practices that produce objective science.

[10] For recent contributions in economics, see Tesfatsion (2002), Tesfatsion and Judd (2006), Velupillai (2010), Chen and Wang (2011), Kirman (2011), Hommes (2013), Colander and Kupers (2014), and Arthur (2015). Rosser (2021) provides an extensive review of the state of the literature.

temperature systems. Second, these individual room temperatures are only "nearly decomposable" from one another because they are affected by the rooms' proximity to one another. Third, because the overall building temperature is different from individual room temperatures, individual room temperatures adjust to this, but their interactive effects cause the overall building temperature to change, which again affects individual room temperatures, etc.

The feedback relationships involved thus reflexively move in two directions between two levels of the system, and the process of temperature determination continues indefinitely. Here is how Simon characterized this:

> Roughly, by a complex system I mean one made up of a large number of parts that interact in a nonsimple way. In such systems, the whole is more than the sum of the parts, not in an ultimate, metaphysical sense, but in the important pragmatic sense that, given the properties of the parts and the laws of their interaction, it is not a trivial matter to infer the properties of the whole. (Simon, 468)

When we model the economy as a complex economic system, this two-way interaction operates between its microlevel, where agents form expectations and interact, and its aggregate macro-level, where we see the overall effects of that interaction. Mainstream models suppress these two-way reflexive feedback effects by ruling out that "the whole is more than the sum of the parts" and by making it "a trivial matter [for agents] to infer the properties of the whole." Agents' expectations are either assumed to be "rational," meaning that they fully (and unrealistically) comprehend the effects of everyone's choices on the economy as a whole, or their micro-level interaction is examined in isolation from its possible effects on the economy as a whole. This makes it possible to assume agents maximize utility in tenseless temporal terms, so that what is true at any given point cannot be upset by what happens later. The economy then ceases to be a dynamic, evolving system, and can be formalized in a highly determinate way.

Realistically, however, "it is not a trivial matter [for agents] to infer the properties of ... whole" economic systems, so agents must continually adapt their behavior and their interaction with other agents causes the overall systems they occupy to change over time. In temporal terms, what may be true when they act need not be true later when their interaction produces its effects on the overall economy. As these overall effects feedback on agents, they must adapt to their new circumstances. Thus, agents are adaptive, and as Simon said, they "satisfice" rather than maximizing utility (Simon, 1956). They may guide their behavior by various rules or principles that have been effective in the past when the economy changed slowly, but they may also abandon these rules or principles and adopt others, but when it changes more dramatically.[11]

Thus, economic agents – and individuals – change with the passage of time just as the economy changes with the passage of time, and consequently they need to be seen to be socially and historically embedded. Indeed, the economies they occupy are not just market processes, but social systems with inherited institutional, legal, and cultural characteristics that make it far from "a trivial matter to infer the properties of the whole" associated with entire economies. These are the entry points of complexity modeling as an open science practice with a view from somewhere understanding of economics as an objective science.

b Mixed Methods Methodological Analysis and Economics' Relationships with Other Disciplines

I treat mixed methods methodological analysis and economics' relations to other disciplines together because they tend to go hand-in-hand when we contrast open and closed conceptions of science in economics. Mainstream economics and other social sciences, then, clearly differ in regard to both the scientific methods they employ and in their respective degrees of openness to methods employed in each other. Other social sciences have adopted some of economics' quantitative methods, but economics has adopted few of other social sciences' methods. Instead, mainstream economics in the postwar period has increased its reliance on mathematical formalization as a method of representation and investigation, and has all but given up the qualitative methods it shared with other social sciences before the war.

To take methods of analysis first, mixed methods research is a methodologically pluralist, pragmatic approach to scientific investigation that combines different quantitative and qualitative methods – for example, surveys and numerical data – in the collection of evidence,

---

[11] This adjustment in decision rules is excellently demonstrated in the Santa Fe artificial stock market analysis (see Palmer et al., 1999).

its analysis, and in the development of theory (Starr, 2014). The main rationale for mixed methods research is that increasing the kinds of evidence and thus the means of analysis sciences employ increases their investigative capacities and reduces the risk that theories are built upon only one, possibly limited source of evidence. Since having different kinds of evidence that different methods produce usually does not generate sharp theoretical inferences, mixed methods research offers a different strategy for theory elaboration. In effect, it creates a forum for theory development in which the contributions of different types of evidence are evaluated and debated in terms of their different theoretical implications. This makes the relationship between evidence and theory open-ended and allows for a continual comparison of entry points and theoretical outcomes.

How, then, does science actually proceed on this more open basis? One influential view draws on the metaphor of triangulation. Should different methods produce a collection of similar theoretical results, this gives further direction regarding what sorts of theories should be investigated (Denzin, 1970; Downward and Mearman, 2007). To put this in terms of the epistemological basis of open science (Table 1.1), the evidence produced by different methods and the theory possibilities they generate reflexively determine one another. To put this in terms of the modeling characteristics of open science (Table 1.2), this calls for a complexity modeling approach that combines different kinds of evidence that (as Simon put it) "interact in a nonsimple way."[12]

In contrast, in mainstream economics' closed science terms, its essentialist epistemological basis (Table 1.1) combined with its reductionist type of modeling (Table 1.2) limits its methodological form of analysis almost exclusively to mathematical formalization. This tends to reinforce its existing theoretical commitments, since placing research weight on further refinements in formalizing theory limits the possible impact that other methods of investigation might have on the interpretation of theory. Thus, the tension between evidence and theory whereby empirical entry points and theory continually act upon and change one another is eliminated.

---

[12] Models, then, are analogous to recipes in which different types of ingredients are combined according to one's explanatory goals rather than some pre-given logical template (Boumans, 1999).

We can distinguish these two science visions according to whether their principle motivation is the representation of ideas or the discovery of new ideas (Schickore, 2018). In the philosophy of science, there is a long-standing distinction between the context of justification and context of discovery (Reichenbach, 1938). Both are part of science, with discovery a constant source of scientific advance and justification a registering and organizing of what that advance is believed to involve. Yet, the specific set of practices a science adopts can tip the balance between the two either toward building existing theory or developing new theory. Emphasis on mixed methods favors the latter; mathematical modeling favors the former.[13]

When we now consider disciplines' relationships to other sciences, we see that when a science borrows from other sciences which uses different methods of investigation, this influences the kinds of evidence it incorporates and thus the weight it places on discovery. Further, since the different methods that different sciences employ reflect the different kinds of phenomena they investigate, borrowing methods from one another also introduces "new" phenomena into a science. This makes its evidence–theory relationship more open-ended. In terms of the Table 1.1 contrast between open and closed conceptions of science, its form of development is dynamic and two-way when it borrows from other sciences rather than static and one-way when it is reluctant to do so.

This is a way to look at the recent uneven rise of heuristics and biases behavioral thinking in economics. The "new" phenomena economics has begun to borrow from psychology – behaviors that have reference points and are influenced by the context of choice – have been described as choice "anomalies" because they do not fit the reductionist modeling method rational choice theory employs. These "new" phenomena have in many cases been introduced through experiments that as a nonstandard method also still have a relatively limited place in mainstream economics. Thus, it can be argued that its closed view from nowhere conception of science acts as a barrier to its further development limiting the role of behavioral thinking in economics. This may change in the future as the overall impact of

---

[13] One way to think about the tension between discovery and justification that builds on Reichenbach is to say "science in the making" is inherently "messy" while the job of philosophy is to replace that thinking with a more ordered account of what it achieves (Schickore, 2020, pp. 484–485).

new kinds of evidence introduced into economics changes it. Yet, this would put at risk its idea that choice is rational with the deep essentialist epistemological basis and the *Homo economicus* view of the individual this relies on. Thus, it is also possible that the mainstream view will ultimately simply be superseded by a new sort of economics with different epistemological foundations and practices. This recalls the question of whether mainstream economics might be a science bubble. Before turning to that question, however, Section c discusses the mainstream's "value neutrality" practice.

c "Value Neutrality" versus Expanding Economics' Value Spectrum

"Value neutrality" as a practice identifying acceptable types of modeling bars ethical or normative values on the grounds that objectivity in economics requires it be positive and free of such values. Even welfare economics and efficiency judgments can be seen to be nonnormative if taken only to register different possible states of affairs and not engage their normative content. Of course, economists say welfare and efficiency ought to be promoted, but for most this only implies people's preferences should be satisfied, because this is seen as descriptive of the behavior people are said to have. Thus, preference satisfaction in itself has no ethical content.[14]

Yet, preferences are still values, so "value neutrality" also means that out of the wide array of human values only the preference value concept should be included in economics. This combination of exclusion of other kinds of values and reduction of the value concept to the preference concept is important to framing the mainstream's essentialist, closed science view from nowhere terms. Further, as a practice "value neutrality" also has a special status compared to these other three practices. Reductionist modeling, formalization, and limiting relationships to other disciplines concern how economics is done, but "value neutrality" concerns what it is about. Thus, one could give up *Homo economicus* and still maintain these other three practices, but if one gave up *Homo economicus* and adopted a richer conception

---

[14] Indeed, the theory ignores the difference between "bad" preferences – immoral, cruel, violent, self-harming, etc. – and "good" ones. This is where the neutrality idea gets its meaning.

of the person it is unlikely one would be able to maintain "value neutrality." That is, "value neutrality" is both necessary to the *Homo economicus* doctrine and also an implication of it. Thus, while these other three practices have fairly wide scientific use, the mainstream's essentialist reduction of all value to preference and its exclusion of millennia of thinking about the diversity of human values is exceptional in social science. What could possibly justify this?

For Aristotle, essentialism was simply a fundamental philosophical mistake and manifestation of intellectual *hubris*. He saw Plato's transcendent forms as an excess and exaggeration of philosophical thinking about science that blinds us from seeing the phenomena science investigates, and that elevates an elite group of "philosopher king" scientists who say what we can and cannot see. In modern philosophy, the later Wittgenstein also criticized his earlier essentialism and saw it as a fundamental error in and abuse of philosophical thinking. He attributed it to an almost religious predisposition people have to believe something simple is always "hidden" beneath the multiplicity of phenomena. His advice, then, was rather than start by asking what is "common" behind all the instances of something being investigated, look instead to see what their many interrelationships were.

Don't say: 'There *must* be something common ... but *look and see* whether there is anything common at all. – For if you look at them you will not see something that is common to *all*, but similarities, relationships, and a whole series of them at that ... a complicated network of similarities overlapping and criss-crossing: sometimes overall similarities, sometimes similarities of detail. (Wittgenstein, 1953, para. 66)

What, then, might we see when we examine the "complicated network of similarities overlapping and criss-crossing" in the wide array of human values? And, if "value neutrality" is required for *Homo economicus*, what does making the wide array of human values central to economics imply about what individuals are? I suggest three things.

First, given the wide array of human values reflects the multiplicity of human social relationships. People should be seen to be social beings with a variety of social identities, not asocial, atomistic bundles of preferences whose connection to one another is mechanically through markets. Second, just as people's social relationships can conflict, so their various values can conflict, in contrast to how the axiomatic interpretation of preferences makes people's preferences logically consistent and ensures smooth substitutions on indifference curves. Third, despite the mainstream's effort to exclude ethical values from economics, an inspection of human history shows that ethical reasoning and debate over what people ought to do is pervasive and a fundamental aspect of people's behavior, economic and otherwise.

Yet, if mainstream economics is as removed from the social world as these points imply, if people are socially and historically embedded individuals rather than utility maximizing *Homo economicus* ones, and if at root of all this is the mainstream's essentialist view from nowhere conception of economics as a science, might mainstream economics be science bubble? I turn to this question.

3 Might Mainstream Economics Be a Science Bubble?

I previously addressed this question using a financial market boom-bust model (Davis, 2017b). Here, I begin by framing that argument in a broad philosophy of science perspective that draws on the history of science and its record of successes and failures. The idea, then, that a science could be like a bubble is suggested by Thomas Kuhn's famous scientific revolutions view (1962/1970). He argued sciences are built upon paradigmatic foundations – idealized conceptual structures – but these foundations are often only weakly constructed and can thus be fragile. Scientific knowledge thus accumulates over time across paradigms, each of which at the time of its development produces one limited vision of that accumulating knowledge.

The history of science shows, then, that successful science paradigms have been consistently abandoned and replaced when new paradigms were constructed upon new foundations. A short list of superseded theories includes in astronomy, the Ptolemaic geocentric theory of the universe and the nebular hypothesis of the solar system's origin; in biology, spontaneous generation, Lamarckism, Mendelian genetics, and recapitulation theory (ontogeny recapitulates phylogeny); in chemistry, alchemy, caloric theory, and phlogiston theory; in physics, Aristotelian theory, Newtonian classical mechanics, and a long list of atomic theories; in geography, flat earth theory, and expanding and contracting earth theories; in psychology, phrenology, and stimulus–response behaviorism. All were thought correct and widely held at one time.

Kuhn did not explain either what fragility in a science's foundations involves or what precipitates their examination and abandonment.

Karl Popper (1959; 1934) had earlier argued that the claims of science are always fallible and potentially subject to falsification should they be contradicted by empirical evidence. However, when empirical evidence was sufficient to do this was unclear since sciences employ a variety of auxiliary assumptions that can be adjusted to protect them from seemingly falsifying evidence. Imre Lakatos (1970) consequently argued that scientific research programs could always insulate their key propositions, their "hard cores," to withstand empirical refutation. Thus perhaps paradoxically, a science could possess fragile conceptual foundations and still endure for long periods of time – though as the history of science shows still ultimately fail were those foundations weak. In effect, such approaches are like science bubbles, exhibiting dramatic expansion in a scientific community but also vulnerable to a collapse in support. What, then, might explain the dynamic by which they survive for a time and then finally fail?

Since bubbles were originally associated with financial phenomena where in many examples in history questionable assumptions prevailed for a period of time only to later fail, often spectacularly, we can look to financial bubbles to model this dynamic of survival and failure. The model that the well-known financier George Soros developed is particularly interesting, because he studied under Popper, adopted Popper's fallibility principle, and added a reflexivity or feedback mechanism principle to produce a dynamic of adoption and abandonment of an investment. Thus, he described a financial bubble as a boom-bust process in which a positive feedback upswing phase in an investment proceeds for a time under a "misconception" regarding the merits of that investment until it comes to be seen as such, after which that investment comes to be seen as over-valued, a negative feedback disinvestment downswing phase takes over, the investment collapses, and the bubble breaks (Soros, 2013).[15]

If mainstream economics, then, is a science bubble, and investment in mainstream principles has the same sort of historical dynamic, roughly the first half of the twentieth century through the 1970s can be seen as a period of continued investment by economists in the foundations of mainstream thinking – equivalent to a positive feedback boom

---

[15] This very highly cited paper appeared in a special issue of the *Journal of Economic Methodology* in which other papers in the issue discussed its methodological meaning and significance.

phase – and the time since then with the appearance of new research programs in economics that contest many fundamental mainstream assumptions (see Colander, Holt, and Rosser, 2006) can be seen as the beginning of a period of increasing disinvestment by economists in those foundations – equivalent to negative feedback bust phase. The "belief reversal" this involves (Davis, 2020a) depends on it being recognized that some "misconception" underlies the assumptions that gave rise to the boom phase. What might that "misconception" be?

What I previously argued (Davis, 2017b) is that mainstream economics' chief "misconception" is that it treats economics as if it is a natural rather than a social science. The mainstream view from nowhere conception of economics' objectivity, then, would provide a further interpretation of this natural science "misconception" in that it associates economists' purported posture of disinterestedness with "value neutrality" as a scientific practice. Thus, if the boom-bust model tells us something about mainstream economics, we need to look for evidence that there exists the beginning of a negative feedback disinvestment bust phase motivated by the conviction that it is a "misconception" that economics is like a natural science and in particular by its commitment to "value neutrality" as a scientific practice.[16]

Consider, specifically, the 1980s emergence of heuristics and biases behavioral economics, often seen as one of the most significant developments in recent economics. Its key assumption is that people's environments influence their choices, or that the context of choice and its reference points matter (Kahneman and Tversky, 1979). Thus, research in this scientific program investigates the many ways in which *how* people make choices influences *what* choices they make – a view from somewhere conception of economics that rejects the mainstream's view from nowhere understanding of pure choice theory built upon a set of abstract axioms governing preferences – most importantly the independence axioms.

Many mainstream economists would no doubt hesitate to say "we're all behavioral economists now" (Angner, 2019), yet the rapid growth of behavioral reasoning in economics can nonetheless be seen as a process of disinvestment in the fundamental "hard core" principles

---

[16] In Davis (2020a), I associate this negative feedback disinvestment process with belief reversals seen as phase transitions on the order of "Minsky moments" in a complexity theory approach with reflexive agents.

of mainstream economics, and as a negative feedback bust phase that regards it as a "misconception" that economics is essentially a natural science. Indeed, when the context of choice matters, people's values matter and thus "value neutrality" becomes untenable. Yet if "value neutrality" is untenable, so also is the "hard core" lynchpin of mainstream theory, *Homo economicus*. When context of choice matters and people's values matter, people cannot be seen as socially and historically *un*embedded individuals.

Most mainstream economists of course do not concern themselves with methodological and historical arguments such as this. In the past, economists were not reluctant to make claims about the foundations of postwar economics, but now few comment on the state of economics or participate in the increasing number of debates about whether there is change in economics. At the same time, a large recent survey of economists' opinions about the state of economics captures considerable ambivalence regarding its direction and character (Andre and Falk, 2021). Perhaps, uncertainty about the state of economics is a sign of concern about possible coming change.

This is one way to understand the recent "empirical turn" in economics (Hamermesh, 2013; Angrist et al., 2017). Data-driven research, innovation in statistical econometric techniques, case-specific experimentalism, etc., can all be pursued without making explicit or even thinking about one's theoretical commitments, so if confidence in the foundations of mainstream economics has declined, the whole subject can be avoided while still recognizing the existence of "change" in economics. Yet, given the oligopolistic structure of the economics profession (Fourcade et al., 2015; Heckman and Moktam, 2020; Hoover and Svorenčík, 2023), it is also possible to say that long-standing theoretical commitments in mainstream economics may continue to survive in unexamined fashion – Kuhn's fragility thesis.

Note that one thing the failed, superseded sciences listed above arguably shared was an essentialism about collections of "hard core" principles that could not be overturned by evidence the phenomena might provide. That is, as effectively view from nowhere closed science approaches, they built fragility into their practices. That commitment to essentialism that I have argued is central to mainstream economics' conception of economics as an objective science could then become the last disinvestment in the mainstream paradigm.

2 | *The Untenability of the Unembedded* Homo economicus

No science has been criticized by its own servants as openly and constantly as economics. The motives of dissatisfaction are many, but the most important pertains to the fiction of Homo oeconomicus.

Georgescu-Roegen (1971, p. 1).

An "economic man", which is to say a constituent robot in an artificial economic system, is typically so constructed as to be perfectly rational (and hence perfectly understandable) in a way that actual people never are.

Lucas (2011, p. 105)

Man has such a predilection for systems and abstract deductions that he is ready to distort the truth intentionally, he is ready to deny the evidence of his senses in order to justify his logic.

Dostoyevsky (1918, p. 67)

"But he hasn't got anything on!" the whole town cried out at last.

Andersen (1837)

1 Identity Analysis and the Individual in Economics: Putting the Cart before the Horse

Identity analysis has many meanings and uses in philosophy. I use it specifically to ask whether the concepts economic theories employ to name and refer to things successfully identify them. I take the successful identification and naming of the things that science is about to be fundamental to its development. In regard to economics, does the most important naming concept in economics, the *Homo economicus* concept, thus succeed in identifying the real-world individuals to which it is said to refer? At issue, is whether economic theories through how they name and refer to things, in effect, "hook" onto the world. If the concepts they use fail to identify the things they name, the question arises: Are those theories simply free-floating, abstract language constructions at best loosely attached to the world and consequently unable to isolate and explain its causal mechanisms?

Epistemology is the philosophical investigation of what knowledge involves. Ontology is the philosophical investigation of what exists, and identity analysis is one kind of ontological investigation. Taking identity analysis seriously involves asking whether theories we develop to provide knowledge about the world successfully refer to and identify the existents they name and are claimed to be about. Thus, epistemology is not independent of ontology. Indeed, in the history of analytic philosophy since the beginning of the twentieth century debates over the theory of reference and nature of meaning have been central to thinking about the foundations of knowledge (Speaks, 2021; Michaelson and Reimer, 2022).

Whether economic theories provide knowledge of the world consequently depends on whether their concepts identify what they refer to. Nonetheless, much of current methodology and philosophy of economics is concerned almost solely with epistemological issues as if ontological issues can be bracketed off and set aside. Its chief subject is what we can know about rationality. This puts the cart before the horse since it leaves unaddressed whether there exists something to which rationality can be ascribed. Indeed, whatever rationality might be depends on what kind of existent might exhibit it. Of course, rationality is assumed to apply to real-world individuals, and the *Homo economicus* rational individual conception is assumed to refer to these individuals. Yet if it cannot be shown that this conception successfully identifies real-world individuals, rationality ends us being an idea that does not apply to anything, or perhaps to anything and everything as the rationality theorist prefers. In that case, it is fair to ask: What "knowledge" about the world does rationality theory provide?

To identify something we name and refer to, we must first ask what kind of thing it is. A "thing" is something distinct and independent from other things – something that has the property of being single. Thus, the kind of thing that *Homo economicus* refers to is single individuals understood to be distinct and independent, first and foremost human individuals but also collections of individuals such as firms that act as distinct and independent economic agents like human individuals. Consequently, we can ask: Does the content of the *Homo economicus* conception as it is generally explained have the property of being a single, distinct, and independent thing? Most economists would say it must because it is the name used to refer to such individuals. However, naming and referring to something is not the same as showing that the ideas you use for this do what you say they do. I will argue below, then, that the *Homo economicus* individual conception does not include content that allows us to say individuals are distinct and independent. Consequently, it fails to identify them in this way and fails what I have called, in identity terms, the individuation criterion (Davis, 2003b, 2011).

The *Homo economicus* conception is also taken to refer to individuals who live extended lives since individuals and firms are said to make choices they expect to affect themselves in the future. Thus, the *Homo economicus* conception also needs to include content that shows us that it refers to the same distinct and independent individuals over time, despite that many of their characteristics change. Again, most economists believe the *Homo economicus* conception refers to re-identifiable individuals. Yet if it fails to show individuals are distinct and independent at one point in time, it cannot show they are at a later point in time and accordingly reidentify them as such over time. I thus argue that this conception also fails what I have called, in identity terms, the reidentification criterion (*Ibid.*).

These two identity criteria, individuation and reidentification, provide a minimal means of testing the referential capacity of individual conceptions in economics and thus a way of evaluating the scientific value of the theories that employ them. This may seem to be a highly philosophical, esoteric issue bearing little on current concerns in economics. However, whether the *Homo economicus* individual conception successfully identifies the individuals whose behavior economics investigates has actually become a key concern for practitioners in light of the emergence of the heuristics and biases behavioral economics research program and the reemergence and appropriation in complexity–computational economics of Herbert Simon's earlier behavioral thinking. In both cases, though in different ways, the preference concept central to the *Homo economicus* individual conception is given up, and individuals use simple rules to make choices and adapt to their environments. This is the idea that choice is context-dependent, an idea ruled out by the *Homo economicus* individual conception whose choices are context-*in*dependent according to rationality theory's independence axioms. Theories of the economy built around adaptive individual conceptions, then, are different in important ways from the theory built around the *Homo economicus* conception. So in fact, a philosophical issue has become paramount in today's economics.

Adaptive individual conceptions, then, are no less subject to the same identity analysis and evaluation as the traditional *Homo economicus* conception. Do they successfully refer to distinct and independent, re-identifiable individuals when we apply the same criteria to them? This chapter applies these criteria to the *Homo economicus* individual conception, and Chapters 3 and 4 apply them to adaptive individual conceptions.

Applying the two identity criteria to both conceptions involves carrying out an analytical examination of candidate individual conceptions. But there is another side to how we think about the identity of individuals in economics. Suppose that when we compare these or any other individual conceptions we conclude that a given conception satisfies both identity criteria, but we see that the way real-world economies are organized limits or prevents many people from behaving as distinct and independent individuals as understood in that conception.

This is the difference between what people are capable of in terms of how they are understood and what they are capable of in terms of what reality makes possible. We could be right theoretically about what people are in economic life and yet because of the way the world is also see that they lack the capability to act fully as independent individuals in whatever way we understand them. For *Homo economicus*, this is a matter of whether people can make free choices; for adaptive individual conceptions, this is a matter of whether they can freely adapt to their circumstances.

Both conceptions frame what individuals are in capability and freedom terms. What may attract many people to the study of economics is their belief in this vision of human life and their perception that it is central to economics as a particular kind of social science. They also soon see when they study economics that its explanations go hand-in-hand with designing policies aimed at expanding people's capabilities, however understood, and advancing human freedom. Contrary to the view that economics is a positive, value-neutral discipline, that it is built around what individuals might become makes it a value-laden discipline. Where many disagreements between economists often come to a head is in regard to what should be done and recommended to achieve this. But this depends crucially on what conception of the individual one adopts.

This chapter only addresses the first, analytical identity issue. The second issue regarding what promotes human freedom begins to be taken up in Chapter 3 in connection with a distinction between what I call "internalist" and "externalist" understandings of individual autonomy. That distinction, and that chapter's discussion of different recent mainstream efforts to reconceptualize what individuals are (provoked by behavioral economics' "reconciliation" problem), begins an examination of what promotes human freedom in regard to how societies are organized, given how individuals are conceptualized.

How is the rest of this chapter organized? The second section begins by evaluating the identity of the standard *Homo economicus* individual conception. It discusses (a) how the identity concept recently came into mainstream economics in connection with George Akerlof and Rachel Kranton's influential view of individual identity; (b) how the idea that the standard individual conception identifies distinct and independent individuals rests on a fallacious inference; (c) what a comparison of the representative agent concept in economics and psychology's social identity theory tells us about the relationship between people's individual and social interests; and (d) what Amartya Sen's alternative conception of distinct and independent individuals involves.

Section 3 of the chapter addresses the issue that divides the *Homo economicus* and adaptive individual conceptions: whether individual choice behavior is context-independent or context-dependent, and ontologically speaking, whether individuals are unembedded or socially and historically embedded economic agents. Since Maurice Allais' criticism of context independence (Allais, 1953), the central role the independence axioms play in securing rationality theory has been extensively discussed. However, this epistemological evaluation needs to be accompanied by an ontological evaluation of the commitments economic theories make about what individuals are. I argue, then, that the independence axioms' grounding in the *Homo economicus* conception is actually inconsistent with the idea that choice behavior is context-independent. This points us toward the adaptive individual conception which makes choice context-dependent.

The short Section 4 of the chapter asks what more there is to what adaptive individuals are besides being adaptive. Sen and Allais provide a starting point for thinking about this question by regarding individuals as reflexive beings who evaluate themselves and their own motivations. Yet what stuff individuals are made up of is left largely open. It cannot simply be collections of preferences since reflexive individuals are beings also able to evaluate their preferences. This issue is taken up in the following Chapter 3 on recent, mainstream strategies for reconstructing economics' individual conception that assumes behavior is context-dependent. Chapter 4 will ultimately propose that the stuff individuals are made up of are their capabilities.

2 The Concept of Identity in Economics

a The Akerlof–Kranton Initiative

Until Akerlof and Kranton's "Economics and Identity" paper imported the concept of social group identity from social psychology into economics (2000; see also Akerlof and Kranton, 2002, 2005, 2010), the concept of identity was hardly employed at all in economics.[1] Psychology, sociology, and anthropology had long employed social identity concepts in decades of empirical research devoted to determining the conditions under which people's social relationships influence their behavior. In psychology's social identity theory, people were shown to often change their behavior when influenced by the social groups to which they belonged. From an agency perspective, group interests then supplant or modify individual interests, and individuals accordingly do not always act as distinct and independent agents. Thus, importing the identity concept into economics came with significant challenges to the mainstream's long-standing commitment to the idea that only individuals are agents.

Akerlof and Kranton creatively addressed these challenges by saying a person's individual identity is their utility function, and then arguing that how people's social group identities mattered to them influenced how they individually maximized utility (Akerlof and Kranton, 2000; Davis, 2007a). People could indeed be concerned about and

---

[1] Sen's use of the concept, the most influential exception, is discussed below. The concept has seen wider use since Akerlof and Kranton's papers.

influenced in their choices by their social identities, or by the different social identity categories they believed applied to them (what Akerlof and Kranton called a person's "sense of self"), but this was simply another individual concern, or type of preference, that could be traded off against others they had in maximizing individual utility. Having social identities could have a place in economics, but in contrast to psychology's social identity theory individuals still always made all their own choices. In identity terms, maximizing one's utility was what identified a person as an individual agent.

In this respect, Akerlof and Kranton followed a well-established path earlier adopted in the social preferences literature that in a similar way had added a variety of different types of social preferences – for example, inequality aversion (Engelmann and Strobel, 2004) – to the utility function alongside the traditional self-regarding ones. However, this literature makes no special claims about the nature of individual identity. Akerlof–Kranton went further in implicitly making an ontological claim that people still had independent individual identities even when their social relationships significantly affected their behavior. Faced with the possibility that people could be strongly socially embedded, they simply fit the identity concept into the individual utility function – a bold, strategic move securing economics' traditional domain of investigation.[2]

Yet surely this does not fully capture how the world works since there are many well-recognized circumstances in which people make other people's choices for them, even when they say those choices are their own. Trivially, parents often make "choices" for their children, who learn to take them as their own. More importantly, across a whole range of social settings people make choices for others when they act as their delegates, representatives, and agents. Economics generally explains this in a way that assumes people still make all their own choices, such as in heroic interpretations of principal–agent theory that dismisses the idea that agents substitute their preferences for their principles' preferences. But in a world of specialized skills in which expertise is unevenly distributed, it seems there are many occasions when people identify with others who they allow to make decisions replacing their own.

---

[2] This also showed that economics seemed able to borrow from other social sciences with their often quite different theoretical commitments without changing or modifying its own theoretical commitments.

Thus, in regarding an individual's utility function as a person's individual identity – or as their personal identity – Akerlof and Kranton open the door to our asking whether the utility function as a conception of individual identity successfully identifies people as distinct and independent individuals. Does being a utility maximizer make one an individual? Why many mainstream economists seem to assume so is because utility maximizers by definition always maximize only their own individual preferences, not someone else's preferences. Yet notice that groups of individuals such as firms are also often said to maximize objective functions akin to utility functions. How, then, can utility maximization name and refer to single individuals and groups of individuals at the same time? Does utility maximization identify both individuals and groups, or either ... or neither?

b The Fallacy of Self-Reference

This calls for us to be clear about how the utility function individual identity conception needs to be stated if it is at least to identify single persons as distinct and independent individuals. Given that in many circumstances, people make choices for others, to say having a utility function makes a person a distinct and independent individual can only mean that their preferences and the utility function a person acts on are always that person's *own* preferences and utility function, not someone else's.[3]

However, this leads to a problem. To say that what distinguishes a person as an independent individual is something specific to that person, which is what using the word "own" does, simply assumes in a circular way the conclusion that needs to be shown. That is, in saying what distinguishes a person as an independent individual is what is specific to that person just says what distinguishes that person as an independent individual is what makes them an independent individual. There are two ways, then, of seeing what the problem is here.

First, the underlying reasoning constitutes an example of a well-known form of fallacious inference known as affirming the consequent.

---

[3] This applies no less to recent philosophical theories of preference, for example, as when seen as "total comparative evaluations" (Hausman, 2012), "overall comparative evaluations" (Engelen, 2017), or belief-dependent dispositions (Guala, 2012, 2019).

Box 2.1   A fallacious inference

If people act on their "own utility functions," they act as independent individuals. [1]

People act as independent individuals. [2]

Therefore, this must be because they act on their "own utility functions." [3]

Affirming the consequent occurs when for "If P, then Q" where Q is assumed to be true, we mistakenly infer that P must also be true.[4]

For the "own utility function" conception of the person, the fallacious inference is given in Box 2.1. We may hold that [2] is true, and that people can act as independent individuals. However, [3] does not follow. Why is straightforward. What inferences that affirm the consequent do wrong is exclude other possibilities that might explain why we might hold something like [2]. For that reason, such inferences are fallacious and are to be avoided. At the same time, this does not mean that we cannot infer something like [2], as I will show below in connection with an example of a valid inference taken from Ronald Coase.

Second, what else is problematic here is that the "own utility function" conception commits a version of what is known as the self-reference problem (Bolander, 2017). In philosophy, logic, and mathematics, self-reference occurs when a concept or conceptual system reflexively refers only to itself rather than what it is supposed to be about and thus fails to generate any explanation of what it is supposed to be about. An example from economics is J.M. Keynes's (1936) famous "beauty contest" where speculators try to determine the value of an investment based on what other speculators think about it. All one gets is a circular set of expectations empty of any determination of value of the investment. Another example from game theory is the "Holmes–Moriarty" problem in which two hyperrational players circularly refer to each other's strategies in determining their own strategies (Koppl and Rosser, 2002). Holmes' strategy is based on Moriarty's strategy, but Moriarty's is based on Holmes' strategy, etc. Self-reference problems, then, not only fail to explain what subjects they are about, but can also generate

---

[4] Affirming the consequent is unkindly called *modus morons* by some logicians.

sparadoxes, such as the famous Cretan liar paradox and "intractability" or "insolvability" of Gödel's incompleteness-type problems.[5]

Generally, then, the names we use refer to things other than themselves. A self-referential expression, however, refers not to something in the world but in a circular way to itself. When we speak of a person's utility function as their own utility function what are we referring to? We are just referring to the idea of a utility function. While the expression is meant to refer to real-world individuals and explain something about them in the content it ascribes to them as utility maximizers, it only refers to that idea itself.

A consequence of self-referentiality is that nothing essentially constrains us from arbitrarily applying this expression to anything in the world that one might like to claim has utility maximizing behavior regardless of whether it does. I suggest this partly underlies the tremendous versatility and appeal of utility function reasoning in mainstream economics. Since the idea does not hook onto the world, it can be applied to whatever economists might want to call an agent: individual people, parts of people, groups of people, other animals, machines, nations, organizations, governments, communities, etc.

As Simon said more generally of rationality theory: "It is a gun for hire that can be employed in the service of any goals we have, good or bad" (Simon, 1983, pp. 7–8). What such expressions in economics need to do to avoid the self-reference problem, then, is be formulated in such a way as to instead refer to things other than themselves. Then, we may ask whether those expressions as they are formulated also successfully identify distinct and independent things. As an example of where this is done successfully, consider how Ronald Coase formulated and defined the firm as a distinct and independent thing.

For Coase, a firm is not defined as a collection of its *own* characteristics, say, its own assets as some might assume, but rather as a "collection of nonmarket exchanges" (Coase, 1937) – an expression that does not refer in a self-referencing way to what it defines. Instead, the idea of "nonmarket exchanges" – how people trade with one another without going through markets – describes something we can observe about the world without referring to firms to do so. Then we can

---

[5] In the case of the Cretan liar paradox, the problem is determining the truth or falsity of the statement made by Epimenides, a Cretan, "All Cretans are liars." If it is true, it is false; if it is false, it is true.

Box 2.2   Coase's inference

If we can distinguish different collections of nonmarket exchanges,
    we can refer to some of them as independent firms. [4]
We can distinguish different collections of nonmarket exchanges. [5]
We can refer to some of them as independent firms. [6]

---

observe there appear to exist distinct and independent collections of
nonmarket exchanges, associate some of them with what economists
call business firms based on the activities they exhibit, and name these
particular collections as distinct and independent firms.

The inference involved in Coase's case is not the fallacious affirming
the consequent inference, but rather the mainstay of inferential reasoning, the valid *modus ponens* inference that affirms the antecedent
(Box 2.2): Here, we affirm the antecedent, not the consequent, and
thus validly infer [6] from [4] and [5]. We can of course debate whether
we observe distinguishable collections of nonmarket exchanges and
also the merits of Coase's definition of the firm as such a collection.
However, in identity terms he provides a good example of a definition
of an independent individual (indeed a multi-person one) that avoids
the self-reference problem.

Coase's example tells us something important about successful
individual conceptions in economics. To avoid self-reference, they
cannot be formulated strictly in terms of individual or "own" characteristics. It follows that they need to make some sort of reference
to people's nonindividual or social characteristics. Coase's "collections of nonmarket exchanges" definition does this by interpreting
the individual firm as essentially a kind of social network. Firms
are independent (multi-person) single individuals because they are
certain kinds of distinct and independent networks of people. The
same reasoning can also be applied to other kinds of things made
up of many individuals, such as institutions, communities, governments, etc.

I hold, then, that this lesson applies to single persons as well as to collections of individuals. A non–self-referential definition of individuals
which successfully identifies them as single persons needs to define them
in terms of other than strictly individual characteristics. Like Coase's
firms, we might say persons are "collections of relationships" that are

different and distinguishable from one another that we can observe in examining the world. When we use the name individual to refer to a person and identify them through these relationships, ontologically speaking we employ a *relational conception of individual identity*, not an *atomistic* one, that makes individuals socially embedded, not unembedded beings. I lay out such a conception for economics in Chapter 4.

One reason perhaps why the "own utility function" individual conception has had so much appeal in economics – an epistemological one – is that it eases construction of formalized explanations and modeling in economics (as discussed in Chapter 1). Since it is formulated only in terms of the concept of preference, it is comparatively simple logically to work out a complete account of behavior based upon elaborating a set of consistent logical axioms governing it. This was done relatively early in the development of formal utility reasoning, culminating in the "von Neumann–Morgenstern utility function theorem" which states that if the axioms of completeness, transitivity, independence, and continuity are all satisfied, any set of preferences is "well ordered" and can be represented by a distinct (monotonic) individual utility function (von Neumann and Morgenstern, 1944).

In contrast, a socially embedded individual explanation is more complicated because it needs to be formulated in terms of two different types of characteristics of people – their individual and social characteristics. How these two types of characteristics are related cannot be explained in a purely abstract, logical "well-ordered" way, and calls for empirical as well as theoretical investigation. This is one way to think about the emergence of experimental economics, which has investigated empirical disconfirmations of the standard axioms underlying the utility function individual conception.[6] But we still need a theoretical understanding of how people's individual and social interests or characteristics relate to one another. A possible pathway that may address this is representative agent theory. In fact, the concept of a representative agent is employed in both mainstream economics and social identity theory, which I compare in Section c.

---

[6] As in early research on the ultimatum and public goods games, see Angner (2012).

c Representative Agents in Social Identity Theory and Mainstream Economics

Social identity theorists argue that, as members of social groups, people may appear to act as individuals and appear to behave independently, but instead often act as others would have them act and as the interests of those groups dictate. They thus act and choose from the perspective of those groups, engage in "in-group" behavior, and function as representative agents of those groups (Tajfel and Turner, 1986). They are still nominally independent individuals, but in acting as representative agents of social groups they put social interests ahead of their individual interests. Empirical research on this dates back in the early postwar period to the famous 1950s "Robbers Cave" experiment, which showed that especially when individuals find themselves in uncertain, zero-sum-type situations, they can act in the interest of social groups rather than as independent individuals (Sherif et al., 1954/1961; Baumeister and Vohs, 2007; Schofield, 2010). Research since then has shown that "in-group" behavior is common and widespread. Compare this thinking, then, to how mainstream economics employs the representative agent concept.

Mainstream macroeconomics' dynamic stochastic general equilibrium (DSGE) model's representative agent concept treats the choices of many individuals as identical and equivalent to the choice of one single representative individual (Lucas, 1976), and heterogeneous agent New Keynesian (HANK) models do the same only with multiple representative agents (Kaplan and Violante, 2018; Kaplan, Moll, and Violante, 2018). Similarly, mainstream microeconomics theory of the firm assumes that firms act as a single agent representing all the individuals that make them up, and the theory of the household assumes that households act as a single agent representing all their family members (Becker, 1981).[7]

---

[7] Hoover (2012) distinguishes noneliminative and eliminative representative agents. Starting with heterogeneous agents and imposing additional restrictions that allow aggregation is a *noneliminative* approach to the representative agent – individual agents are not eliminated, but are just restricted in such a way that their aggregate behavior is *as if* there were only one agent. In contrast, simply assuming there exists a single representative agent is an *eliminative* approach – it eliminates individual agents from the model altogether. I thank Wade Hands for alerting me to Hoover's distinction. On the representative agent concept, see Kirman (1992).

This representative agent thinking is quite different from that employed in social identity theory. The mainstream concept is primarily a model-simplifying device that aggregates together many particular individuals in order to treat them together as a scaled-up or generalized utility maximizing agent. No reference to social groups or social interests is then needed, because the collection of individuals which the representative agent stands for is simply replaced by that agent. Moreover, because representative agents are taken to adequately stand for many particular individuals, this assumes that these collections of individuals have no properties over and above those of the representative individual.

The rationale for this is that if all individuals are essentially alike, aggregating them as a single representative individual is only a formal simplification without substantive meaning. Yet, the evidence we have from "Robbers Cave" and social identity theory research is that sometimes when a collection of real-world individuals perceive they share social group identities, and do not behave as independent individuals. Then these collections of individuals have additional social group properties that the aggregative representative agent concept does not capture, and it would not be the case that independent individuals can be represented as a single representative agent with the same characteristics. So, although the mainstream takes the representative agent idea to be a model-simplifying device, behaviorally speaking it is more a means of blocking off the idea that like individuals have social interests that go along with their individual interests.

The issue of whether aggregations of individuals should be understood in this reductionistic way has not been entirely ignored in the mainstream, as shown, for example, by the literature on how information cascades operate across individuals (e.g., Banerjee, 1992; Bikhchandani et al., 1998). In that literature, if real-world individuals are assumed to be like one another in some important way and also know this, this can result in social group or "herd" behaviors when they take others' choices into account in making their own choices. Yet, in contrast to social identity theory where people identify with others, cascade theory maintains the Akerlof–Kranton assumption that people's individual identities are solely their utility functions. They accordingly do not identify with others but instead draw on other individuals' information. That is, cascades are information cascades, not identity cascades.

Thus, while there are social aspects to what the representative agent literature models, like the social preference and Akerlof and Kranton's initiatives, those aspects still presuppose the standard self-referential individual conception. How, then, can we make individuals' social involvements and interests a factor in explaining individual behavior or what individuals are? In Section d, I discuss how Amartya Sen goes about doing this.

d Sen's Alternative Account of Individual Identity

Sen first advances his conception of individual identity in his "Goals, Commitment, and Identity" paper (Sen, 1985), published fifteen years before Akerlof–Kranton's first paper. As the latter point out (Akerlof and Kranton, 2000, ftn. 1), Sen did not make identity an argument in the individual utility function but used the identity concept in a different way. He allows that people can act on utility functions – and distinguishes three types of utility functions in terms of their degrees of "privateness" – but also says people can make commitments to others that ignore personal gain or loss. Commitment to others for him involves identifying with them as that idea is understood in social identity theory (Davis, 2007b). Indeed, Sen's concept of commitment includes identification not only with social groups but also with other individuals through one's social relationships such as friends, family members, coworkers, etc.[8]

Sen thus divides the individual into four different types of selves that a person has and can act on. The three utility function types progress from narrower to wider forms of individual interest or self-regardingness: self-centered welfare, self-welfare goal, and self-goal choice. Commitment goes beyond the last in replacing even the broadest individual interest with social interest. For Sen, acting on social interests also takes us into the domain of ethics which deals with what people believe they ought to do rather than what they want or prefer to do.[9]

---

[8] Social psychologists distinguish categorical social identities, involving social groups a person identifies with, and relational social identities, involving other individuals a person identifies with in social relationships, for example, in families, places of employment, communities, etc. (see Brewer and Gardner, 1996). These two types of social identification need not be consistent with one another (see Davis, 2021).

[9] This reflects his belief that ethics and economics are connected in many ways (Sen, 1987).

Box 2.3   Sen's inference

If we observe different collections of selves, we can refer to them as
  distinct and independent individuals. [7]
We observe different collections of selves. [8]
We can refer to them as distinct and independent individuals. [9]

If people have multiple selves, can they nonetheless still be regarded as single individuals? I argue that Sen's reasoning parallels Coase's. Coase's premise was that if can we distinguish different collections of nonmarket exchanges, we can refer to them as independent firms (Box 2.2). Sen's premise is that if we can distinguish different collections of selves, we can refer to them as independent individual persons (Box 2.3). Both Coase and Sen say we can distinguish such collections, and conclude we can refer to them as independent firms/individual persons.

This of course leaves open for both why we would want to refer to these different collections as independent firms/individual persons, and this is where their theories of individuality come into play. For Coase, arguably implicit in his argument is that what makes different collections of nonmarket exchanges independent firms is that people are involved in managing and organizing them as such. There is no circularity in this inference since it does not employ the firm's *own* characteristics to say what firms are. Rather, the idea that people engage in such activities and exhibit what might be called a capacity to do so comes from thinking about people generally.

If a capacity is what Coase has in mind, he is not explicit about it. However, Sen is explicit about the sort of capacity involved, and thus about why we should think different collections of selves can function as independent individual persons. The capacity human beings possess to manage and organize the different kinds of selves people exhibit is what he calls a "reasoning and self-scrutiny" capacity (Sen, 2002, p. 36). Then, the single "self" is what reasons about and scrutinizes these selves. As he puts it:

Our choices need not relentlessly follow *our* experiences of consumption or welfare, or simply translate perceived goals into action. *We* can ask what *we* want to do and how, and in that context also examine what *we* should want and how. (*Ibid.*; emphasis added)

That is, Sen simply holds that human beings possess a specific kind of cognitive capacity which goes beyond simple instrumental calculation, and involves how any person can take a stance toward their different goals and compare and relate them to one another. That is, what makes this specifically a human capacity is its reflexive character. If animals have capacities to recognize objects in their environments, people also have that capacity including being able to examine their different goals as objects in their environments. Again, there is no circularity in this inference since it does not employ the individual person's *own* characteristics to say what individuals are. Rather what underlies the inference is a capacity human beings are said to have.[10]

Simply being able to exercise this reflexive capacity, then, even if a person does not always do so, is what in Sen's multiple selves individual conception individuates and identifies people as distinct and independent individuals. We are as human beings in principle always able to "ask what *we* want to do and how, and in that context also examine what *we* should want and how." But does Sen's individual conception also allow us to reidentify individuals through change? If people have a capacity to manage and organize their different selves, but over time fail to use it, then we cannot reidentify them as distinct and independent individuals.

For Sen, then, this is a difference between what people can be and do in terms of their capacities, and what capabilities they develop based on their capacities for what they are and do. As argued above, it means that individuality is not just something we explain analytically, but is also something that needs to be realized employing a normative analysis that investigates how societies are organized to influence what people can be and do. In effect, while Sen's conceptual analysis explains what individuals are by describing how they stand outside and evaluate themselves, a normative analysis emphasizing realization of individuality focuses on our standing outside how societies function and evaluating how they succeed or fail in promoting this realization.

Sen does not make significant use of the idea of individuals being adaptive in regard to how people move back and forth between their different individual selves. Nonetheless, that on one occasion a person

---

[10] Thus, for both Coase and Sen anthropological assumptions underlie their individuation arguments. For the anthropological emphasis in Sen's capability thinking, see Giovanola (2009) and Erasmo (2021, 2022).

might be self-regarding in some way and on another occasion instead be other-regarding tells us that the circumstances people face influence them and they can be seen to adapt to them. To say people are adaptive is basically just to say that their environments affect their choices and behavior. In terms of rationality theory, context matters implying we must give up the standard independence axioms if we are to replace *Homo economicus* with a more realistic conception of the individual in economics. Section 3 turns to this issue.

3 Context Matters: Putting the Horse Back before the Cart

The *Homo economicus* individual conception employs two independence axioms, one for riskless choices – the independence of irrelevant alternatives (IIA) axiom – and one for risky choices – expected utility theory's independence (IA) axiom. The axioms and the idea that choice is context-independent are logically required for the *Homo economicus* conception, since according to the von Neumann–Morgenstern utility function theorem, utility functions only exist when the standard axioms governing preferences are satisfied (von Neumann and Morgenstern, 1944). Once this axiomatic bedrock associated with the idea of people having "stable, well-ordered preferences" is given up, the *Homo economicus* conception falls back into its traditional informal asocial, unembedded individual meaning that predated economics' postwar logical turn. As argued above, that conception rests on a fallacious inference regarding individuals being distinct and independent, defines individuals self-referentially in terms of their own utility functions, and fails to identify the real-world individuals it claims it names.

   Much of the recent literature on preferences and in behavioral economics gives up the independence axioms, if not always noting this or that doing so undermines the basis for the *Homo economicus* conception. It thereby develops new thinking about economic behavior without an account of who or what that behavior belongs to, or risks inconsistency in ascribing that behavior to the traditional asocial individuals view. If this seems putting the horse before the cart, then what is called for is a serious examination of what economic individuals are and what sort of individual conception can explain the economic behavior that is observed. That is, it calls for first revisiting *Homo economicus* and putting the horse back before the cart.

This section gives two reasons, one associated with each axiom, for why these axioms in themselves should be abandoned. I argue in Section a that the IIA riskless choice axiom is conceptually incoherent and in Section b that the IA risky choice axiom is highly unrealistic. The IIA axiom is in some ways more fundamental because it embodies in a simple way the idea that choice is purely subjective. The IA axiom is important because most choices are risky choices so the axiom underlies much mainstream economics research.

The purpose of the section is to help build the philosophical foundations of an embedded individual conception that goes beyond *Homo economicus*. This discussion also introduces Chapter 3's review of four recent mainstream strategies for reconstructing what individuals are that attempt to revise *Homo economicus* but assume choice is context-dependent – two that address the IIA axiom and two that address the IA axiom.

a The Incoherence of the Independence of Irrelevant Alternative Riskless Choice Axiom

There are different formulations of the IIA axiom, but an often-used, clear way of stating it is: If x is preferred to y, introducing a third option z cannot make y preferred to x. Consider what the axiom requires. If we rule out that the introduction of some z changes the comparison of x and y, then that comparison has to stand no matter how the world might be organized. This implies either that people just subjectively stick with their comparisons no matter what, or that they factor in all imaginable effects of additional possible options being introduced. Both responses ignore the evidence that how choices are "framed" influences choice, as illustrated by how the ordering of food items in cafeteria lines often changes what people prefer (Thaler and Sunstein, 2008), or what has been called the decoy effect (or asymmetric dominance effect) studied in business marketing, where a person, say, selling something can manipulate another's choice buying something, by structuring a menu of choices in the former's favor (Angner, 2012, pp. 38–42).

At the heart of the IIA assumption is the idea that people determine their preferences in a completely private way without any reference to factors external to them. My argument that this is incoherent is adapted from Ludwig Wittgenstein's famous critique of the idea of a private language (Wittgenstein, 1953, §§243–271; see Candlish and Wrisley, 2014). Before he advanced it, many philosophers had believed that the way people understood language was to associate the meanings of words with sensations they privately experienced. One knew that "dog" referred to what people called dogs because one associated this with the private sensation one had of seeing dogs when the term "dog" was used. Language thus worked through a kind of private–public interaction – private sensations and public language working together through some sort of associational psychology. Wittgenstein argued, however, that this view made no sense.

> The words of this language are to refer to what can be known only to the speaker; to his immediate, private, sensations. So another cannot understand the language. (Wittgenstein, 1953, §243)

That is, if sensations are truly private, then they cannot be associated with public meanings, and an "inner" private psychology provides no basis for language.

With the IIA axiom, then, subjective preferences are essentially private sensations since the axiom requires that the comparison of any x and y must occur apart from the presence of anything external to this comparison in the form of another option z. These comparisons must thus constitute a "private language" that is neither meaningful nor language. More generally, from a contemporary philosophical point of view, the whole idea of private sensations and an "inner" private psychology on which the subjective preference idea is modeled is a throwback to a now discredited theory of perception built around the private "sense data" concept (Hatfield, 2021). Indeed, the modern concept of preference not only solidified in the 1930s ordinalist neoclassical economics, but also in disregard to any attention to what its philosophical foundations might be.

Yet, concern about the problematic nature of the private preference concept has not been entirely absent from economics and found prewar expression in Paul Samuelson's insistence that choice theory should be "freed from any vestigial traces of the utility concept" (1938, p. 71). In his alternative revealed preference theory, any particular bundle of goods a person selects only needed to be seen to be "revealed preferred" to any other bundle they could select (see Hands, 2014). Samuelson was skeptical that a theory of choice based on a psychology of the unobservable workings of the mind was scientific.

He did not argue in the manner of Wittgenstein that the idea of private preference is incoherent, but his emphasis on observability has the same basis as Wittgenstein's understanding of language as shared meaning.[11]

Since the 1970s, the revealed preference theory has been a research workhorse of economics' demand theory. Oddly, until the 1980s and 1990s emergence of new behavioral economics' emphasis on reference dependence, the IIA axiom and context-independent choice remained a mainstay of traditional utility function reasoning and economics instruction as if it were consistent with revealed preference theory and its underlying assumptions were unproblematic.

Consider, then, how the concept of context operates in Wittgenstein's argument. For him, language meaning must be socially shared meaning. He expressed this in his definition of meaning in terms of use.

For a *large* class of cases – though not for all – in which we employ the word "meaning" it can be defined thus: the meaning of a word is its use in the language. (1953, §43)

The concept of use has an ancient but straightforward understanding. What has a use and is useful are the means people employ to achieve their goals. Yet, whether something works well in achieving a given goal also depends on the context in which it is applied. Thus, to say the meaning of a word or an expression is its use in language presupposes both shared experience about how meanings are used and incorporating how the context of application influences the meaning of a word or an expression. That is, how a system of socially shared meanings is tied to their use is always context-dependent.

Any choice over some x and y, then, since it is motivated by the goal of utility maximization, considers their comparative usefulness for that goal. That is, the meaning x and y have is their use. But on Wittgensteinian argument above, use presupposes both socially shared experience about what usefulness means in regard to achieving any goal and also an ability to incorporate how the context of application influences what usefulness means in regard to that goal. Yet, the context independence principle limits choice to the comparative

---

[11] Samuelson also argued against the risky choice IA version of the independence axiom (see Moscati, 2016), so he was also skeptical of the independence idea *per se*.

usefulness of x and y, ignoring how any contextual z may influence their comparative usefulness.

Thus, the IIA axiom misrepresents the nature of choice and relies on incoherent conceptual foundations. Wittgenstein's critique of private language allows us to diagnose its failing as deriving from a confused understanding of subjectivity as intrinsically private. This does not imply nor would we want to say that people do not have subjective experiences. It only implies that the meanings they use to describe them which make it possible for them to choose between options are socially shared, where that comes with a sensitivity to the contexts on which they depend.[12]

b The Unrealisticness of Expected Utility Theory's Risky Choice Independence Axiom

A different argument regarding why context matters applies to risky choices (or gambles) and the independence axiom (IA), or "sure thing" principle, underlying expected utility theory (EUT). A serious challenge to the IA was mounted early on by Maurice Allais who designed a choice problem counterexample to the IA showing that how people were likely to make choices is inconsistent with the axiom and EUT predictions (Allais, 1953; see Heukelom, 2015). Allais presented the problem to Leonard Savage, whose *The Foundations of Statistics* (1954) had codified EUT. When Savage failed to choose as his theory predicted, he responded that one ought to adopt a normative stance toward the IA, where to be rational people ought to choose in such a way as to avoid the sorts of choices Allais described (Moscati, 2018, pp. 294ff). What Savage believed important was explaining the world in terms of rational behavior.

Most commentators on the "Allais paradox" have interpreted Allais' argument in epistemological–methodological terms as potentially an empirical falsification of the IA and in some respects rationality theory itself. However, Philippe Mongin (2019) showed that Allais was also skeptical about the IA and EUT on ontological grounds, because this assumed a "rational man" individual conception he believed did not

---

[12] I return to how a socially embedded subjectivity has and can be explained in Chapter 8. I regard the mainstream's philosophically primitive view of human subjectivity as one of its great weaknesses and a reason for it to worry about being a science bubble.

represent the "real man" individual conception he thought economics should employ. Mongin argues that whereas a "rational man" makes choices in an all-things-considered kind of way that ignores context, for Allais a "real man" is a "reasonable and prudent" person who answers for his choices however they may turn out and respects general rules of conduct. Allais did not further develop his view of the person, but the idea of answering for one's choices and paying attention to general rules of conduct is like Sen's emphasis on reasoning and self-scrutiny and the idea that one can stand outside oneself and reflexively evaluate one's individual interests and commitments to others.

What lies behind the difference between Allais' "real man" who sometimes sees a need to answer for past choices and Savage's "rational man" who does not? Savage follows Frank Ramsey (1926) and Bruno de Finetti (1937) in seeing probability judgments as thoroughly subjective. They consequently cannot be second-guessed. Therefore, people ought to choose as the theory has rational people choose. It follows that a "rational man" is a person who is always unhesitatingly willing to undertake gambles. Allais agrees people make subjective bets on the future when they make choices, but since he assumes they sometimes see a need to answer for them, he injects a principle of caution into what is involved in taking risky gambles.

At issue here are two conceptions of subjectivity and action. Note that whereas the riskless choice IIA axiom concerns the nature of people's preferences, the Allais–Savage exchange over the IA risky choice axiom focuses on individuals' subjective willingness to act. This understanding of subjectivity avoids the private language incoherence problem that applies to the preference-based IIA axiom, because it is not built upon an inner world private psychology. Instead, subjective willingness to act concerns how individuals see their life chances in light of their choices. Allais emphasizes caution and the need to be able to second-guess our choices. Contemporary Bayesian decision theory that derives from Savage offers one response to Allais in how decision-makers can adjust to unexpected circumstances through updating their prior probabilities to generate posterior ones as new information becomes available. Does this sufficiently address Allais' concern?

At issue is whose view provides a more realistic understanding of human action. That issue is inseparable from the issue of what the world is like – also an ontological matter. How people make decisions and act depends on the possibilities the world creates for them. People have a capacity to act and achieve goals, but it is not unlimited. Bayesian theory's response to this is its information updating principle. Yet this principle does not address circumstances in which a Keynes–Knight-type uncertainty prevails, where there is no way of knowing many things about the future, and people may have no grounds at all for assigning probabilities to future events (Keynes, 1921; Knight, 1921).

Savage recognized that Keynes–Knight uncertainty did not fit his risky choice theory. He differentiated between "small" worlds where his theory applies and "large" ones where it does not. Allais could then say that we were often in "small" worlds but that we are not always in them means we ought to be cautious, be prepared to second-guess ourselves, and perhaps pay attention to general rules of conduct. Savage did not accept this, because he argued when we encounter "large" worlds we can figure out how to treat them as "small" worlds. He referred to two proverbs – "look before you leap" and "you can cross that bridge when you get to it" – and essentially argued that when decision-makers encounter circumstances which were not immediately like small worlds, they can reconstruct them as small ones. After all, assigning probabilities to future events was a subjective matter, and it was thus up to the decision-maker to determine how the circumstances encountered should be valued.

Thus for Savage, and for most Bayesians today, large worlds really do not exist. Savage might have moved toward Allais had he not died young since his treatment of the two proverbs was informal. Kenneth Binmore (2009) suggests this and argues Bayesianism has become an unbounded philosophical principle extending Bayesian decision theory in ways Savage would not have intended. Indeed, it is hard to ignore the evidence that decision-makers often fail dramatically to anticipate unexpected events – especially in cases such as "black swans" (Taleb, 2007) in the 2007/2008 financial crisis. In those sorts of circumstances, decision-makers, practically speaking, find they need to put aside exclusive focus on scenarios they believe possible, and try – counterfactually – to imagine what they thought all but impossible (Feduzi, et. al., 2022). Then, for example, they might reconstruct the small/large world distinction by forming analogies to past cases (Gilboa and Schmeidler, 2001). Or in game theory terms, they might adopt different "frames" for interpreting their shared circumstances – a "variable frame" theory (Bacharach, 2006) – where which frames people adopt are determined by salience cues (Larrouy and Lecouteux, 2018).[13]

It consequently seems fair to say that there are two implications of all this: Context matters and individuals are adaptive. The IA axiom neither shows choice is context-independent nor provides a realistic understanding of human action. That is, it fails in both epistemological and ontological terms. The IIA and IA axioms raise different philosophical issues, but put together those issues make the argument that context independence is not a reasonable foundation for explaining choice behavior nor supposing people are *Homo economicus* individuals. What can we say, then, about what embedded individuals are?

4 What the Individual Is Matters, or Should in Economics

When context matters, individuals are adaptive and adjust to changes in their circumstances. Heuristics and biases behavioral economics expresses this by making choice reference-dependent (Kahneman, 2003). Simon captures it with the idea that choice "is shaped by a scissors whose two blades are the structure of task environments and the computational capabilities of the actor" (Simon 1990, p. 7). Yet, what does being adaptive tell us about what individuals are? The idea of being adaptive by itself does not tell us much. Indeed, proponents of the utility function conception of individuals might also want to say people adapt to their choice opportunities.

Sen and Allais, we saw, provide us something more to think about regarding what being adaptive involves. Reasoning ontologically, for them being adaptive involves people being able to take positions toward themselves. This reflexive capacity makes them more than just instrumentally motivated *Homo economicus* types of individuals. Saying people have this capacity gives us a reason to think of them as embedded in the world since taking positions toward themselves involves them seeing themselves in the world.

This understanding of what individuals are also tells us that people cannot be conceived of as simply collections of preferences. Individuals

---

[13] One thing such imagining exercises depends on is whether the distribution of the phenomena is normal or not, such as in "fat tails" types of cases that the 2007/2008 financial crisis made famous.

have preferences but they are more than that. I turn to what more this might be in Sen's thinking in Chapter 4. In Chapter 3, I first discuss four strategies for reconstructing what individuals are that take choice to be context-dependent, yet continue to essentially regard individuals as collections of preferences. At issue in this discussion is whether maintaining this standard view of what people are made up of still commits one to the utility maximizing conception of the individual. Given the self-referentiality problems this conception faces, it is then fair to ask whether these strategies ultimately end up maintaining the idea that people are unembedded subjective beings despite their giving up the independence axioms.

3 | From the "Reconciliation Problem" to an Individuality Reconstruction Problem

There was a time, not long ago, when the foundations of rational-choice theory appeared firm, and when the job of the economic theorist seemed to be one of drawing out the often complex implications of a fairly simple and uncontroversial system of axioms. But it is increasingly becoming clear that these foundations are less secure than we thought, and that they need to be examined and perhaps rebuilt.

Sugden (1991, p. 783)

Humpty Dumpty had a great fall.

English nursery rhyme

1 The "Reconciliation Problem"

The much discussed "reconciliation problem" is a product of psychology's influence on economics and behavioral economics' challenge to neoclassical economics. The problem is this: If behavioral economics provides new foundations for positive economics, positive and normative economics are no longer consistent with one another and need to be reconciled (McQuillin and Sudgen, 2012). Positive economics describes the behavior of economic agents; normative economics evaluates economic outcomes in welfare terms. In neoclassical economics, welfare recommendations are based on preference satisfaction. If agents' preferences exhibit various decision biases and heuristics and individuals often fail to act rationally, should policy recommendations be based on satisfying the preferences agents would have were they rational or satisfying their observed preferences?

One way of proceeding retains the traditional individualist welfare framework, modified as a new "Behavioral Welfare Economics" (Bernheim, 2008, 2016; Bernheim and Taubinsky, 2018), and argues it is the preferences agents have when rational that should count. This requires the standard individual conception be reconstructed to show

53

how people can still be seen to be rational beings. The argument is as follows. First, given that people do not always act rationally, we should distinguish their rational preferences when they do from the preferences they exhibit when they do not. Second, we should identify people's rational preferences with their "true" selves. Third, in making welfare recommendations we should set aside people's observed preferences and formulate those recommendations so as to satisfy the preferences agents would have were they rational.

The crucial second step reaffirms the standard utility function individual conception, modified now with a two-tier treatment of preferences to produce a "dual selves" reconstruction of individuals. Whereas Akerlof and Kranton equate individual identity with the standard utility function, the dual selves approach equates it with the utility function of an "inner" rational self. In effect, the dual selves approach inserts the neoclassical *Homo economicus* individual inside behavioral economics' *Homo sapiens* individual (Thaler, 2000), but makes the former the true self, thus restoring rational behavior as the foundation of economic policy.

What underlies this dual selves individual conception is an insistence that how people behave needs to be understood in terms of how they ought to behave (Hands, 2012a). How they ought to behave is a matter of what being rational entails, which is a matter of behaving as *Homo economicus* individuals. This recalls how Savage, when confronted by Allais with evidence that his choices were inconsistent with what his subjective expected utility theory predicted, asserted that his theory still held because it explained how people rationally ought to choose. What justifies this response? Only the claim that people ought to be regarded as rational *Homo economicus* individuals. Contrary to the long-held idea that economics is a value-neutral, positive science, this proposed rescue of *Homo economicus* and traditional welfare economics rather requires that positive economics be normative.[1]

The dual selves initiative preserves the key axiom underlying the utility function individual conception discussed at the end of Chapter 9, namely, that people's preferences, or now their "true" inner preferences are context-independent. In light of the evidence that people's

---

[1] I examine the nature of economics as a normative discipline and how it revolves around two different views economists have about individuals in Chapter 7.

preferences are context- or reference-dependent, to preserve the standard view one needs to analytically remove from their description any factors associated with their being context-dependent. Much is at stake here since if preferences are context-dependent and the *Homo economicus* explanation of behavior is jeopardized, traditional economic thinking is also suddenly at risk. How would one explain supply-and-demand equilibrium reasoning without assuming people are rational?

Nonetheless, there is considerable evidence that people's preferences exhibit context dependence, and this has also stimulated development of a number of new strategies that instead seek to replace the *Homo economicus* individual conception altogether with a *Homo sapiens* one. This chapter's main task is to review and evaluate four of these strategies for reconstructing economics' individual conception which assume in one way or another that economic behavior is context-dependent.

Section 2, however, begins by laying out Douglas Bernheim and Antonio Rangel's Behavioral Welfare Economics answer to the "reconciliation problem" where in contrast to the strategies that seek to replace *Homo economicus*, their goal is to rescue it. I look at (a) their dual selves response to the problem of present bias and weakness of will that creates a special challenge to rationality theory and the standard view of the individual; (b) how their "an inner rational agent" view entails what has been called a "preference purification" program and what this assumes.

Section 3 transitions to the strategies that seek to replace *Homo economicus* by comparing two broad approaches to the concept of individual autonomy. Whereas the individuation and reidentification criteria I use establish minimal requirements for how we conceptualize individuals regarded as distinct and independent beings, the concept of individual autonomy concerns what is involved in saying for individual conceptions that meet these criteria that individuals can also act freely. I label the two approaches I distinguish "internalist" and "externalist" views. For the first individual, autonomy derives from private subjectivity; for the second individual, autonomy derives from how economic and social institutions are structured.

Section 4 reviews the new strategies for explaining what individuals are. They all assume choice is influenced by context, adopt the "externalist" position, and make individual autonomy depend on how the economic and social world is structured. The four strategies are

(a) Roland Bénabou and Jean Tirole's *Homo sapiens* reconstruction of the individual that takes present bias, weakness of will, and the problem of self-control as its starting point; (b) Robert Sugden's analysis of teams and Michael Bacharach's "variable frame theory" of individual identity; (c) Richard Thaler and Cass Sunstein's libertarian paternalism view; (d) mechanism design's performing the economy theory.

All four strategies still regard people as collections of preferences, though their subjectivity is influenced by their social interaction. Here, there is a parting of ways between the heuristics and biases behavioral economics program and Simon's earlier behavioral economics program with its two blades of a scissors idea and rejection of the utility maximization concept. For Simon, people's choice environments require a much broader understanding of context than the heuristics and biases reference dependence approach. People's choice environments can be highly changeable, are always evolving, and are fundamentally uncertain – thus are more like Savage's large worlds. Chapter 4 turns to what this implies about what individuals are.

Section 5 briefly takes stock of what the new strategies discussed here accomplish and fail to address. Essentially, their commitment to a preference-based understanding of individuals limits their ability to develop an "externalist" approach to individual autonomy. I suggest this points us toward a nonsubjectivist, "externalist" conception of individuals that I associate with Simon's thinking. That is the entry point of the Chapter 4's elaboration of an alternative adaptive individual conception.

2 Behavioral Welfare Economics' Dual Selves View of Individuals

a Present Bias and Dual Selves

The heuristics and biases program has shown people's observed preferences exhibit a variety of psychological biases, show preference reversals, and demonstrate a lack of self-control. Especially problematic are present-biased preferences. Present bias exists when people myopically overvalue the present and undervalue the future, and make choices in the present they regret in the future – a problem termed weakness of will and *akrasia* in classical philosophy (Ainslie, 1992). When people express regret regarding their past choices implies they regard those earlier choices as mistaken or irrational. When their later selves regret their earlier selves' choices, they also effectively break up into multiple selves with conflicting interests as if they were different people.

Needless to say, people make many future-oriented choices including regarding insurance, pensions, savings plans, purchases of long-lasting goods, human capital investments, etc., that involve expectations of future effects. They are also usually assumed to be single selves, not collections of different people. Neoclassical economics and standard rationality theory, then, simply rule out present bias and assume people value all time periods equally. Paul Samuelson (1937) showed this requires a constant (or exponential) time-consistent rate of discount in which the valuation of future periods always falls by a constant factor. Behavioral economists, in light of considerable evidence that individuals display present bias (Frederick, Loewenstein, and O'Donoghue, 2002), employ what is termed a quasi-hyperbolic rate of time discount (approximating a hyperbolic discount function), irrationally preferring smaller, earlier gains to ultimately larger, later gains (Laibson, 1997).[2]

Bernheim and Rangel's Behavioral Welfare Economics adopts both discount rates. They allow people to behave irrationally and exhibit time-inconsistent behavior but assume that their inner rational selves behave in a time-consistent way. That is, people have psychological

---

[2] In fairness to Samuelson, though he saw the theoretical benefit of assuming a time-consistent rate of discount, he was skeptical that it was a realistic assumption, and believed it had "serious limitations ... which almost certainly vitiate it even from a theoretical point of view" (p. 159). More fully,

it is extremely doubtful whether we can learn much from considering such an economic man, whose tastes remain unchanged, who seeks to maximize some functional of consumption alone, in a perfect world, where all things are certain and synchronized. For in any case such a functional would have to be dependent upon certain parameters which are socially determined; 'effective' desire for social prestige, length of human life, life cycle of individual economic activity, corporate structure, institutional banking and investment structure, etc. In general, there is strong reasons to believe that changes in such parameters are not of an equilibrating nature. Even to generalise concerning these can only be done in terms of a theory of 'history' (in itself almost a contradiction in terms). In any case, this would seem to lie in the region which Marshall termed Economic Biology, where the powerful tools of mathematical abstraction will little serve our turn, and direct study of such institutional data would seem in order.(1937, p. 160)

Thanks to Wade Hands for drawing my attention to this passage.

selves and rational selves – a dual selves view of the person in which their rational selves are their "true" selves. It might seem that this is a kind of multiple selves view, but that is not the case. Their two-tier treatment preferences do not refer us to a person's different selves but are rather a means of setting aside people's observed preferences and identifying them with their rational preferences. This argument in its broad outline provides the underlying rationale for a variety of different dual selves models in economics (see Brocas and Carrillo, 2014). What they all share is the idea that individuals possess both rational and less-than-rational preferences, that the individual's rational preferences are the individual's "true" preferences, and that the individual's less-than-rational preferences are like noise from a rationality perspective. This idea that, in effect, preferences must be "laundered" to determine which are the individual's "true" preferences has been aptly termed "preference purification" (Hausman, 2012).

There are two main issues here: how people's rational preferences can be identified or elicited and what justifies regarding them as their "true" preferences. For Bernheim and Rangel (2007, 2008, 2009), people's "true" preferences are identified or elicited through a process of learning that justifies regarding them as their "true" preferences.[3]

b Bernheim and Rangel: "An Inner Rational Agent … Trapped Inside a Psychological Shell"

For Bernheim and Rangel, then, people face what they term a "generalized choice situation" in which there is a distinction between their real objects of choice and "ancillary conditions" surrounding choice. The latter concern a whole range of context-dependent psychological factors that distort choice by making it unclear what the real objects of choice are. When people form preferences on this basis, they fail to identify their "true" preferences and make mistakes in their choices. In effect, the "ancillary conditions" surrounding choice conceal people's

---

[3] An arguably more promising route to addressing dual selves issues involves embracing the idea that people possess different types of cognitive processing or selves that are engaged in intrapersonal and intraneural conflict (Grayot, 2019, 2020). Below in Chapter 8, I adopt a related view of intrapersonal processes but one instead premised on the idea of a human psychology situated and embodied and distributed in the world.

"true" preferences within these apparent but actually false preferences. Context-independent choice, consequently, is what people would engage in were they to learn that the "ancillary conditions" surrounding their choices are irrelevant to their determining their "true" preferences. There are two serious problems with this argument.

Since context-dependent preferences reflect psychological features of individuals but context-independent preferences are free of such features, this assumes that the former are psychologically motivated, but the latter are not. This leaves unclear how individuals would engage in a learning process that moves them from a psychological state to a nonpsychological state (Kahneman, 1996; Sugden, 2015). Indeed, though there is a vast body of research in education and social science on the nature of human learning processes, none of this plays a role in the dual selves view. In fact, there really is no theory of learning here at all, and the idea that people "learn" what their true preferences are acts more as a means of simply claiming they have rational preferences than as an account of a learning mechanism.

Even more seriously, it is unclear why acting on context-independent preferences is rational. The basis for the idea that acting on context-independent preferences is rational is the assumption that acting on context-dependent preferences is irrational. Yet, it is nowhere explained why acting on context-dependent preferences is irrational. Indeed, one could say that one's "true" preferences are context-dependent, as argued by proponents of the ecological rationality idea that decision-making is adapted to rather than independent of the decision-maker's environment (Berg and Gigerenzer, 2010). Even present bias can be seen as evolutionarily advantageous in a world in which satisfying immediate needs is often paramount for survival.

What justifies, then, saying people's context-independent preferences are their "true" preferences? The answer to this question, I believe, is tied up with the idea central to both the dual selves and the standard neoclassical views of the individual that only if a person's choices are taken to be context-independent can that person be regarded as autonomous individual. The concept of individual autonomy is of course much debated in philosophy and political theory, but surely, going back to J.S. Mill (1859), it includes the idea of being self-governing (see Buss and Westlund, 2008). In the case of *Homo economicus* asocial view of the individual, then, it seems basically to mean that a person makes choices free of interference from others.

I take up what individual autonomy is in the next section, but note that if people's choices are context-dependent, for proponents of *Homo economicus* we cannot be certain their choices are their own. This issue arose in Chapter 2 in connection with the neoclassical–mainstream understanding of representative agents. Accordingly, if people's choices are context-*in*dependent, because they derive from their own "true" preferences, presumably we can confidently say they are free of interference from others and must be their own. From this perspective, the image of the individual in dual selves theory is of "an inner rational agent ... trapped inside a psychological shell" (Infante, et al., 2016, p. 6; Sugden, 2015) where that "psychological shell" is a space in which a person is not safe from having their choices psychologically manipulated by others. Thus, people's context-independent preferences must be their "true" preferences.

The dual selves "inner rational agent" reconstruction of the individual thus derives individual autonomy from private subjectivity. Yet, it is not uncontroversial that a person's existence as an autonomous, independent being lies solely in their possessing a private, subjective existence. One might be free in one's private world but quite unfree in the public world. People's autonomy as individuals, then, has also been seen as socially determined. Indeed, if free private subjectivity is seen to be important to individual autonomy, this could be because human societies and social institutions have been developed to make it so. I turn, then, to two views of what individual autonomy involves.

3 Two Views of Individual Autonomy

Chapter 2 discussed whether individual conceptions successfully refer to distinct and independent individuals in identity terms. Whether individuals are autonomous concerns their agency and whether they choose and act freely. This issue is central to distinguishing the dual selves plan for rescuing *Homo economicus* and the four strategies for reconstructing what individuals are in the next section.

I suggested above that what justifies saying people have inner rational preferences is that this secures individual autonomy. When we associate this with having a private subjectivity, this gives us what I call an "internalist" view of individual autonomy. Yet, we can also say that people might be free in their private subjectivity but quite unfree in the public world. When we say economic and social institutions are what enable people to choose freely, we have what I call an "externalist" view of individual autonomy. Consider what each of these alternative views involves.

a The "Internalist" View

"Internalist" views assume that possessing a private subjectivity, understood in neoclassical theory and dual selves models as having stable, well-ordered rational preferences, is necessary and sufficient to explain individual autonomy. It is necessary because without this, a person could be influenced by others' preferences and their choices and actions reflect others' preferences. It is sufficient because if people possess a private subjectivity, what economic and social institutions exist is irrelevant to their being autonomous beings.

Key here is saying a person's preferences are private, where this means that each person has unique access to their preferences. The idea is they can say what their preferences are but others can only say what they are through what the person's reports or shows by what they do. However, this understanding of subjectivity is hardly uncontested, for example, in recent philosophy of mind and cognitive science that treats subjectivity as embodied and situated in the world (see Clark, 1997; Clark and Chalmers, 1998). I discuss this literature in Chapter 8 in connection with an alternative understanding of subjectivity, but here simply extend Wittgenstein's critique of private language discussed in Chapter 9 to the idea of a private subjectivity.

Thus, just as the idea of a private language as a kind of inner language is inconsistent with what we understand about language and meaning, so is the idea that a person has a unique, inner language regarding their preferences. Language and meaning, whatever their subject matters, concern how people communicate, and are thus inherently public in nature. If something cannot be communicated, it does not qualify as language and we have no basis for ascribing meaning to it. Individuals can certainly speak about what they each feel and prefer – indeed they have a relatively unique access to their own experiences – but the sort of privacy this involves, and how it is communicated, depends on its being expressed in a shared, public language. Thus, the idea of a private subjectivity cannot explain individual autonomy. Consider, then, an "externalist" grounding of individual autonomy.

b The "Externalist" View

In an "externalist" grounding of individual autonomy, economic and social institutions are the means by which individuals choose and act freely. Institutions are relatively settled, long-lasting sets of social relationships that take the form of laws, customs, norms, implicit and explicit rules, rights, practices, regulations, systems of social governance, etc. One example of an institution thought to promote individual autonomy is the market system and the laws that exist to enforce it. Another are liberal constitutional orders that promote individual rights.

It is not difficult to see that having social institutions believed to promote individual autonomy is often thought both necessary and sufficient for achieving this. Yet, it is unclear just what the argument is for thinking this. Obviously, the long and continuing human history of autocratic, undemocratic societies shows that economic and social institutions can limit rather than promote individual autonomy. Also, institutions that promote individual autonomy can do so for some and not others. So, institutions *per se* are not sufficient for promoting individual autonomy, nor in light of their complex and different effects on people is it clear what characteristics they need to have to make them necessary.

Thus, at best "externalists" can argue that institutions can promote individual autonomy when organized in certain ways, and then investigate what this involves. If we frame this in terms of which of their characteristics do this and which do not, we need to distinguish between autonomy-promoting and autonomy-limiting types of institutions and focus on conditions that favor the former. Looking forward, Chapter 5 discusses how societies stratified by social groups employ autonomy-limiting types of social institutions that constrain people's free capability development. In contrast, Chapter 6 argues that the United Nations Development Programme for expanding people's capabilities is built around autonomy-promoting types of economic and social institutions.

En route to Chapters 5 and 6, this one continues with discussion of four "externalist" strategies that all draw on behavioral economics heuristics and biases program for reconstructing what individuals are that makes their social relationships essential to their choosing and acting freely as single individuals. The lessons this review produces are the basis of one further "externalist" strategy for reconstructing what individuals are that draws on Simon's behavioral economics and Gerd Gigerenzer's recent ecological economics that open Chapter 4.

4 Four "Externalist" Strategies for Reconstructing Economics' Individual Conception

The four "externalist" strategies for reconstructing economics' individual conception discussed here all respond to the reconciliation problem. If individuals are present-biased and weak of will, how do we need to change our thinking about them to say they do not fragment into multiple selves? Determining this would "reconcile" positive and standard (welfare-based) normative economics and would escape the "true" preferences-observed preferences dilemma, because it would allow us to say what preferences count in policy recommendations. How these four strategies then proceed is to show how people act as single, unfragmented individuals in virtue of their social relationships. Thus, not only is individual behavior context-dependent, but individuality is as well, or rather, individuality is socially dependent.

The entry point for this overall strategy is the rejection of the standard view that economic behavior is context-independent. While each strategy assumes behavior is context-dependent, each approaches context dependence differently and works with a different understanding of how "social" is employed when referring to social relationships. This reflects whether what is objectionable about context independence is primarily the IIA riskless choice axiom or primarily the IA risky choice axiom. The first two strategies focus on the IIA axiom; the second two focus on the IA axiom.

a Social Interaction as a Model for Self-Regulation

Bénabou and Tirole's *Homo sapiens* reconstruction of the individual takes present bias, weakness of will, and the problem of self-control as its entry point. People have multiple temporal selves but exercise self-control and act as unified, single individuals through a process of self-regulation that harmonizes their different selves' competing interests (2002, 2003, 2004; see Davis, 2011, pp. 50–61). Their key assumption is that these different temporal selves can be modeled as if they were different people. Their "unified approach to social psychology" they offer consequently employs the same "underlying 'fundamentals' whether the individual is engaged in self-regulation or interacting with others" (Bénabou and Tirole, 2003, p. 159).

How they see social psychology's explanation of interaction between different people is similar to how economists understand principal–agent relationships.

> The common thread running through a variety of social situations is that one agent (or more) is trying to get another one (or more) to perform a certain task ... [while] the other party is interested in determining ... "what is in it" for them. In such settings, which economists refer to as principal-agent relationships, psychologists have studied two types of interactions (going in opposite directions) between an individual's self-view and his social environment. (*Ibid.*)

In the first type of interaction (going in one direction), between "an individual's self-view and his or her social environment," people try to influence others' opinions of themselves. In the second type of interaction (going in the opposite direction), others try to influence a person's self-view. For example, children may try to get their parents to see them in a certain way, while parents also try to influence their children's views of themselves. Consider, then, this social interaction explanation as a model for explaining the relationship between a child's present and future selves.

Children often lack self-control and are present-biased. Suppose the reason is that they lack confidence about what they can achieve. In effect, they doubt their future selves will abide by plans their present selves make. However, when treating these selves as if they are different people, imagine that a child's present and future temporal selves seek to influence one another and engage in "a game of strategic communication" (Bénabou and Tirole, 2002, p. 875). The child's present self wants its future self to honor its plans; its future self wants to judge those past plans as it chooses. Then in their "communication" these different temporal selves could signal each other regarding the value to them both of having shared plans – a kind of cooperative game – and were this signaling successful, each could become more confident about committing to those shared plans. The child's different selves would create a shared personal asset in the form of the overall person's self-confidence. For Bénabou and Tirole, high levels of self-confidence reduce present bias and weakness of will, and cause multiple selves to act together as single selves.

Of course, Bénabou and Tirole know a person's different temporal selves do not actually engage in "a game of strategic communication" with one another. Nonetheless, people do learn self-control, so something like a communication between a person's different selves could be said to occur. Factor in now that parents seek to teach children to become confident in themselves to teach them self-control. Since Bénabou and Tirole's "unified approach to social psychology" employs the same "underlying 'fundamentals' … whether the individual is engaged in self-regulation or interacting with others," we can say that "a game of strategic communication" between parents and children effectively causes children to engage in an imagined "game of strategic communication" between their different selves. Extending this argument beyond children and parents, friends assist their friends in this sort of way as well, so Bénabou and Tirole intend their theory to be a general solution to the weakness of will problem. With respect to any individual person, though there may not be something like a "game of strategic communication" between a person's different temporal selves, social interaction effectively guides people to learn the lessons of such games as if there were.

Bénabou and Tirole thus show how social relationships and social interaction could help individuals overcome present bias and exercise self-control. This involves giving up IIA (irrelevant alternatives) axiom, since parents and friends influencing someone's lack of self-control would essentially change the context in which that person chooses.[4] However, as a solution to the multiple selves problem, their strategy still has a significant problem. It leaves open that others and social interaction might work to exploit for their own benefit a person's weakness of will and instead reinforce their multiple selves fragmentation (Davis, 2011, pp. 59–61).[5]

This problem arises because they explain individuals strictly in terms of preferences. As collections of nothing but preferences, individuals

---

[4] In effect by introducing a third option that changes the person's ranking of their first two options.

[5] This is the problem of asymmetric dominance, called the decoy effect, where one party incentivizes another to change their preference between two options when a third option – the decoy – is introduced in a way that is to that party's advantage (see Angner, 2012, pp. 39–41). This practice is pervasive in marketing practices, and one of the reasons behavioral thinking has been successful in management theory. Thus, behind the veil of neoclassicism's context-independent world, we find the hard realities of business' context-dependent world.

have no other basis for evaluating themselves or others in making their choices. The preferences of a person's future self are just as important as those of their present self, and the preferences of parents and friends are just as important as those of who they influence. Self-control and being an unfragmented individual is a goal that accordingly can only have an accidental place in a world seen as simply collections of preferences. Note the difference between how Bénabou and Tirole explain self-control and how Sen explains it. Sen's conception of the identity of the person has multiple selves, but also invests people with a capacity to determine which of their selves they act on. People have preferences, but they are not only collections of preferences. Their capacity for reflexively evaluating their preferences means that their social relationships and social interaction with others have another dimension. Thus, what is "social" in individuality needs more structure than Bénabou and Tirole give it.

b Individuals as Teams and Team Reasoning

A second individual reconstruction strategy also addresses whether individuals fragment into different selves, but in this case into different social selves or different social identities. Thus, people make different kinds of choices in different social settings (households, work, etc.) and can appear to be entirely different individuals. Yet that they can distinguish what is required of them in one social setting compared to another and behave appropriately in each suggests they are still single individuals across those different social settings. There are two linked questions here. First, since social settings can vary considerably, how do people know how to act when moving from one to another? Second, if people's social interaction is important to what they are, how are they still single individuals?

The first question is dealt with by Sugden in his analysis of teams (Sugden, 2000, 2003). His examples of teams are tightly organized sports teams, but his analysis can be generalized to individuals' involvements in other kinds of social groups. Individuals on teams, then, are said to have "team preferences" reflecting the roles they have on a team. Accompanying these preferences is a kind of team-specific reasoning, whereby a person "endorse[s] a principle ... which prescribes acting as a team member conditional on assurance that others have endorsed the same principle" (Sugden, 2003, p. 165). All team members know what each team member should do, and all individual team members fulfill their roles on this understanding – a game theory common knowledge-type assumption with a prescriptive component.

Thus, the answer to the first question regarding how people know how to act in moving from one social setting to another is that each social setting frames a person's preferences according to a team-specific reasoning specific to that setting. Players know what their roles/positions require because everyone on a team understands what is required of them. In the case of less structured social groups, these mutual expectations regarding roles/positions also exist but may be less sharply defined than in the case of sports teams. Thus, people know how to act in any given social setting because the contexts they create convey the information needed to do so. Thus, the IIA axiom does not hold, because moving from one social setting to another introduces new options that influence choice.

This second question is if people belong to different teams and social groups, how are they single individuals? Bacharach, who was also interested in people's involvement in social groups, addressed this question in his general "variable frame theory" of social inter-action (Bacharach, 2006; also see Gold and Sugden, 2007; Larrouy and Lecouteux, 2018). He reported he had been puzzled by the discrepancy between what the standard prisoner's dilemma predicts and that people in everyday life seem to regularly escape the dilemma. His hypothesis was, confronted with the dilemma, people simply ask themselves "what should we do?" instead of "what should I do?"

To explain how this could work, Bacharach drew explicitly on psychology's social group identity theory that postulates that when people identify with social groups (and act as representative agents of those groups) they reflexively "self-categorize" themselves as members of those groups (Turner, 1999). Self-categorization ties "what should I do?" and "what should we do?" together, and also presupposes the person or "self" who does the self-categorizing. This thus makes people single individuals and at the same time social beings in virtue of their group involvements.

Bacharach further filled out his view as follows. On analogy to how teams are made up of many people, he argued the individual is also a team made up of the person's many different social group identi-fications. Consequently, just as on teams people work together, so individual people are teams in which a person's many social identifications work together. Self-categorization is the principle by which this person team functions. It involves a kind of reflexive reasoning capacity people employ in social settings. It complements Sugden's team endorsement principle that involves the reasoning needed to participate in teams/groups. Clearly again context matters and the IIA axiom does not hold.

Thus, whereas the utility function individual conception describes individuals self-referentially in terms of only their own characteristics, here individuals are described in terms of something additional to their own characteristics, namely, their social group identities. The individuation argument Coase makes works for this view, because we could observe people behaving as if they were distinguishable collections of teams, and then refer to those collections as different single individuals.

Bacharach thus goes beyond Bénabou and Tirole who describe people in terms of just personal preferences. He also adds to Sugden's idea that people engage in team-reasoning the idea that they engage in self-categorization reasoning. What is left unexplained is how and under what circumstances people are actually able to exercise this self-categorization capacity. Are there circumstances in which they instead defer to others to make decisions for them – an in-group-type behavior in which they cease to be distinct and independent individuals?

The inference in the last section is that social institutions and the social relationships can promote people being distinct and independent individuals if autonomy-promoting institutions have greater weight than autonomy-limiting ones. Thus, what else Bacharach's analysis requires is something about how social institutions are structured that makes this the case. If people can sustain their individuality in and across their different social settings, what does this imply about social institutions?

The two strategies discussed next for reconstructing economics' individual conception move to how institutions structure social relationships and affect individual behavior. This makes the IA axiom that concerns risky choice important, because how institutions affect behavior overall involves considerable unpredictability. Indeed, how a combination of autonomy-promoting and autonomy-limiting institutions affects individuality can be quite unclear until we observe how people behave. When our goal is promoting individual autonomy, we thus need to ask, if such and such institutional arrangements exist, what does this imply about how individuals are described?

c Libertarian Paternalism: Constructing Freedom

The autonomy-promoting institutional structure Thaler and Sunstein proposed (Thaler and Sunstein, 2003, 2008) called for policymakers or choice architects to design choice settings to "nudge" people into making rational choices when they fail to make them on their own (see Hands, 2020; Hausman, 2023). Libertarian paternalism, also termed "asymmetric paternalism" (Camerer et al., 2003), accepts the evidence that people's preferences often fall short of being rational preferences, but rather than locating a rational self within the person, choice architects reconstruct how markets work to "make choosers better off, *as judged by themselves*" (Thaler and Sunstein, 2008, p. 5; their emphasis) – or better off as they would judge when seeing what their best interests are.

People have a capacity to be rational despite present bias and weakness of will, as reflected in their only needing modest encouragement, or nudges, to behave rationally. This makes rational choice a socially rational choice, reflecting both the social point of view of choice architects and individuals themselves. People do not have isolated *Homo economicus* inner rational preferences, but instead the rational preferences of social *Homo sapiens* individuals.

That much depends on people coming to appreciate what is in their best interests puts emphasis on their changing their expectations of the future. They may be susceptible to a variety of mistaken beliefs about what is good for them, and overcoming these beliefs can be influenced by choice architects who better understand the long-term consequences of people's choices. Thus, it is the IA risky choice axiom that no longer applies. Choice is not only reference-dependent but socially reference-dependent as well.

On my reading of what Thaler and Sunstein, what they are doing is revising John Stuart Mill's (Mill, 1859) classical liberal understanding of the relationship between individual autonomy and freedom. Mill's view is "internalist" but makes self-direction rather than private preferences its foundation. For him, individual freedom (F) stems from the individual being autonomous (A) which requires they be self-directed (SD):

SD → A → F

Mill, then, was concerned that government exercise of power infringes individual autonomy, and argued that governments ought only to interfere in individuals' lives when they might harm others.[6]

Consequently, government ought to never limit individual freedom to prevent individuals from harming themselves. His grounds for saying this was his belief that individuals are always in the best position to know their own interest, because (i) they are the most interested in their well-being; and (ii) they know more about their best interest than anyone else. Respecting these two conditions would ensure people are self-directed (SD) and thus autonomous (A) and free (F).

While libertarian paternalists do not contest the condition (i), they offer considerable evidence that condition (ii) fails and people often do not know more about what is in their best interest than others. This is thus where choice architects come in, assumed to be rational – and benevolent – and as experts better informed than individuals themselves about what is in their best interest. Thaler and Sunstein can accordingly be seen as modifying Mill's harm principle to allow choice architects, and governments, to act in ways aimed at preventing people from harming themselves. This produces a modified understanding of individual autonomy (A'), derived from a modified or "nudged" view of individual self-direction (SD'), and a revised conception of individual freedom (F'):

SD' → A' → F'

If for Mill individual freedom derives from the self-direction alone, for Thaler Sunstein it derives from how others influence individuals' "self"-direction. That is, moving from SD to SD' effectively embeds others in a person's "self" who share in that person's "self"-direction.

Classical liberals as pure internalists are likely to deny that SD' counts as self-direction, reject A' as a concept of individual autonomy, and reject F' as a concept of individual freedom. Thaler and Sunstein reply by saying nudges make people "better off as *judged*

---

[6] His famous "harm" principle is:

the only purpose for which power can be rightfully exercised over any member of a civilized community, against his will, is to prevent harm to others. His own good, either physical or moral, is not a sufficient warrant. (Mill, 1859, p. 22) *by themselves.*" Who are they actually referring to? They cannot be referring to people subject to various psychological biases, because they believe that people who make irrational choices fail to judge how they are better off. Rather, they must be referring to people's "rational" selves in their new way and how people would judge what would make them better off if free from those biases. It follows for Thaler and Sunstein that choice architects only facilitate people's self-direction and do not interfere with it.

On this benign view of choice architects, libertarian paternalism should be seen less as paternalist and more as libertarian. If so, Thaler and Sunstein's concept of freedom F' is not as different from Mill's F concept of freedom as it seems. Still, Thaler and Sunstein's SD' idea clearly differs from Mill's SD idea since it explicitly embeds others in a person's "self"-direction. How can their individual freedom concept be like Mill's when their self-direction concept is quite different?

One strategy is to focus directly on what having a personal identity involves and explain this in terms of learning people do about their preferences in "self-constituting" themselves as reasoned sets of preferences (Dold and Schubert, 2018). This strategy recognizes the importance of "educational and cultural institutions" while tying learning to preference formation.[7]

Thaler and Sunstein do not take up this strategy, but Sunstein suggests one way to proceed is to substitute default rules for nudges and emphasize the idea of people "choosing not to choose" (Sunstein, 2015; see Davis, 2018b). In the case of nudges, choosers are not involved in the construction of the new choice settings. In the case of default rules, people choose to have others – experts in certain types of decision-making – make decisions for them. Then, "their" choices are nudged by those they choose to make decisions for them, though how they are nudged is broadly still their choice. The most general case involves what Sunstein calls "impersonal" default rules (ones that apply to everyone and most would elect), whose characteristics are as follows: The context of choice is confusing, technical, or unfamiliar; people typically prefer not to choose; learning is not important or useful; people are not particularly heterogeneous (Sunstein, 2015, p. 18).

---

[7] I return to learning in the Chapter 4 in connection with the idea of boosts as opposed to nudges, but do not make learning a matter of preference formation.

Where these characteristics obtain, default rules would be expected to make people "better off as *judged by themselves*."[8]

This raises the question of how the alternative individual freedom concept this involves differs from Mill's individual freedom concept. Consider Mill's two conditions for his harm principle. If behavioral economics shows people often do not know their own best interest, contrary to his condition (ii), a default rules approach provides a way in which Mill's condition (i) – that individuals are themselves the people most interested in their well-being – can be strengthened in compensation for giving up his second condition.

However, it is fair to ask: Might this trade-off nonetheless weaken individual freedom? If we interpret Mill's individual self-direction as a capacity people possess, then his argument is that their individual freedom relies on exercising this capacity. Sunstein's understanding of individual freedom is one in which the individual's ability to act freely is expanded by adding the capacities of others to act in the person's interest. Default rules for him strengthen rather than weaken individual freedom.

This makes F' foundational rather than self-direction which is foundational for Mill. Accordingly, Sunstein's choosing not to choose libertarian paternalism should be represented as follows:

$$F' \rightarrow A' \rightarrow SD'$$

Individual freedom is expanded when people adopt default rules and rely on others, in "externalist" terms a person's individual autonomy then rests on their relationships with others, and their self-direction enlists the guidance of others.

Let me summarize where this takes us. Like Benabou and Tirole and like Sugden and Bacharach, Thaler and Sunstein's libertarian paternalism shows how social relationships can assist people in overcoming present bias and weakness of will. They go farther in framing social relationships in institutional terms in their ideas about choice architectures and default expert relationships. Still, this institutional analysis is modest at best. For institutions to enable people to consistently behave in a more rational manner, surely much more needs to be said about

---

[8] For example, when people go to doctors, the default rule they put in place is that the doctors choose their course of treatment. By defaulting to the doctor to make such choices, the person is adopting the "choosing not to choose" default rule. Clearly, people rely on experts in a variety of circumstances in life.

them. That Thaler and Sunstein think little about this is evident in how casually they assume choice architects are generally benevolent.

However, there is a deeper issue associated with their libertarian paternalist reconstruction of the individual. To say people are able to behave rationally when social institutions are structured for this calls for an understanding of what having an ability involves. Yet, nudge/default analysis has little to say about ability. Indeed, Thaler and Sunstein largely ignore how people are able to adjust to new choice situations and understand adjustment in the standard subjective expected utility way: New choice situations simply activate new preferences. Yet, there is really nothing in this about what ability people might have to adjust to new choice situations. People miraculously know however things might change what they then prefer. The barrier, then, to explaining ability to adjust is that *Homo economicus* individuals are still only made up of private preferences. Thaler and Sunstein believe people are able to behave in a more rational manner, but if people are just collections of preferences, they lack any way of thinking about how changing choice architectures would actualize this ability.

While Thaler and Sunstein's reconstructing individuals by reconstructing freedom approach offers us little regarding how institutions affect individual autonomy other than that they matter, I argue in the following section that mechanism design theory takes their "reconstructing individuals by reconstructing freedom" approach via institutional change quite seriously. Here, mechanism design means comprehensive institutional (re-)design. The focus is on how economic and social institutions ought generally to be structured in such a way that autonomy-limiting institutions are replaced with autonomy-promoting institutions. Yet, the criterion for the latter is that people behave consistently as utility-maximizing individuals, ultimately leaving unexplained whether either individuals or freedom has been reconstructed.

d Performing the World: Mechanism Design Theory

Mechanism design theory is now a well-established economics research program with a wide range of applications including kidney exchange programs, hospital–residents matching, school choice systems, spectrum wavelength auctions, emissions trading schemes, voting systems, etc. (see Nir, Roth, Neeman, 2013). This method is to start from a desired set of objectives in strategic settings, and then design the mechanisms that would realize them – "the 'inverse' of traditional economic theory, which is typically devoted to the analysis of the performance of a given mechanism" and then determines policy recommendations (Hurwicz and Reiter, 2006, p. 30). Since mechanisms are mathematical structures intended to model real-world institutions, they can be developed for all sorts of interactive settings. Some of the theory's applications aim to improve the functioning of existing markets, where individuals, for example, are weak of will and short-sighted, but many aim to create markets where they do not exist or where nonmarket-based allocation mechanisms operate, for example, kidney exchange programs and school admission allocation programs. Thus, a guiding assumption of the theory is that only competitive markets allocate resources efficiently, so the standard competitive market model should be applied and extended wherever possible. Mechanism design aimed at changing institutions thus means designing them to function in a market mechanism fashion.[9]

Mechanism design theory involves another, different kind of response to behavioral economics' reconciliation problem. If people are subject to various psychological biases and the idea of an inner rational self is problematic, its individual reconstruction strategy is to institutionally reconstruct economic systems to motivate people to behave as rational individuals – a real-world reconstruction of individuals which makes the inner rational self the person's only self.

This goes well beyond libertarian paternalism's piecemeal, one-by-one approach to changing people's decision environments through nudges and default rules. The point in mechanism design theory is not to offset people's periodic expression of less-than-rational preferences. Rather, it is to engage in a far-reaching institutional redesign of the economic and social world to prevent such preferences from even existing. People would then no longer fragment into multiple selves whose status as rational individuals depends on choice architects and experts. Rather, once the policies of mechanism design architects have been implemented, they would function as rational individuals in virtue of their own choices.

---

[9] In the methodology literature on mechanism design, see Boldyrev and Ushakov (2016) and see Kyu (2016).

Thus, the relationship between mechanism design theory and context is complex. On the one hand, the evidence from behavioral economics that many choices are context-dependent is taken seriously. On the other hand, the aim is to restore context-independent choice through the market-based redesign of choice settings to ensure people only behave rationally. Systemically, this makes people's choices context-dependent or dependent on mechanism design architects, but at the level of behavior it makes choice context-independent.

We can explain this by saying that mechanism design theory is a performative type of theory whose response to the reconciliation problem is to give up science's traditional descriptive role that separates positive and normative economics, and describe the world as the theorist believes it ought to be explained. As in dual selves models, people ought to be seen to behave as *Homo economicus* utility-maximizing individuals. Thus, when economic systems are designed and implemented so that people are compelled to act as rational individuals, the evidence will then exist showing people can be described as behaving in that way. At this point, science's traditional descriptive role reemerges, albeit in a new way, since the evidence confirming the theory is no longer given by the world as in the traditional understanding of the relationship between evidence and theory, but is the product of the theory's intervention in the world. Thus, as a performative approach to science, mechanism design theory works in a self-confirming or self-fulfilling way whereby the theory produces policies that produce outcomes that – when those interventions are successful – produce evidence confirming the theory. As Michel Callon influentially put it, economics then "performs, shapes and formats the economy, rather than observes how it functions," so that the "real economy is embedded not in society but in economics" (Callon, 1998, pp. 2, 30).

However, in one carefully studied example, the Black–Scholes–Merton option pricing model, things did not work out this way. At first, the model was widely adopted in financial markets, and the resulting evidence appeared to confirm it. Yet, the model–evidence relationship subsequently broke down, and the model was abandoned, modified, or became just one more among many methods in financial traders' toolkits. Donald Mackenzie, in his careful investigation of the history of the Black–Scholes–Merton model and financial markets, shows that how models are adopted is complicated by their interpretation, how their adoption affects how they work, how this affects how markets then adjust, and a whole host of back-and-forth interactions between the model and the world which make idea that economics can simply "perform" the economy unrealistic. He characterizes Callon's view as a strong performativity thesis, or as a "Barnesian performativity" view, and distinguishes what he calls "counterperformativity," in which the uptake of economics in the economy feeds back on economics, often causing economic processes to be less rather than more like the way they are represented in economic models (Mackenzie, 2007; see also Brisset, 2016). We might thus say following Uskali Mäki that one reason why is that the "economy performs economic theory" as well (Mäki, 2013) – an interaction between an economics that aims to be performative and an economy that does its own performing.

Accordingly, if the relationship between economics and the economy is more like a two-way street in which each "performs" the other, then it seems mechanism design theory should similarly model the relationship between individuals and their environments in a two-way street manner. What individuals do affects their environments, and this can cause them to behave differently, which can affect their environments in new ways, which can again cause them behave in new ways, and so on and so on in continual sort of two-way street interaction between them and their environments. Further, if this sort of dynamic applies generally, then mechanism design theorists would need to regularly redesign their models, since as their revised models elicited further adjustments on the part of real-world individuals and changes in markets, they would need to do so again and again in a continual tinkering that inserts themselves as ongoing participants into the processes they design.

Thus, mechanism designers – and this also applies to choice architects and other experts – are reflexively part of the processes they seek to influence rather than standing outside it (as if with a view from nowhere). Not only does this show that the contexts economists construct are fundamental to the choices people make, but it also makes economists themselves part of the contexts they construct. People never make context-independent choices, but are always socially and economically embedded in their constructed contexts and the plans of those who create them.

Mechanism design theory, like the previous three individual reconstruction strategies, aims to show how people can be reconstructed as autonomous individuals. Its market design program makes it "externalist," but its *Homo economicus* basis paradoxically puts its strategy in service of an "internalist" understanding of individual autonomy. There is no escape from this dilemma. As long as people are simply collections of preferences, no other reconstruction of what they are is possible. Like libertarian paternalism, mechanism design theory assumes people have an ability to adjust to newly designed market structures, but again its subjectivism rules out including ability in its reconstruction of individuals.

5 Rethinking How Context Matters

The reconciliation problem is specifically a problem with the subjectivist utility maximization individual conception. Behavioral economics shows people's observed preferences are often context-dependent and they can fragment into many context-dependent selves, making it unclear who standard normative economics applies to. The response to the reconciliation problem in all four strategies above involves explaining how utility-maximizing individuals can still be seen to be single individuals once we address how context matters to them. All four individual conception reconstruction strategies say social interaction matters, where the two latter strategies add an institutional dimension to this via roles for choice architects and market designers.

These strategies share the assumption that people have an ability to adjust to changes in their circumstances. Yet when individuals are made up only of subjective preferences, adjustment is a black box that cannot be opened since we can never say how a person comes to prefer one thing to another when this is a subjectively private matter. Thus, if we suppose people being able to adjust to their changing circumstances is essential to their being autonomous beings – since otherwise we have no reason not to think they are simply conditioned by them – then these strategies will not tell us how people choose and act freely; however, we think about social interaction and institutional settings.

In terms of Savage's subjective expected utility theory, all four strategies seek in one way or another and assure us that people occupy small world environments in which current Bayesian decision theory applies, because this seems to be where choice is best explained. However, there is nothing in Bayesian theory that makes choice free choice. Surely, moreover, it is unrealistic to suppose people only inhabit small manageable worlds and never encounter large worlds with unpredictable uncertainties. To confine our thinking about individuals in this way thus seems to give us a very pessimistic view of individuality. If we cannot explain how they are able to adjust to new and unfamiliar circumstances, it seems we have not really reconstructed economics' conception of individuals.

The conclusion of this chapter and the first part of this book is that we cannot make much progress as long as we conceive of individuals as made up solely of subjective preferences. We need instead to see them as somehow made up of abilities, or as Chapter 4 will argue, capabilities. To introduce this alternative entry point, Chapter 4 begins with Simon's behavioral approach and the ecological economics of Gigerenzer and others, which employ a wider, large world conception of context that treats individuals' decision environments as changeable, evolving, and uncertain. This makes ability to adjust central to people being able to choose and act freely, and takes us away from a purely subjectivist individual conception toward a nonsubjectivist one. What more is then needed is an explanation of how adjustment works. I make the concept of reflexivity central to this and examine what this tells us about the nature of the person.

PART II

Building a Socially Embedded Individual Conception

This part of the book moves from the first part's critique of the standard atomistic individual view to an alternative conception of individuals as socially embedded, adaptive, and reflexive. A key difference is that people are made up of sets of capabilities, not collections of subjective preferences, and that their choices and actions aim at developing their capabilities. They may desire or prefer to develop certain capabilities rather than others, but what observably explains their behavior is their goal of developing their capabilities. At the same time, given an externalist understanding of individual autonomy, social and economic institutions, particularly when societies are undemocratic and favor some social groups over others, limit many people from fully developing their capabilities. I argue this produces two kinds of capability shortfalls, both of which can be targeted with economic and social policies designed to promote people's capability development, and also allows us to think about enhancing people's capabilities in the long run, which involves another level of policy thinking.

Chapter 4 lays out the book's adaptive, reflexive capability view of socially embedded individuals. An important reason we ought to see people as adaptive is that this provides a basis for explaining how they make choices and act in changing, often highly uncertain environments – large worlds rather than small Bayesian ones. When we accept that choice is context-dependent, we need to be able to explain individuals' behavior in the most demanding circumstances they can face. An implication of this framing is that, as in Simon's procedural rationality view, behaviorally speaking there is really no maximization – only continual adjustment over time. To capture all this, I use a *stock–flow, state description/process description* characterization of adaptive individuals and then model their behavior more specifically as a capability-choice/action-capability pattern of behavioral adjustment that works via a reflexive feedback loop. Given that this individual conception also needs to satisfy the two identity criteria I used in Part I to evaluate the standard *Homo economicus* individual conception,

I then show how an adaptive, capability individual conception successfully individuates people as distinct and independent. In light of how undemocratic economic and social institutions limit people's capability development, I also discuss the circumstances under which they can be reidentified as the same individuals over time.

Chapter 5 turns to social embeddedness, describes this in terms of two kinds of *social identities* people have, and explains how a world stratified by social groups produces two kinds of *shortfalls* in the capability development of people in disadvantaged social groups. First, a micro-level mechanism, social group stigmatization, or social identity stereotyping operates in *relational social identity settings*, limits stigmatized individuals' ability to develop their capabilities, and results in what I call *capability devaluations*. Second, a macro-level process, sorting people over club goods and common pool goods types of social economic locations, produces *social group inequalities* especially by race/ethnicity and gender, limits lower ranked groups' capability development, and results in what I call *capability deficits*. How these two kinds of capability shortfalls combine and reinforce a hierarchical ordering of social groups is explained using a basic complexity theory analysis from Simon. Combatting these two capability shortfalls – motivated by the goal of creating nonhierarchical, democratic societies that promote individuals' capability development irrespective of social identity – is associated with policies to eliminate social discrimination in the case of capability devaluations and to advance social group reparations in the case of capability deficits.

Chapter 6 moves from combatting capability *shortfalls* to expanding people's capability development through capability *gains*. In addition to promoting people's *basic capabilities* for what they can be and do, we can also promote their potential *enhanced capabilities* when societies are democratic and reduce social inequality. I argue this calls for envisioning the economy as a *capability generation process* rather than as income generation process (or preference satisfaction process) as the mainstream sees it. I address the relationship between democracy and capabilities, explain democracy in the social contract tradition as a system of public reason, discuss the nature of collective capabilities in terms of the idea of people forming collective intentions, and argue that this all entails seeing democratic societies as "open political systems" that allow for constant innovation and evolution in how diverse kinds of people settle upon and consent to rules that govern the decision-making practices they find functional to living together. Finally, since this is all inconsistent with the mainstream conception of private subjectivity, I discuss the idea of a person's self-narratives as a personal identity capability and suggest understanding it requires we rethink how subjectivity is socially embodied and socially situated – a topic taken up in Part III.

4 | Adaptive Reflexive Individuals
A Capability Conception of the Person

Life can only be understood backwards, but it must be lived forwards.

Kierkegaard (1843, vol. 18, p. 306)

...substituting a process description for a state description of nature has played a central role in the development of modern science ... [and] the correlation between [them] is basic to the functioning of any adaptive organism, to its capacity for acting purposefully upon its environment.

Simon (1962, p. 481)

There is no reason to suppose that most human beings are engaged in maximizing anything unless it be unhappiness, and even this with incomplete success.

Coase (1988, p. 4)

1 Individuals and Ability in Large Open Worlds

In Chapter 2, we saw that what Savage called small worlds – the domain of probabilistic, risky choice (later, Bayesian decision theory) – requires the risky choice independence axiom. In Chapter 3, we also saw that the heuristic and biases behavioral economics research program, with its reference dependence treatment of choice, gives up both the riskless and risky choice independence axioms and makes context an important determinant of choice. This led to the much-discussed reconciliation problem between positive and normative economics. The four strategies reviewed in Chapter 3 respond to it by reconstructing what individuals are in order to explain how they make context-dependent, socially embedded choices. These strategies implicitly assume people have the some sort of ability to make such choices, but because they still see people primarily as utility maximizers made up of bundles of subjective preferences, they say little about what their abilities are or how they are able to exercise them.

This is a significant problem. Contexts of choice can change and differ significantly from one to the next, and so what makes choice possible in one setting may be of little use in another. What is it, then, that explains how people are able to make new choices when contexts of choice change? How do we know that they even make choices?

Consider what is at issue when we allow that people occupy not only Savage's predictable small worlds but also Keynes–Knight uncertain large, open worlds. What any given context of choice involves, how and when small and large world contexts differ, and what is involved in moving from one kind of context to another is quite complicated. Simon's framework for investigating choice makes this an issue in saying rationality is bounded by not only our limited cognitive capacities but also by the character of our environments. "Human rational behavior ... is shaped by a scissors whose two blades are the structure of task environments and the computational capabilities of the actor" (Simon, 1990, p. 7). The heuristic and biases behavioral research program puts aside the second blade to focus on "the computational capabilities of the actor" blade of the scissors. But if people's behavior is only bounded by being less than rational, they effectively occupy only small worlds, where nudge/default sorts of choice architectures can be designed to more or less address them. Still left unexplained is not only how people negotiate the boundaries between small and large worlds but especially how they make choices in the latter.[1]

Simon's framework, with its additional "structure of task environments" scissors blade, led him to argue that the best people can do is engage in a "satisficing" behavior aimed at broad aspiration levels (Simon, 1955). What is important for the argument of this chapter is

---

[1] On the critique of Bayesianism as bound by small worlds, see Zappia (2018). One way the literature has developed on this is to focus on the special characteristics of choice behavior in large worlds (see Binmore, 2009; Gilboa and Schmeidler, 2001; Gilboa, Postlewaite and Schmeidler, 2009; Larrouy and Lecouteux, 2018). Savage, who is often taken as the starting point, cited a pair of maxims regarding how people move between small and large worlds and on how people ought to behave when they find themselves in ostensibly large worlds. His maxim in the first case was: "Look before you leap." His maxim in the second case was: "You can cross that bridge when you come to it" (Savage, 1954, p. 16). One interpretation of the latter is that one ought to figure out how small world probabilistic thinking can be applied in large worlds. A second less charitable interpretation is that one simply should focus on worlds that are clearly small and ignore those that are not.

his judgment that in worlds in which environments are highly uncertain people cannot optimize, so "no 'utility function' needs" – indeed ought – "to be postulated" to explain their behavior (Simon, 1956, p. 138). This line of thinking, and the idea that people are instead adaptive beings, has been pursued in the evolutionary ecological behavioral research program following Simon's lead as developed by Gerd Gigerenzer and his colleagues (Berg and Gigerenzer, 2010; Gigerenzer, 2008, 2019; Gigerenzer and Selten, 2001; Gigerenzer and Todd, 1999), and also by Vernon Smith (2005, 2008).[2]

Yet if people are "satisficers" and not subjective beings in Savage's and the mainstream utility theory sense, nor only boundedly subjective beings in the heuristic and biases program sense, how are they to be understood? Subjectivity still matters for Simon since both it and the environments people occupy explain choice, but in giving up utility functions it needs to be understood differently, not as some fully private capacity but somehow as a subjectivity embedded in the world. Chapter 8 discusses how the idea of an "embodied" subjectivity has been developed in an extensive literature on embodied, situated cognition, but here I focus on how Simon's satisficing concept and reference to broad aspiration levels can explain how people behave as adaptive beings.

Saying that satisficing aims at broad aspiration levels may suggest it does not target specific outcomes, and that consequently it does not explain how people make particular choices. However, we can also say that satisficing and broad aspiration levels refer instead to an array of specific outcomes – intermediate targets – that are bundled in that general characterization. For example, one might say: "I plan to visit a friend, but exactly when and how that visit occurs depends on what an array of possible routes will allow where I cannot predict in advance which I will adopt." That is, the idea of broad aspiration levels is shorthand for managing a set of intermediate targets, and we speak in general terms about our goals because, given uncertainties we face, we often cannot know in advance which of these targets we will choose. Satisficing, then, frames our goals in general terms because of the complications involved in acting upon them.

---

[2] Antecedents of this thinking can be found in the Veblenian evolutionary institutionalist tradition. Mayhew (1998) associates it with Veblen's theory of recurring novelty or recurring variation.

Regarding what this tells us about being an adaptive being, the process of achieving a goal through a series of intermediate steps then involves being able to adjust one's plans according to the extent to which those steps contribute to that goal. Assessing the adequacy of a series of steps and adjusting one's behavior underlie having an ability to make choices in uncertain circumstances. It involves reasoning about the world and making judgments that are comparative in nature across potentially quite different circumstances. Indeed, I will argue below that this can involve counterfactual reasoning and thinking.

Simon, then, when we focus on adjustment behavior, can be seen to have opened the black box associated with saying people have an ability to make context-dependent choices. Inside that box is all that explaining adjustment involves. One thing it involves is how the general characterization of the goals people have evolves as they act on the steps that bring it about. Not only do people adjust their pathways in achieving their goals, but they also adjust what exactly their goals are in the process. Satisficing consequently aims at broad aspiration levels because people's goals are general until filled in.[3]

I argue that this filling-in process essentially works in terms of feedback effects. As a person's goals are filled in, this feeds back on the intermediate steps they take and fills them in as well. That is, these feedback effects work in both directions: goals and steps acting on each other. Thus, the specific ability people have to make context-dependent choices in uncertain circumstances is what I characterize as a reflexive adjustment ability. Let us further frame this in temporal terms.

Simon has argued that in the sciences of behavior we need to "substitute[e] a process description for a state description of nature" to be able to explain the "basic to the functioning of any adaptive organism [in] its capacity for acting purposefully upon its environment" (Simon, 1962, p. 481). This distinction refers us to the two conceptions of time distinguished in Chapter 1, the before–after one appropriate to sequences of state descriptions and the past–present–future one appropriate to process descriptions. In large, uncertain worlds, arguably the latter view of time is what is needed. A succession of

---

[3] I say more about how Simon sees aspiration levels evolving in Davis (2023b).

states descriptions might tell us what happened in the past, but people need to make choices about the future. In Kierkegaard's words in the first epigraph: "Life can only be understood backwards" – where this concerns what possibilities people thought they faced – "but it must be lived forwards" – where this concerns choice and action (Kierkegaard, 1843, vol. 18, p. 306). In reflexivity terms, every forward-looking choice reflexively includes a backward-looking reassessment of the choices that preceded it that sets up that forward-looking choice – a continual dynamic of feedback loops between the past and the future in which we occupy the present.

This chapter further develops these ideas in advancing a conception of individuals as adaptive beings. In a series of steps, Section 2 (a) uses the behavioral economics distinction between nudges and boosts to emphasize the importance of the idea that people are made up of abilities, not preferences; (b) develops a stock–flow temporal representation of adaptive individual's behavior as a process of adjustment involving a "correlation" between point-in-time state and through-time process descriptions of individuals; (c) describes this as an ability–action–ability pattern of behavioral adjustment that works via reflexive feedback loops; (d) argues people's abilities should be regarded as capabilities in Sen's sense; (e) describes how adaptive adjustment behavior often relies on counterfactual reasoning and counterfactual thinking.

Section 3 applies the identity criteria I use to evaluate individual conceptions in economics to this adaptive individual conception, and asks whether adaptive individuals can be individuated and reidentified as distinct and independent. It argues they can be individuated at different points-in-time, but whether they can also be reidentified as such over time depends on economic and social institutions promoting people's individual capability development. To the extent that they do, that development includes people developing a personal identity, self-narrative capability by which they keep track of who they are amidst all the changes in their lives.

Section 4 briefly summarizes where Chapters 5 and 6 in Part II go from here. On the "externalist" understanding of what influences individual autonomy, we can distinguish socially stratified and democratic economies according to whether they limit or promote capability development. I associate the former in Chapter 5 with capability shortfalls and the latter in Chapter 6 with capability gains.

2 An Adaptive Individual Conception

a From Nudges to Boosts

An obvious problem with nudges in libertarian paternalism is that while on the libertarian side they are meant to increase people's freedom by making choices possible they would believe make them better off, on the paternalism side nudges are carried out behind people's backs by others, limiting their self-direction. One way of addressing this is to reinterpret the nature and scope of desirable nudges in such a way as to both limit others' agency and expand individuals' own agency. This has been argued by proponents of the idea that, instead of nudges, we ought to think in terms of "boosts" or changes in people's environments that increase their ability for employing adaptive heuristics (Grüne-Yanoff and Hertwig, 2016; Hertwig and Grüne-Yanoff, 2017; Grüne-Yanoff, Marchionni, and Feufel, 2018). In effect, policy should be focused on empowering decision-makers rather than manipulating their choices.

Note an important difference between nudges and boosts. Nudges alter the choice context people face, given their existing capacities for making choices, and implicitly employ a static view of the person. In contrast, boosts assume people can learn, and thus employ a dynamic view of people. This calls for a distinction between capacities and abilities. Capacities can be understood as potentials that may be actualized as specific abilities. The problem with nudge or default rule types of interventions, then, is that they include nothing about whether people can learn nor about how capacities they possess could become actual abilities they exercise. Two points can be made.

First, emphasizing that people have capacities and abilities introduces a new way of thinking about individuals. Since the standard subjectivist understanding of individuals invests people with a single, given capacity for making choices, it lacks a way of explaining how they are able to exercise it across different contexts of choice. We might say that its understanding of a person's potentiality is closed. In contrast, on the boost view (and in evolutionary ecological behavioral approaches), people's potentialities are open, inviting us to investigate what abilities people might possess and develop given their capacity for making choices.

Second, the boost view allows us to investigate people's behavior in both small worlds and large worlds, since it is open to their developing new decision-making abilities. Especially important, because they have been largely ignored in mainstream economics, are the abilities needed in large worlds where people need to learn how to make choices in changeable, evolving, and uncertain environments. Their unpredictable nature thus shifts our attention from what capacities people have to what abilities they could have, or environmentally need to have. This emphasis on ability to learn thus calls for a general understanding of how people adapt and adjust to different contexts of choice. Adapting and adjusting are processes occurring in time, so we need to determine how people can be modeled as adaptive beings who adjust in time.

b Making Time Matter: Agents Understood in Terms of Stocks and Flows

The mainstream "internalist" view of individuals is formulated in terms of subjective states of the person. Saying a person is in a certain state places the person at a point-in-time – a "state description" in Simon's words (1962, 481). They make choices about future points-in-time and thus about themselves being in future states, but since time is understood only as a succession of points-in-time, the person can only be understood as an unexplained succession of temporal states.[4]

Missing from this succession of states representation of time is the through-time, passage of time idea that connects different points-in-time – the "process description" for Simon. Representing people in terms of states they occupy is important, since it is the basis of comparative analysis of their condition over time. However, to fully understand their behavior, the states they occupy need to be connected via the temporal processes linking those states. As Simon puts it, "the correlation between [state and process descriptions] is basic to explanations the functioning of any adaptive organism, to its capacity for acting purposefully upon its environment" (*Ibid.*).[5]

---

[4] This raises the problem of future contingents, Aristotle's sea battle problem, discussed in Chapter 1.

[5] Linking state and process descriptions to identify the former within the latter is the subject of a now extensive operations research literature modeling discrete event simulation (DES) pioneered especially by Sheldon Jacobson and his colleagues. DES identifies distinct events in continuous flow systems for comparative analysis of states of a system over time (e.g., a flow of transportation activity can be decomposed into loading, departure, arrival,

This points us to the fundamental advantage of an adaptive individual conception. The concept of adapting, as an activity (or action term), links states at particular points-in-time from which something adapts to states at a subsequent points-in-time that result. On the one hand, adaptive individuals are understood in terms of the succession of states they occupy. On the other hand, since when we speak of them as adapting and see them as purposive, their movement from one state to another is also understood in terms of a process they initiate, as agents, through actions they undertake. Thus, for adaptive individuals, "states descriptions" and "process descriptions" of their behavior are inherently connected. We need to explain the states they occupy, but to understand their movement from one state to another we also need to explain the through-time processes by which this happens.

This combined state–process thinking, then, has long been standard and widely employed in business, finance, and economics in stock–flow terms. Stock–flow reasoning links particular stocks as a point-in-time concept and flows as a through-time concept as two connected dimensions of an economic process. That is, stocks and flows are two sides of a coin in that stocks produce flows that in turn produce new stocks that then produce new flows in a continuously repeating manner over time. Needless to say, stock–flow thinking is fundamental and pervasive in economics: income and capital, revenue and productive capacity, GDP and national resources, etc. Indeed, it constitutes one of the primitive conceptual and ontological foundations of economic thinking arguably dating to even its prerecorded earliest origins.[6]

Given this, it is fairly straightforward to transfer this state–process, stock–flow thinking to what adaptive individuals are and how they behave when we see them as made up of abilities. Then, the particular stocks that make them up at a given point-in-time are the abilities they possess at that point-in-time, the stocks that subsequently make them up are the abilities they develop, and the flows that connect these two sets of abilities/stocks are the actions they undertake: an

unloading, etc., type states/events). For an application to health-care systems integrating patient flow data and event-based health-care decision-making, see Jacobson, Hall, and Swisher (2006).

[6] For a review of the modern history of economic thinking about the stock–flow distinction, see Harrison (1980).

ability$_x$/ability$_y$ sequence linked by action$_{xy}$. Abilities are stocks because they are something held at a point-in-time used through-time to achieve goals. Actions are flows because they concern adapting understood as an activity linking points-in-time.

Of course, a resulting ability$_y$ will typically not correspond exactly to what intended in an action$_{xy}$. If we differentiate small, probabilistic worlds where this correspondence can be relatively high from large, uncertain worlds where it can be low, the ability/stock$_x$ – action/flow$_{xy}$ – ability/stock$_y$ sequence applies to both types of worlds and provides a general characterization of adaptive individuals combining state and process descriptions of their behavior.

The key role Simon's second scissors blade idea plays in an adaptive individual conception should now be clear. Since our environments – institutional structures, social relationships, others' actions, etc. – affect what we aim to achieve, our behavior cannot be modeled as simply a succession of destinations rationally achieved. Stock–flow analysis, of course, is modeled in mainstream economics using utility functions. However, the single blade strategy in the neoclassical utility function-unbounded rationality approach and the heuristics and biases-bounded rationality approach essentially restricts time to successions of points-in-time and suppresses the process, through-time concept. In effect, optimization closes off each choice episode from previous and later choice occasions as if it were complete in itself, thus making the passage of time only a succession of point-in-time exercises. This makes optimality or near optimality a behavioral idealization that sets aside how people are continually engaged in adjusting their behavior, sometimes significantly, as they move from one choice context to another.

What this two-blades representation of adaptive agents does not address is how individuals adjust their later choices in response to when the results of their previous choices fail to correspond to their intended goals. When we look at stock–flow reasoning behavior in business, finance, and economic decision-making, we see that short-run planning is always embedded in a long-run planning. The latter is built around how past goals and actions are regularly evaluated and strategies for their revision planned in order to respond to expected unforeseen contingencies. Section c describes how this reflexive assessment, adjustment process can be explained as a central aspect of individuals' adaptive behavior.

c Reflexive Adaptive Behavior

While the concept of reflexivity has many meanings and applications in science, philosophy, logic, and the humanities, when it concerns action and behavior it is the idea of something acting upon itself.[7] One important interpretation of this concerns the relationships between scientists and what they investigate. Thus, reflexivity is associated with the observer or "Hawthorne effect" where social scientists' observation of individuals caused them to modify their behavior – the observer thus acting upon and affecting the observation (Landsberger, 1958). In cultural anthropology, it concerns how Western observers read their own perspectives into observation of other cultures (Clifford and Marcus, 1986). In the sociology and economics of scientific knowledge, reflexivity concerns how social theories apply to those who construct them as well as to what they explain (Davis and Klaes, 2003). In theories of financial behavior, reflexivity operates when judgments of investments are influenced by how speculators judge them (Keynes, 1936; Soros, 2013).[8]

In economics, Oskar Morgenstern (1928) used the reflexivity concept to argue that prediction and forecasting are impossible. To make a correct public prediction P_1, a forecaster must anticipate the "absorption" by economic agents of the theory underlying the prediction and thus their reaction R_1 to P_1. This requires the forecaster to replace P_1 with an adjusted prediction P_2. But this implies a further reaction by economics agents, R_2 to P_2, leading to further adjustment of the forecaster's prediction, and so on in a continuous interplay of prediction and anticipated reaction that takes the form of an infinite regress or a "Morgenstern Process" (see Lehmann-Waffenschmidt, 1990, p. 149).[9]

---

[7] In Chapter 2, reflexivity was defined more broadly in terms of self-reference in conceptual systems and something referring to itself. Here, the concept specifically concerns something acting on itself.

[8] Reflexivity is also associated with feedback relationships within theories rather than between theorists and theories. This is the sense I used in Chapter 1 where I argued that reflexivity operates as a methodological principle in complexity modeling in open science economic approaches (see also Davis, 2018a).

[9] Emile Grunberg and Franco Modigliani responded to Morgenstern that, using Brouwer's fixed point theorem (the idea for which they credited Simon) there exist formal conditions under which a Morgenstern process converges, so that prediction and forecasting do not produce an infinite regress (Grunberg and Modigliani, 1954; see Hands, 1990). Simon similarly made the fixed point argument (and in turn credited Grunberg and Modigliani for suggesting the fixed point theorem!) in regard to predictions of election outcomes (Simon, 1954).

A related, recent influential example of reflexivity reasoning is the Lucas critique in macroeconomics, in which traditional Keynesian fiscal policies using government expenditure to increase GDP are argued to have feedback effects on total expenditure that offset those policies (Lucas, 1976). As Marcel Boumans explains it: "The underlying idea, known as the Lucas Critique, is that estimating what were previously regarded as structural in econometric analysis of policy actually depended on the economic policy pursued" (Boumans, 2001, p. 439). According to Lucas, what was regarded as structural and independent of policy then turns out not to be when the effects of the policy feedback upon that structure and undercut the policy's planned effects.

In science generally, then, the concept of reflexivity is often used to explain a type of causal process exhibiting some sort of feedback mechanism. If the simplest idea of causal action is where something acts on and only affects something else, a reflexive causal process is where something acts on and affects something else and itself as well. The part of the action's effects that act upon itself are its feedback effects, which can then partially or even fully offset the action's effects on something else (as in the Lucas critique). In directional terms, the "feed*back*" idea suggests a circular or loop type of movement traveling in the reverse direction from and the forward direction of an action, or back from the effects of that action to affect how that action itself works.

In a micro, behavioral setting, reflexivity can explain how and why economic agents adjust their behavior over time, such as in how they may respond to the "unintended consequences" of their actions. When the cause of unintended effects is seen (in part or in whole) to be an unanticipated feedback effect of their own actions, agents may then choose to prevent or strengthen this effect, depending on its desirability. Robert Merton (1936) examined feedback effects on agent action and distinguished different types of adjustment responses agents adopt according to the nature of those effects. Agents can choose to ignore, moderate, or fully counteract how those effects operate. Merton also investigated how micro-level reflexive behavior can have macro-level consequences in his examination of self-fulfilling prophecies.[10]

---

[10] His famous example is the bank run, inspired by the 1930s depression experience, in which depositors withdraw their funds from banks upon coming to believe that an unintended consequence of having previously placed their funds in banks is that they might lose those funds (Merton, 1949; see Davis, 2020a).

Box 4.1   A continuous reflexive feedback loop pattern of behavioral adjustment

People's choices have intended and unintended effects →
The latter feedback on and may cause them to revise their
later choices →
These choices feed forward having new sets of intended and
unintended effects →
The latter again feedback on and may cause them to revise
their later choices →
etc.

There is now a rich literature on reflexive agents in agent-based computational complexity economics that examines how agents evolve as their interaction evolves (see Chen, 2012, 2016; Kirman, 2011; Rosser, 2021; Tesfatsion, 2006).[11] When reflexive adaptive behavior is the foundation of what agents are, both they and the economies they occupy coevolve over time. The economy is thus a complex system in virtue of the interdependency that operates across agents and processes through which they interact.

Behaviorally, Box 4.1 is a simple representation of the adjustment process agents undergo seen as a continuous reflexive feedback loop pattern. Its basis is large, open world choice settings in which agents' adaptive behavior is built around the need for adjustment strategies.

Box 4.1 does not address how agents are able to make a succession of adjustment choices in response to what they learn about their past choices. Over time and across a succession of choices, they acquire experience and learn about how successfully or unsuccessfully they responded and adjusted their behavior to past unintended effects. New choice contexts limit what this experience tells them, but it nonetheless provides a basis they rely on in making new choices. Thus, this experience generates a sort developing ability stock they employ in adapting their choices over time to changes in context. How a reflexive feedback loop pattern of behavioral adjustment operates over time then depends on the nature of the ability agents develop.[12]

---

[11] My recent contributions to this thinking include Davis (2018a, 2020a, and 2023b).

[12] Veblen's evolutionary thinking explained reflexivity in terms of unintended consequences. As Mayhew puts it: "in Veblen's analysis, individuals, their

---

Box 4.2   An ability/stock$_x$ – action/flow$_{xy}$ – ability/stock$_y$ pattern of reflexive adjustment

People's choices have intended and unintended effects →
The latter feedback on their interpretation of their ability/stocks$_x$ →
Re-interpretating ability/stocks$_x$ feeds forward in action/flow$_{xy}$
terms into their new choices →
These new choices have new intended and unintended effects →
This again feeds back on their interpretation of their
ability/stocks$_y$ →
etc.

Box 4.2 translates Box 4.1 into an ability/stock$_x$ – action/flow$_{xy}$ – ability/stock$_y$ adjustment sequence.

Note how this adaptive individual adjustment process differs from how adjustment is explained in both the neoclassical and heuristics and biases individual conceptions. In the former, learning occurs through a Bayesian updating in small worlds. New facts inductively and mechanically change the basis on which agents act. Nothing is said about individuals' ability to organize information or about how agents might learn to make successions of choices in less tractable, uncertain worlds. In the heuristics and biases program, Bayesian updating learning is assisted by choice architects who signal new facts for boundedly rational individuals. Again, nothing is said about agents having an ability to organize information or learn to make choices in new unfamiliar circumstances.[13]

In contrast, ascribing ability–action–ability adjustment behavior to agents seen as adaptive allows us to describe how individuals make choices across different contexts of choice where those contexts may vary significantly in character (as *per* Simon's environments scissors blade and ecological behavioral approaches). An ability conceptualization of the stocks that people accumulate also allows us to develop new types of economic and social policies that specifically address learning, as in the boost alternative to nudges. To help think about the

---

goals and their understanding are affected by unintended consequences so that the next round of pragmatic and purposeful action is different from previous rounds" (1998, p. 455). For Veblen, over time this involved a cumulative process akin to developing an ability stock.

[13] Nor is anything really said about choice architects' learning processes.

basis for such policies, I turn next to why people's abilities are better understood as capabilities in Sen's sense.

d Individuals' Abilities as Their Capabilities

The ability concept above is quite general and can be used to explain adjustment behavior in human and nonhuman kinds of agents. In the case of human individuals, ability needs to be understood in terms of how people understand their abilities and how over time they seek to develop them. Sugden (2018) makes abilities central to what people are in describing them in terms of opportunity sets. The opportunity idea includes both the ability concept – "being able" as the opportunity to become something – and that people seek to develop over time in acquiring new opportunities. Thus implicitly, his framework employs Box 4.2's ability–action–ability thinking with an opportunity interpretation of ability. Yet, he does not map out how the abilities/opportunities people have at any point-in-time form the basis for actions they undertake, or how the results of those actions create new sets of abilities/opportunities as the basis for their later actions.

Sen's capability concept is also an ability concept, but has the advantage that it is formulated in terms of capabilities people have in the specific social settings they occupy. A person's capabilities are the "person's *actual* ability to do the different things that she values doing" – "the *actual opportunities* a person has" (Sen, 2009, p. 253; original emphasis). What these abilities/capabilities are consequently depends on the resources at their disposal and the constraints operating upon them in using those resources in those environments.

Different people can have quite different opportunities for converting income and other primary goods into characteristics of good living and into the kind of freedom valued in human life. Thus, the relationship between resources and poverty is both variable and deeply contingent on the characteristics of the respective people and the environment in which they live. (*Ibid.*, 254)

Sen's concept of people's "*actual opportunities*" thus refers to people's socially embedded capabilities. In contrast to the abstract idea of ability *per se*, capability always needs to be understood as what a person can be and do at any time in their particular circumstances, and accordingly he emphasizes that what capabilities people have reflects their heterogeneities, diversities in their physical environments, variations in their social climates, and differences in their relational perspectives (*Ibid.*, 255).

Specifically, Sen distinguishes functionings, what people can actually be and do, from capabilities, the functionings they can develop and what they may be able to be and do. In terms of the point-in-time and through-time relationship above, a person's functionings and the "*actual opportunities*" or the capabilities people actually have provide the point-in-time basis for the actions they undertake to further develop their capabilities.

How they pursue this development, and the actions they choose to undertake, is then a matter of the judgments they make about themselves regarding the particular state of their capabilities at any point-in-time. We saw in Chapter 2 that Sen distinguishes different, competing kinds of selves people have, and argues people engage in a process of "reasoning and self-scrutiny" (Sen, 2002, p. 36) in determining the basis on which they choose to act. This reflexive self-assessment is thus a point-in-time act of judgment that connects "the capabilities people actually have" with possible actions they undertake specific to those capabilities to develop their capabilities.

The emphasis in Sen's *Development as Freedom* (1999) is on people's continual development of their capabilities. It combines state descriptions of what their capabilities are at successive points-in-time and a process description of how over time those capability states are connected through their ability–action link. Box 4.3 reinterprets Box 4.2 to make people's ability–action–ability reflexive pattern of adjustment a capability–action–capability pattern of adjustment.

Box 4.3 does not address two matters. One is the role habit plays in this adjustment process. In social psychology, there is an extensive literature on habit as a type of cognitive representation (see Fleetwood,

---

Box 4.3   A capability–action–capability pattern of reflexive adjustment

People's choices have intended and actual effects →
The latter feedback on their interpretation of their capabilities →
Reinterpretation of their capabilities feeds forward on their actions →
These actions have new intended and unintended effects →
This again feeds back on their interpretation of their capabilities →
etc.

2021) and habit is also central to the Veblenian evolutionary institutionalist tradition (Hodgson, 2004, 2010). What attention to habit provides in explanations of reflexive adjustment is way of accounting for persistence and flexibility regarding attachment to past courses of action.

Another matter is how people understand the scope of their opportunities and reason about what may be possible for them at future points-in-time regarding developing their capabilities, especially in highly uncertain worlds where the future is often obscure. This bears on factors underlying habit, and I turn to this in connection with adaptive individuals' counterfactual reasoning and counterfactual thinking which concern how people think about possibility.

e Adaptive Individuals' Counterfactual Reasoning and Counterfactual Thinking

If in small worlds people are conventionally thought to systematically update in a Bayesian way their prior probabilities as they acquire new facts, in large uncertain worlds there are two barriers to doing this. First, the facts they have are insufficient to account for all possible future states of the world people face (especially for "one-off" types of choices). Second, Bayesian thinking assumes random phenomena are normally or bell-shaped distributed and possess determinate means and finite variance properties, whereas large worlds can exhibit "black swan" phenomena (Taleb, 2007) and have Cauchy distributions, the family of "fat-tail" distributions in which means and variance are undefined (Davis, 2013b).

Thus, not only do people often not have all the facts they need, but the facts they have may not be probabilistically distributed such that they can act upon them. I address the first problem in terms of how adaptive individuals develop contrary-to-fact information and engage in counterfactual *reasoning*, and the second problem in terms of how they rely on "close counterfactuals" in counterfactual *thinking* (see Table 4.1).[14]

---

[14] I distinguish counterfactual reasoning and counterfactual thinking to reflect the different ways philosophers and psychologists understand counterfactuality. Philosophers are primarily concerned with how we reason logically (Starr, 2019); psychologists are concerned with how people actually think and behave (Davis, 2018c; Davis and Koutsobinas, 2021).

Table 4.1 *Limitations of small world and large world strategies*

Limitations of small worlds thinking in large worlds	Large world choice strategies
Facts are insufficient	Counterfactual reasoning: contrary-to-fact, depth, and "what if" information
Non-normal probability distributions	Counterfactual thinking: "close counterfactuals"

i Counterfactual Reasoning: Contrary-to-Fact, Depth, and "What If" Information

When the facts people have are insufficient for making choices, they may make inferences based on what is not the case but could be the case, or on contrary-to-fact information. Bayesian reasoning derives conclusions from premises by the *modus ponens* "if-then" rule, where if p implies q and p is true, then q is true. New information in the form of some new p that is true allows us to infer updated probabilities and that a new q is true. In counterfactual reasoning, however, people acquire information about the world without employing *modus ponens*. Consider famous Oswald–Kennedy example.[15]

If Oswald didn't kill Kennedy, someone else did.

Assuming it is true Oswald killed Kennedy, the "if" clause "Oswald didn't kill Kennedy" is false or contrary-to-fact, but the inference is still valid and the conclusion still true (Starr, 2019). Despite the false premise, this inference remains informative because it tells us something about our understanding of the nature of the possibilities involved in the Kennedy assassination (namely, that we believe the assassination was an intentional act on someone's part).

Moreover, counterfactual reasoning also provides us information about the world when we *in*validly infer false statements from false premises. Thus, someone might also say:

If Oswald had not killed Kennedy, someone else would have.

---

[15] The example is originally due to Adams (1975).

Here, again assuming that Oswald killed Kennedy, not only is the "if" clause false and contrary-to-fact, but many people would also say the inference and conclusion are false as well (*Ibid.*). Had Oswald not killed Kennedy, it does not follow that someone else would have. Despite this, this second statement is still informative, because it reflects something in our thinking about the possibilities and causal relationships surrounding the Kennedy assassination (perhaps in this case that it is believed the assassination was not part of a conspiracy).

The linguistic difference between the two statements is that the first is an indicative conditional and second is a subjunctive conditional. Both employ counterfactual reasoning but differ in that the latter makes explicit use of the subjunctive mood, which (in English) employs terms such as "would," "might," "could," etc. In natural languages, of course, speakers move comfortably across both indicative and subjunctive forms, and this tells us they understand subtle differences in counterfactual reasoning such as between the two statements. This facility is not easy to explain analytically (especially compared to the relative simplicity of Bayesian updating) and until relatively recently (Kripke, 1980) possible worlds semantics and modal logic which such language concerns had been regarded as philosophically intractable. All I argue, however, is that economic agents use counterfactual reasoning to acquire information to make inferences when what they know to be true is insufficient for the choices they need to make.[16]

An argument regarding what this involves was made by the philosopher Jaakko Hintikka in regard to a classic problem regarding the nature of deduction. The problem is that while deductive inference is thought to be informative, formally speaking deductions do not convey new information beyond what their premises contain. To address this, Hintikka distinguished between "surface" information and "depth" information, and argued that a valid deductive inference actually conveys new information because it employs "depth" information implicit in the inference (Hintikka, 1973; see Davis, 2018d). This is arguably how we find ourselves reasoning in the Oswald–Kennedy examples, where "depth" information we find ourselves relying on concerns such

---

[16] Debates over what possible worlds are go beyond my concern here with the behavior of adaptive agents. But see Lewis (1973, 1986) and Stalnaker (1968, 1976, 1987).

things as our implicit beliefs that the assassination was an intentional act and not part of a conspiracy.

A related kind of argument was developed much earlier by Charles S. Peirce in regard to "what if" and "if only" thinking that he treated as a method of searching for possible causal relationships in science. In what he called abduction (as contrasted with deduction and induction), the way we reason can be set out as follows (Peirce et al., 1931–1958, vol. 5, p. 189; see Tohmé and Crespo, 2013):

> The surprising fact C is observed.
> But if *A* were true, C would be a matter of course.
> Hence, there is reason to suspect that *A* is true.

The surprising fact that C is observed suggests that there may exist a previously unrecognized causal relationship between *A* and C. Yet, we still only "suspect" that *A* is a cause of C and whether it is requires additional investigation.[17]

However, economic agents do not have the luxury of not acting and must often make choices whether or not they are able to further explain their basis. How, then, do they actually manage uncertain environments with many possibilities?

ii Counterfactual Thinking and "Close Counterfactuals"

Turning from philosophy to psychology, whereas philosophers are concerned with counterfactual reasoning, or how we can make logical inferences from contrary-to-fact states of affairs, psychologists are concerned with counterfactual thinking, or how people actually behave in highly uncertain environments. A key step in this literature, then, was to say that counterfactual thinking is a functional rather than dysfunctional type of thinking. Daniel Kahneman and Amos Tversky (1982) took this position and argued that counterfactual

---

[17] In current philosophy of science on the nature of causal explanations, many now think in terms of "what if things had been different" types of explanations, making counterfactual reasoning central to explaining causality (Woodward, 2003). Philosophers of economics who have recently investigated "what if" and "if only" questions as "how-possibly" types of explanations (Marchionni and Ylikoski, 2013; Ylikoski, 2014) go on to argue that the candidate causal relationships this can generate are still subject to testing and additional examination via robustness analysis that any other sort of theoretical conjecture involves (Kuorkoski, Lehtinen, and Marchionni, 2010; Marchionni and Ylikoski, 2013).

thinking allows people to explore possible sequences of events that have not occurred but could have occurred. For individuals specifically seen as adaptive, when people fail to meet their goals and need to make new choices, this thinking activates a "what if" type of thinking like Peirce's abduction.

Ruth Byrne has influentially argued that "what if"-type thinking employs a specific kind of human mental model she labels "rational imagination" (Byrne, 2005, 2007, 2016). While imagination is popularly often seen as a type of fantasy, she treats it as a rational capacity for investigating the nature of events based on people thinking: "if only" such-and-such were to have occurred, how might events have played out differently? Then, when people imagine how events could have played out differently, this "lead[s] them to judge that a strong causal relation exists between an antecedent event and the outcome," which they may subsequently rely upon in their future choices (Byrne, 2007, p. 439).

This formulation ties people's counterfactual thinking to familiar choice scenarios they could reasonably face, albeit not actually involving normally distributed phenomena, but normally distributed-like phenomena. Their focus is on imagined possibilities realistically available to them, not on possibilities that are remote and altogether unlikely. Thus, if we treat these as their choice portfolios, they are built around choice contexts immediate to their experience. These portfolios can then be described in terms of sets of "close counterfactuals," or "cases in which 'X almost happened' [and] X could have happened" had things been only a little different (Kahneman and Varey 1990, p. 1101) – thus, "if only" kinds of scenarios which could potentially be acted upon.

Consider a standard example from the literature. A person studies less for an examination than they thought they could have. That they did not is a fact tied to something contrary-to-fact, namely, that they could have studied more. This link between the fact and what is contrary-to-fact expands the information base relevant to the person's choice setting – a "close counterfactual" bearing on what might have happened if they had studied more.

In contrast, non-"close counterfactuals" involve circumstances where a contrary-to-fact state of affairs is unlikely and unrealistic (if not impossible): for example, were a person to say: "if only I had been Albert Einstein, I would have done better on my exam." The information that nonclose counterfactuals convey usually has little practical value, and thus falls outside the domain of a rational imagination and adaptive individual behavior.[18]

Psychologists, then, broadly distinguish different types of "close counterfactuals" choice scenarios as involving *downward* and *upward* counterfactual thinking (Roese and Morrison, 2009). Downward counterfactual thinking concerns how things could have been worse if a person had acted differently, and is often associated with errors or mistakes that were avoided. In the exam case, one might say: "I would have gotten a lower grade if I hadn't studied as much as I did." Functionally, downward counterfactual thinking is treated as an affective "coping" mechanism, where people regard themselves as fortunate that their actions turned out as well they did. Upward counterfactual thinking concerns how things might have been better if a person had acted differently, and is often associated with opportunities missed. For example, one might say, "I would have gotten a higher grade if I had studied more." Upward counterfactual thinking, then, is characterized as an affective "preparative" mechanism which can put people in position to better achieve their goals in the future.

These two kinds of counterfactual thinking, then, correspond to two different ways the reflexive adjustment process works when we take into account people's goals. When their abilities are seen as capabilities, as in Box 4.3, downward counterfactual thinking involves maintaining a set of capabilities and upward counterfactual thinking it involves further developing them. In a larger social setting, this can be illustrated with how capability development is understood in the main international framework devoted to this, the United Nations Development Programme (UNDP) Human Development Index (HDI).[19]

Suppose, then, that economic development in a country is stagnant and levels of education are not increasing. Then, when choices are

---

[18] However, non-"close counterfactuals" are, as many can testify, an important source of humor, so they are not entirely empty in practical value.

[19] The HDI evaluates capability development in terms of health, education, and income. In the case of education, since 2010 education has been measured by a country's average adult years of schooling and by expected years of schooling for children. What levels countries achieve in these two measures depends not only on their overall levels of social and economic development and policies they adopt to promote education, but also on people's behaviors regarding pursuit of education.

Table 4.2 *Counterfactual thinking and capability adjustment*

Kind of counterfactual thinking	Behavioral mechanism	Type of capability adjustment
Downward	"Coping"	Capability maintenance
Upward	"Preparative"	Capability development

made regarding further education, people may exhibit downward counterfactual thinking and emphasize "coping" strategies – a type of capability adjustment that can be termed *capability maintenance*. Compare this with a situation in which economic development in a country is advancing and levels of education are increasing. Then, choices made regarding further education may exhibit upward counterfactual thinking and emphasize "preparative" strategies – a type of capability adjustment that can be termed *capability development*.[20]

Table 4.2 shows how these two types of cases involve two main kinds of counterfactual thinking where people's goals are understood in terms of how they seek to reflexively adjust their capabilities.

This application of counterfactual thinking to the UNDP's HDI shows how counterfactual thinking can be tied to imagined "close counterfactuals" in large policy settings. When people's abilities are seen as capabilities, adaptive agents can be expected to adjust their behavior over time to what they think is possible according to their particular social and economic environments. These capability maintenance and capability development scenarios in large social settings are the focus of the chapters to follow.

3 The Identity of Reflexive Adaptive Individuals

Can reflexive adaptive individuals, when we see them as made up of capabilities, be individuated as distinct and independent beings and also reidentified through-time? Or might the idea of being adaptive be inconsistent with this? If adaption is understood only in flow terms, and everything is thought to be connected to and part of everything else, this would seem to follow. However, when our treatment

---

[20] The distinction between capability maintenance and development is the basis, respectively, of Chapters 5 and 6.

of time combines points-in-time, state descriptions and through-time, process descriptions, the former are individually distinguishable while also embedded in the latter (as in stock–flow analysis). Thus, point-in-time, stock state-type descriptions individuate what they refer to as long as they are not defined self-referentially. This is generally how stocks are typically described, namely, in terms of characteristics they possess, not in terms of who or what they belong to.

When we additionally interpret people's stocks of abilities as their capabilities, we might be tempted to say this is self-referential if we emphasize that a person's capabilities are their "own" capabilities. However, Sen understands capabilities as "the *actual opportunities* a person has," and the opportunities concept refers to opportunities a person would have were they in a position that comes with certain opportunities. That is, when the capabilities people have are defined in terms of the positions they occupy, this defines capabilities, like the stock concept, in terms of characteristics positions possess apart from who occupies them.

This still leaves open whether people seen as distinct and independent individuals at any one point-in-time are re-identifiably the same people at any later point-in-time. That they are different sets of capabilities at different points-in-time means they could be seen as having different selves over time. Indeed, whether a person's different selves over time are somehow connected is central to debates over the nature of personal identity in philosophy. Perhaps, the most influential view of the matter is Derek Parfit's (1984), who rejects the idea that a person seen as having multiple selves can be reidentified as the same person over time, arguing, however, that those multiple selves can still be seen as "connected" – a novel view of what personal "identity" involves.

Parfit's connectedness idea – call it a weak sense of the concept – is based on a state description view of people, so it is not surprising that it is difficult to see he accepts a multiple selves view of the person. Suppose instead we see state descriptions and process descriptions as always linked. We can then explain connectedness between different states of something in terms of their embeddedness in processes – call this a strong sense of the connectedness idea. However, this understanding is not open to Parfit, because he sees the states of people as characteristics they possess – not as sets of agent characteristics that they act upon. Yet, it is these agent action characteristics which provide the basis for an abilities/stocks$_x$–flow/process–abilities/stocks$_y$ understanding of how distinguishable states of something are connected in through-time processes.

There is a hint of such an understanding in Parfit's claim that what "matters" to people regarding personal identity is the connectedness of their different selves, where "matters" suggest a concern with who we might be through-time. But whose concern? For Parfit, "us" probably refers to what he believes philosophers think matters regarding personal identity. Perhaps, however, we ought rather to ask ourselves what we think people generally believe matters when it comes to what connects the different states of their lives.

I suggest, then, that when the different states of people's lives are over time seen as a succession of sets of capabilities linked by actions they undertake, what matters to them regarding how they are connected is whether they are able to act to develop their capabilities over time, particularly as called for in light of their frequently changing circumstances. Being able to act and do something is an agency idea that ties states to processes. Thus, what matters to people regarding how the different states of their lives connect is their agency (and the extent of it) in directing the process involved.

Note that when we say being able to act and do something is what matters to people, we ascribe to them a point of view they take toward themselves – one that has an oversight, evaluative nature. In Chapter 2, I discussed Sen different types of selves people have (self-centered welfare, self-welfare goal, and self-goal choice types of selves), and how he characterizes a person as someone able to evaluate "one's own reasoning and self-scrutiny" (Sen, 2002, p. 36).

A person is not only an entity that can enjoy one's own consumption, experience and appreciate one's welfare, and have one's goals, but also an entity that can examine one's values and objectives and choose in light of those values and objectives (*Ibid.*).

Being able to evaluate "one's own reasoning and self-scrutiny" is also an ability, or better a capability in the sense of something one can acquire. It also operates on a different level from all the particular functionings and capabilities people employ to achieve their goals. Rather than a capability to achieve things, it is a capability to manage one's capabilities to achieve things.

I have called this special capability a personal identity capability (Davis, 2009a, 2011; Davis and Wells, 2016), an idea also developed by Pierre Livet (2006). Though like other capabilities it is something that needs to be acquired, its reflexive nature makes it more complex and arguably difficult to acquire. At the same time, it seems fair to say it plays an essential role in adaptive individuals' reflexive adjustment behavior. That is, the interpretation and reinterpretation of their capabilities people are described in Box 4.3 as continually engaged in presumably depends on their regularly asking, "how am I developing my capabilities as I choose." Reflexive adjustment of one's choices involves reflexive self-assessment.

Thus, though Sen believes a person can, in principle, evaluate "one's own reasoning and self-scrutiny," just as success in developing capabilities varies across people, so success in developing this special capability also varies across people. Clearly, a key factor involved in this is whether a person's social circumstances promote or limit their acquiring it. This then is also a factor determining whether we can reidentify people over time as the same distinct and independent individuals. To the extent that they acquire this personal identity capability and can successfully address the different choice contexts they encounter in life, they can be. To the extent that they do not acquire it, they are vulnerable to fragmenting into different selves and, as Parfit sees it, a succession of unconnected states of themselves.

What more can we say about this personal identity capability? I previously described it as a self-narrative capability built around having a self-concept (Davis, 2011, pp. 183–189; cf. Schechtman, 1996). A self-narrative is how a person explains their life. Ivan Mitrouchev and Valerio Buonomo (2023), in their critique of psychological theories of identity in economics, distinguish narrative theories from sociological theories of personal identity and characterize a self-narrative personal identity capability as a hybrid psychological–sociological approach. Indeed, narratives of all kinds are both individual and social phenomena, just as are all kinds of capabilities. This points us toward a further examination of what is socially involved in people individually acquiring this capability, but I reserve this discussion to Chapter 8 on socially embedded subjectivity and the psychological and social foundations of self-narratives, as pioneered by Carl Rogers (1951, 1959).

4 A Capability Conception of the Person

The conclusion of this chapter is that in the large, open worlds we occupy adaptive individuals' different points-in-time selves can be regarded as distinct and independent, but whether they are distinct and independent individuals overtime depends on their developing a personal identity self-narrative capability. Since we value individuality, we ought to then examine what this depends upon and see addressing that as a central social goal of society. Or rather, we ought to examine what barriers exist to people being able to direct their lives as they understand their capabilities and themselves – Mill's famous self-direction idea of freedom.

On the "externalist" view of individual autonomy taken in Chapter 3, whether people are distinct and independent, autonomous individuals depend on whether social institutions and social relationships promote or constrain their choices. Thus, when social institutions and relationships systematically work to the disadvantage of some people and the advantage of others, as in socially stratified societies, individual autonomy is constrained rather than promoted, and not only should we expect people not to develop the capabilities they would in democratic societies, but we should also expect them to be less successful in managing their existing capabilities. Social stratification, that is, both limits capability development and fragments people into sets of disconnected selves.

In Chapter 5, I discuss how social institutions and social relationships in socially stratified economies limit people's capability development, and produce capability shortfalls relative to would be the case in the absence of those institutions and relationships. In Chapter 6, I discuss how social institutions and social relationships in democratic economies promote people's capability development, instead producing capability gains. Thus, the argument of Chapters 5 and 6 is that what a "person's *actual* ability [is] to do the different things that she values doing" or what "the *actual opportunities* [are] a person has" (Sen, 2009, p. 253) depends on how societies are organized and the nature of people's social embeddedness.

5 | A General Theory of Social Economic Stratification
Stigmatization, Exclusion, and Capability Shortfalls

Actors do not behave or decide as atoms outside a social context.... Their attempts at purposive action are instead embedded in concrete, ongoing systems of social relations.

Granovetter (1985, p. 487)

The conception of the individual as a very "private" person – unconcerned about the rest of the world – has been seen, in my judgement rightly, as both empirically unrealistic and theoretically misleading.

Sen (1985, p. 9)

Claims about the defectiveness of a group with outcast/caste status are an ideological mask that absolves the social system and privileged groups from criticism for their role in perpetuating the condition of the dispossessed.

Darity (2005, p. 144).

1 Social Stratification versus Democracy

In externalist views of individual autonomy, whether people function as distinct and independent individuals depends on whether social institutions and social relationships promote or limit their choices and actions. "Social institutions and social relationships" constitutes a very broad framework. I employ one general way of characterizing it: whether they are structured so as to reinforce and sustain hierarchical orderings between large social groups defined in terms of people's different social identities, especially race, ethnicity, gender, religion, and sexual orientation (and combinations of these).

How societies and economies are structurally stratified by social groups was central to classical economics, has long been studied in sociology, and is now the basis of stratification economics. Social group hierarchies create greater opportunities for people in higher ranked social groups and lesser opportunities for people in lower ranked social groups. Social institutions and social relationships that reinforce and sustain these hierarchical orderings then cause people's social identities to work to their advantage or disadvantage according to their social group positions and either promote or limit their individual autonomy. Addressing this thus modifies the adaptive individual analysis of the last chapter by socially embedding people in institutional–relational contexts.

While there are degrees in which and considerable variability regarding how social group hierarchies operate in societies, in order to give one externalist explanation of individual autonomy, I focus on how social stratification works in the US case in connection with race and gender. While social stratification in the US has its own distinctive characteristics, it nonetheless illustrates how social stratification works in many places in the world today. I use this case, then, to generally characterize socially stratified societies as ones where social group position limits individual autonomy. I regard societies where this does not occur, or where in socially stratified ones it does not, as broadly democratic. To examine what this involves, Chapter 6 discusses strategies for capability development in democratic societies that limit social and economic stratification.

Chapter 4's adaptive individual capability conception advanced an explanation of people's individual/personal identity. This chapter adds people's social identities to that conception, making people more clearly both individual and social. People are both individual and social when we see them as made up of capabilities since capabilities are inherently social phenomena. When we are also explicit about their social identities as being important to what they are, they are also both individual and social because they can act both independently of and/or on the basis of their social identities. If we put this on a spectrum from their being primarily representative agents of themselves to their being primarily representative agents of the social groups to which they belong, one thing that inclines them toward the latter (according to evidence from social psychology reviewed below) is whether individuals feel they are at risk on their own and seek the security of social groups. One way this occurs is when social institutions and social relationships are organized around social group hierarchies that significantly limit individual autonomy for some. Thus, what sorts of social institutions and social relationships exist has an influence on both the makeup of people's individual/personal identities and how people determine the balance between their individual/ personal identities and social identities.

Section 2 begins by linking social identity to social embeddedness and by distinguishing weak and strong conceptions of social embeddedness in economics. Weak social embeddedness might be said to occur when individuals understood in utility function terms act on other-regarding interests, though I argue this is still a conception of socially *un*embedded individuals. Strong social embeddedness is explained using social psychology's in-group/out-group explanation of individuals acting as representative agents of social groups. The main part of the chapter goes on to address strong social embeddedness using the adaptive capability individual conception and distinguishes micro-level mechanisms and macro-level processes at work in socially stratified societies.

Section 3 distinguishes two types of social identities in the social psychology literature in order to model a micro-level mechanism that operates in socially stratified economies I term *selective stigmatization*. Individuals with higher ranked social identities in positions of power over individuals with lower ranked social identities stigmatize only a subset of the latter's social identities. This works to the former's advantage and the latter's disadvantage, acts to reinforce and sustain existing hierarchical social group relationships, and in capability terms produces capability shortfalls for the individuals with stigmatized social identities I term capability *devaluations*.

Section 4 uses stratification economics to explain how *exclusion by social group identity* works as a macro-level process to generate two types of socially and economically different economic and social destinations for individuals depending on their social group positions: a "club" good-type location and a "common pool"-type location. The existence of these two types of destinations reinforces and sustains hierarchical social group relationships, and in capability terms produces a second kind of capability shortfall for individuals I term capability *deficits* that reflect average differences between social groups.

Sections 3 and 4 examine how micro-level mechanisms and macro-level processes each work to sustain social group hierarchies and limit the capability development of individuals with lower ranked social identities. Section 5 examines how they interact and are interconnected. It describes this interaction using a bottom-up/top-down complexity theory approach and provides a simple formalism to describe its dynamics. Section 5 then identifies two kinds of social policies aimed at combatting social stratification: one that targets stigmatization as a micro-level mechanism and one that targets social exclusion as a macro-level process. Their shared goal is to promote people being able to act as distinct and independent individuals who seek to develop their capabilities. Section 6 briefly concludes the chapter.

2 Social Embeddedness, Social Identity, and Social Stratification

In mainstream economics, if one were to say people are socially embedded, this would mean social relationships affect their behavior understood in utility function terms, for example, as when people's social identities (Akerlof and Kranton, 2000) or their social preferences (Fehr and Fischbacher, 2002) are included in their individual utility functions. This is a weak sense of social embeddedness, because if people are still individual utility maximizers, their social relationships and regard for others only count for as much as they individually prefer. More accurately, they are socially *un*embedded in that concern for others is optional, and people remain essentially independent of their social relationships.[1]

Social embeddedness can also be understood in a strong sense when people are viewed first and foremost as social beings. As Karl Polanyi (1944) argued, markets are embedded in social relationships rather than the reverse, and social relationships play a fundamental role in determining people's choices. Individual agency on this view is modified by a person's social relationships, and people can act on others' choices even though their choices are nominally their "own" and are expressed as their "own" choices. While the idea of social embeddedness in this strong sense appeals to many, the absence of a conception

---

[1] To take one example, in health care the principal–agent interpretation of provider–patient relationships makes the providers' concern for patients instrumental to the utility satisfaction of the former, so that care in a noninstrumental ethical sense is reduced to an externality (Davis and McMaster, 2017). While the provider–patient relationship appears to socially embed providers, their utility function characterization belies this.

of the individual alternative to the utility function one has limited its adoption in economics.

However, strong social embeddedness has been extensively investigated in social psychology's social identity theory where individuals act as representative agents of social groups with which they identify and behave in a pro-in-group/anti-out-group manner (Tajfel and Turner, 1979; Postmes and Branscombe, 2010). Essentially, people make choices they believe are in the group's interest their own choices. People are still individuals and still make choices independent of their social identities when those identities matter little, but act as representative agents of those groups when they matter more. But why do people identify with social groups in the first place? Why not always act as independent individuals, as mainstream economics assumes?

To answer these questions, Realistic Conflict Theory (Baumeister and Vohs, 2007; Schofield, 2010) identifies conditions under which people form and join social groups. Those conditions were first explored and explained in the now famous Robbers Cave experiment (Sherif et al., 1954/1961; Sherif, 1956) that showed that when individuals find themselves in risky, uncertain, zero-sum-type circumstances, they often organize themselves into competing social groups, act as they perceive their own groups require, and cease to act as independent individuals.

The Robbers Cave experiment, and much subsequent social psychology research on social group formation and affiliation (Platow and Hunter, 2012; Haslam, 2018), has shown that social group members often share some set of characteristics, such as race, ethnicity, gender, or religion, but that groups can also form from sets of heterogeneous individuals who see themselves as sharing a common purpose, such as we observe in many social movements. Thus, what is key to group formation are the conditions under which it occurs, specifically, when individuals perceive they face risky, uncertain, zero-sum-type circumstances. Later social network theory has built on this conclusion to show that people's social ties, whatever their basis, tend to cluster around relatively well-defined or distinguishable social groups (Wasserman and Faust, 1994). Membership in groups thus acts as a behavioral anchor individuals regularly fall back upon when they find themselves in risky zero-sum worlds.

This chapter uses the strong sense of social embeddedness to show how economies stratified by social groups, as explained in stratification economics, structurally limit the capability development of individuals in disadvantaged social groups while promoting it for individuals in advantaged social groups. It uses the idea of capability development developed in Chapter 4 to characterize the effects on individuals and social groups of social stratification. Section 3 examines a micro-level stigmatization mechanism that generates capability shortfalls I term capability devaluations.

3 Social Stigmatization and Capability Devaluations

When we explain social embeddedness in social identity terms and focus on societies stratified by social groups, this introduces power and conflict into our analysis of people's choices since in these circumstances groups compete with one another and individuals' choices reflect this. However, social identity analysis distinguishes two types of social identities: people's categorical or group social identities and their individual-to-individual relational social identities. To explain the effects of stigmatization at the micro-level, I show how these two types of social identities interact in social role settings, such as in employment, households, schools, and clinics. I characterize these as *hierarchical social role settings* in which some individuals exercise authority over others, and it can be in their social group's interest to reinforce their social group's relative positions.

In this analysis, I explain how individuals in positions of authority in hierarchical social role settings are motivated to:

(i) *selectively stigmatize* and disfavor out of all subordinates' social group identities those social identities that are most important to maintaining a society's main social group hierarchical relationships;

(ii) *selectively favor* out of all subordinates' particular social group identities those that have the appearance of reducing a society's hierarchical character.

This dual targeting is contrary to what supervisors' roles in these social settings functionally require in ordinary efficiency terms, and contrary to what subordinates' capability development requires. To illustrate, I interpret recent evidence regarding race and gender in the US as a practice of *selective stigmatization* that disfavors some subordinates' social group identities and favors others, and thereby works to sustain existing race and gender hierarchical social group relationships.

I then explain how this practice produces measurable shortfalls in the capabilities people can develop. I term this particular kind of capability shortfall a capability *devaluation*, because it results from the actions people undertake to devalue others' capabilities. I distinguish two micro-level substitution effects this involves: a distortion effect and a burden effect.

a Two Types of Social Identity

In social psychology, people have two types of social identities: "identifications of the self *as* a certain kind of person" – role-based identities – and social identities involving "identifications of the self *with* a group or category as a whole" – collective identities (Thoits and Virsup, 1997, p. 106). In each case, they make others a part of themselves and socially embed others in themselves. Social psychologists treat these two social identifications as "two levels of [people's] social selves – (i) those that derive from interpersonal relationships and interdependence with specific others and (ii) those that derive from membership in larger, more impersonal collectives or social categories" (Brewer and Gardner, 1996, p. 83; Brewer 2001; Reynolds et al., 2003).

The first type of social identity is a *relational social identity* and the second a *categorical social identity*. Relational social identities exist where people occupy positions in a "relational web" (such as in family, friendship, employment, and service relationships), and identify with others in specific ways. They involve differentiated relationships with others with whom they are in relatively close contact (e.g., employers and employees, parents and children, students and teachers, caregivers and care-recipients, etc.). Categorical social identities exist where people find themselves "sharing some categorical attribute" with other like people (race, ethnicity, gender, religion, age, disability, language, class, nationality, sexual orientation, etc.), and socially identify with others as all representative of that shared category (Brubaker and Cooper, 2000, pp. 15ff). Categorical social identities involve shared relationships with many people one typically does not know or may never encounter (e.g., those of the same race or gender). See Table 5.1 (also Davis, 2011, pp. 201ff).

Note, then, that in social role settings people have both categorical and relational social identities. For example, "employer" and

Table 5.1 *Two types of social identity*

Type of social identity	Mode of identification	Basis of identification	Proximity to others
Relational	Social roles	Linked differences	Relatively close
Categorical	Social groups	Commonalities	Often distant

"employee" social roles create an "employer–employee" relational social identity, but "employers" and "employees" also constitute categorical social group identities. Social role settings thus create potential conflicts of interest between people's relational and categorical social identities when what a role requires and what social group interest requires conflict.

Conflicts also exist between individuals' different categorical social identities and between their different relational social identities. Feminist intersectionality theory investigates conflicts between individuals' different categorical social group identities, such as between race and gender (Crenshaw, 1991; Lykke, 2010; Allen, 2016), and feminist economics has extensively investigated conflicts between individuals' different relational social identities, such as between household and market relationships (Peterson and Lewis, 1999; Barker and Feiner, 2004). I focus on conflicts between people's categorical and relational social identities specifically in hierarchical relational role settings, where one set of individuals exercises authority over another, because this allows us to directly link stigmatization as a micro-level practice and macro-level social stratification.[2]

Social roles in relational settings, when they are hierarchical, have a dual nature. On the one hand, they involve a division of responsibility and delegation of activities that is primarily functional in character and as such normatively unobjectionable. A person in a supervisory capacity is justified in directing another person's activities if experience and knowledge justify it. On the other hand, hierarchical social roles also create opportunities for individuals to exercise arbitrary

---

[2] I thus set aside here complicated issues regarding how intersectionality, or having multiple social group identities, operates in hierarchical societies, though it can be argued contrary to what might be expected that it generally does not moderate social stratification (Davis, 2015b).

power over others which lacks a functional basis and is normatively objectionable. This is the case with which I am concerned.[3]

In individualistic mainstream economics, the cause of this is simply individuals' self-aggrandizing behavior – an inefficient sort of principal–agent relationship – that says nothing about how society is organized. However, when individuals are seen as strongly socially embedded and society stratified by social groups, it is in the interest of individuals in positions of authority in higher ranked social groups to act to reinforce their group's relative positions. Selective social stigmatization targeting specific social group identities of subordinates is a means of achieving this.

b Selective Stigmatization as a Means of Reinforcing Social Inequality

Previously, I explained social stigmatization as a broad social practice that works through stereotyping, discrimination, social prejudice, harassment, and vilification of individuals according to their social group identities, and reinforces and sustains a society's hierarchical organization around race, gender, religion, sexual orientation, and ethnicity (Davis, 2014, 2015c). When a person is stigmatized, they are reduced to an "attribute or characteristic that conveys a social identity" shared by many others (Goffman, 1963, p. 505). Stigmatization is also known as stereotype threat or social identity threat (Steele, Spencer, Aronson, 2002). Moreover, while individuals stigmatize individuals, stigmatization is not simply "a set of feelings which members of one racial group have toward the members of another racial group," since this ignores – for example, in the case of race – "the collective process by which a racial group comes to define and redefine another racial group" (Blumer, 1958, p. 3; see Darity, 2009, pp. 803–805). Consequently, stigmatization needs to be understood in terms of intergroup dynamics and differences in power between social groups, not in an individualistic, subjectivist manner as in the neoclassical "taste for discrimination" approach (Becker, 1957).

---

[3] There is an extensive literature on the relationship between social position and power. See Lukes (2005), Fleming and Spicer (2007), Lawson (2019), and Martins (2022).

Consider, then, the evidence regarding social group inequality in connection with race in the US. As shown in an extensive study of intergenerational income mobility and persistence of income disparities across racial groups for the period 1989–2015 (Chetty et al., 2018), black Americans have substantially lower rates of upward mobility and higher rates of downward mobility than white Americans, reinforcing long-standing income and wealth disparities by race in the US (see Darity and Mullen, 2020, ch. 2). However, at the same time, there is very little difference over this period in income mobility rates between black women and white women (though to be clear, black women still have lower incomes than white women).[4] Thus, lower income mobility for black Americans overall relative to white Americans can be explained by black men's income mobility relative to white men outweighing black women's relative income mobility relative to white women.

This tells us that individuals in a dominant social group in positions of authority in employment settings can help sustain the relative social group positions of whites over blacks by stigmatizing black men but not black women, or by disproportionately stigmatizing the former. This tends to (i) reinforce the most important racial social group inequalities by depressing income and employment for black Americans overall; (ii) create an opportunity for those in positions of authority to claim they oppose discrimination, using black women as evidence.[5]

Consider now the evidence regarding social group inequality in connection with gender in the US. Just as there is a persistent black–white income gap so there is also a persistent gender income gap. Yet, there is also significantly less of a gender income gap when women and men of the same education and levels of experience work equally long hours

---

[4] As Chetty et al. emphasize, the absence of differences in mobility rates is conditional on family income or where family income levels are the same. Thus, income levels and income mobility are separate measures, and potentially addressed by different public policies.

[5] Not stigmatizing black women in employment settings does not mean black women are not stigmatized culturally and socially. Nor does it not mean black women are not stigmatized in employment settings at all. The argument is that racial stigmatization primarily targets black men. The interpretation offered here of the Chetty et al. results is only meant to address that black women and white women have essentially the same income mobility, not the same income levels or social standing.

in their places of employment – a phenomenon called "overwork" that has become increasingly common in the US since 2000 (Weeden et al., 2016).[6] However, since women have the main responsibility for household activities, most women do not take positions that involve long hours.

How does a strategy of selective stigmatization work here? If long hours are not stigmatized whether women or men work them, then (ii) it appears discrimination by gender does not occur, again minimizing discrimination in the workplace as a public policy issue. Yet, the effect of this is (i) to stigmatize women who, given the traditional household division of labor, are less likely to work long hours, thus reinforcing the overall income gap between women and men, and perpetuating traditional household social roles. Indeed, since women's education levels have risen relative to men's in the US, the emergence of "overwork" acts counter to social forces that would tend to reduce gender inequality.

Selective stigmatization with its two connected goals thus sustains social stratification and creates a narrative denying it at the same time. In the case of race, discrimination appears to be absent if black and white women have the same income mobility. In the case of gender, discrimination appears to be absent if women who overwork do as well as men. These narratives ignore how selective stigmatization manipulates people's intersectionality by favoring certain social group identities and disfavoring others. Note also that to succeed black women need to reduce their identities to being women and suppress their identities of being black, and women who overwork need to reduce their identities to being people who work long hours and suppress their identities of being women. The overall effect in each case is to reinforce the main social group inequalities regarding race and gender.

Selective stigmatization, moreover, can operate in any hierarchical social role setting in societies organized by social groups where individuals in positions of authority exercise power over others – besides employment, housing, education, public services, etc. Mainstream economics suppresses analysis of this, since not only does it ignore

---

[6] Historically, the establishment of overtime compensation rates aimed at discouraging long hours, and the 40-hour workweek was taken as a social norm. In effect, if long hours were previously stigmatized, in an "overwork" economy normal hours are stigmatized.

Box 5.1   A "microeconomics" of selective stigmatization

Categorical social group identities are ranked hierarchically in
  society
Relational social identities link social roles
It is the interest of those in positions of authority to reinforce social
  group hierarchy
Selective stigmatization in relational settings:

 (i) strengthens the most important social group inequalities
(ii) may reduce less important social group inequalities

---

power and conflict, but it attributes differences in economic outcomes
between individuals to individual human capital differences. This
feeds into popular derogatory views of lower ranked social groups –
a "science"-level practice that dovetails with real-world prejudice.
Then, as stratification economist William Darity puts it, "claims about
the defectiveness of a group with outcast/caste status [become] an ideological mask that absolves the social system and privileged groups
from criticism for their role in perpetuating the condition of the dispossessed" (Darity, 2005, p. 144).

Box 5.1 summarizes this micro-level account of how stigmatization
reinforces social hierarchy.

c *Selective Stigmatization and Capability Devaluations*

Selective stigmatization reinforces social and economic inequality in
societies hierarchically organized around competing social groups by
manipulating intersectionality. It has two specific distorting effects.
From an economy-wide perspective, as with any discriminatory activity, selective stigmatization limits how well functional roles can be
performed, thereby reducing potential economic output. From an
individual's perspective, it limits how people develop their capabilities causing them to act differently from what they would choose and
rather as stigmatizers prefer. I call these effects capability *devaluations*,
because stigmatization involves someone actively devaluing someone
else's capabilities by disfavoring certain social identities they possess
and by reducing some of their individual characteristics to disfavored
group characteristics.

This devaluation exploits intersectionality. In the case of the US, the evidence tells us that when black and white women have the same income mobility and black Americans overall have downward income mobility, selective stigmatization favors a black woman being a woman and discourages her from being black. She possesses both social identities, so her capability development should depend on how she combines and organizes both, but since being black has been reduced in value, she is pressured to develop her capabilities minus her identity of being black – a forced social identity *substitution effect*.

In the case of gender, we saw when women and men both overwork their incomes appear nondiscriminatory but that overall women still earn less than men. Selective stigmatization, then, favors a woman being an over-worker and suppresses her being a woman. If absent stigmatization, her capability development depends on how she combines and organizes her social identities, when it is present in employment settings, she is likely to develop her capabilities minus her identity as a woman – again, a forced social identity *substitution effect*.

In strong social embeddedness terms, in both cases the stigmatized individual loses agency to the stigmatizer. I characterize these capability devaluations as measurable capability shortfalls in which the stocks of capabilities people develop are reduced from what they would develop were they to develop their capabilities as they choose. How can such capability shortfalls be measured? I suggest they can be benchmarked by the measurable capabilities people would have according to what their social roles would require were stigmatization absent.

In relational social settings, then, criteria for fulfilling social roles according to what those roles require are set out in terms of specific sets of activities they involve. That is, social roles can be described functionally in terms of agreed-upon sets of activities, and those activities then require that people have specific capabilities for performing them. For example, operating various types of equipment requires one understand technical manuals and user protocols, and this entails having various capabilities for understanding and using those materials. In effect, the capability set is determined by task activity requirements. Thus, though capabilities are often understood in fairly general terms as associated with the development literature idea of basic capabilities needed to escape poverty, the concept of capability can also be employed in relational settings where productive activity occurs, as reflected in how it is commonly used in business organization models (e.g., Greski, 2009).

Activities required and capabilities paired with them, then, are often well specified in employment settings, since there they are closely connected to wage-setting. In nonemployment household and community settings, extensive time-use studies of household production and community cooperative activities demonstrate that the activities and capabilities involved there are quite specific as well.

Benchmarking capability shortfalls by activity–capability standards, then, allows us to explain how the capability substitution effect that stigmatization involves takes two forms. A pure *distortion effect* results when the activities and capabilities appropriate to a social role are replaced by activities and capabilities less appropriate or even inappropriate to it. A *burden effect* results when the activities and capabilities required in a role are inappropriately shifted from the stigmatizer to the stigmatized. The pure distortion effect is arguably more technical in character because it is especially tied to efficient methods and technologies used in productive activity, yet social values regarding how people work together are still important. The burden effect, however, especially incorporates social values and normative views in a significant way in regard to responsibility sharing, which in turn involves social justice issues.

An important line of research in stratification economics examines combinations of distortion and burden effects in connection with how people adapt their identities and consumption choices under stigmatization using a concept of negative identity production externalities (see Stewart, 1995). In terms of the framework here, these effects redirect people's capability development away from what it would otherwise be.

Generally, then, in employment settings, the activities that social roles require depend on the nature of the production involved. A cost of discrimination perpetuated by stigmatization is more easily determined in this case than in the case of household and family settings, where the division of responsibilities is highly gendered and social values play an important role. However, a burden effect resulting from stigmatization can still be benchmarked by how social roles are allocated according to prevalent social values. It follows that this benchmarking would produce different results under alternative social values and accompanying institutional arrangements.

This section, then, explains one way a social identity-based micro-level analysis built upon strong social embeddedness can explain people's interaction in relational settings when an economy exhibits significant social group stratification. Section 4 moves to a macro-level analysis to discuss how stratification economics explains social group stratification in the economy as a whole.

4 Stratification Economics: Social Exclusion and Capability Deficits

Stratification economics draws on social psychology and other fields to analyze intergroup inequalities organized around hierarchical orderings of social groups, particularly by race, ethnicity, gender, and class (see Darity, 2022; Darity et al., 2015). Research in stratification economics examines how the cumulative, cross-generational effects of wealth inequality across social groups are related to a number of socioeconomic measures of well-being (Ali, et al., 2021). A fundamental issue for stratification economics is how social group hierarchy is systematically perpetuated, and why such hierarchies do not break down over time. Like institutional and evolutionary economics, stratification economics investigates the nature of the structures that institutionalize inequalities in order to identify strategies aimed at their elimination.

Here, I first address what stratification economics adds to realistic conflict theory to explain intergroup inequality, and then argue that socially stratified economies function as systems of social of exclusion in which an economics of abundance operates for socially privileged social groups and the economics of scarcity for those in socially disadvantage social groups. Finally, I argue that social stratification produces a set of capability shortfalls termed capability *deficits* distinct in nature from the capability devaluation shortfalls that stigmatization produces.

a Stratification Economics and Realistic Conflict Theory

Stratification economics shows how social relationships within different domains of society – employment, education, housing, health, etc. – generally reflect intergroup conflict, and how this results in superior economic opportunities and outcomes for individuals in dominant social groups and inferior ones for individuals in dominated groups (Chelwa et al., 2022; Chester and McMaster, 2023; Darity 2005, 2022; Darity et al., 2006, Darity et al., 2017; Davis, 2019c, 2022; Darity and Mullen, 2020; Obeng-Odoom, 2020; Stewart 1995, 2008, 2010). Intergroup conflict within any given domain tends to work to the advantage of more powerful social groups, but their advantages in any one domain spill over into others, thus building on and reinforcing intergroup conflict across them all (Ali et al., 2021). For example, discrimination in housing and education have well-known spillover effects on employment and health. This locks in social group hierarchies and makes them the foundation of the overall economic process.

Whereas in mainstream macroeconomics the income generation process is driven by competition between individuals, in stratification economics it is driven by competition between social groups. Stratification economics is like classical political economy and contemporary heterodox theories that explain growth in terms of distribution (Dutt, 2017), but its focus is on social groups rather than income classes such as labor and capital. Inequalities in income and wealth exist by class, but class in contemporary capitalism also needs to be understood in terms of social group identity.

Thus, if in realistic conflict theory individuals organize themselves into social groups in the risky, uncertain, zero-sum-type circumstances as identified in the Robbers Cave experiment, what specific form do these circumstances take in contemporary capitalist economies according to stratification economics? I argue that in the case of the US since the 1970s and 1980s two developments are especially important:

(i) Income and wealth inequality are rising;
(ii) Relatively large numbers of people face either a downward intergenerational income mobility or little income mobility at all.

Both are characteristics of US capitalism since the 1970s and 1980s. First, there is clear evidence that overall income inequality in the US has worsened significantly since the 1970s (Piketty and Saez, 2003; Saez, 2021), and that over the same period overall wealth inequality has increased significantly in the US as well (Saez and Zucman, 2014). In the case of race, the evidence for the US is also clear (Darity et al., 2018; Darity and Mullen, 2020). A 2018 US Bureau of Labor Statistics study shows that household income clearly varies significantly by race and ethnicity (Noël, 2018). A 2013 Urban Institute study shows that not only is wealth inequality significant across Hispanic, black, and white households but it is also increasing (McKernan, Ratcliffe, Steuerle, and Zhang, 2013). In the case of gender, a 2016 US Bureau of Labor Statistics study shows that women in general earn less than men, and that this difference has narrowed very little over time for most women (US Bureau of Labor Statistics). A 2017 study shows that women's wealth gap is significant and far greater than the gender income gap (McCulloch, 2017). Further, black–white and female–male income inequality have both risen as a result of the Great Recession (Arestis et al., 2014; Addo and Darity, 2021).

Second, regarding intergenerational income mobility, it has been shown for the US that "absolute" income mobility, defined as "the fraction of children earning or consuming more than their parents," has fallen "approximately 90% for children born in 1940 to 50% for children born in the 1980s" (Chetty et al., 2017). At the same time, as noted above, income mobility for black Americans is consistently worse than for white Americans (Chetty et al., 2018; Darity and Mullen, 2020, ch. 2).

I will argue, then, that this allows us to argue socially stratified economies operate as systems of social exclusion and that stratification economics is also an economics of exclusion (Davis, 2019c).

b Stratification Economics as an Economics of Exclusion

A socially stratified economy creates different kinds of economic destinations or positions for different people that produce different qualities of employment, education, housing, and health care. The broad mechanism by which this occurs is segregation that operates in employment, housing, education, purchase of goods, access to government programs, credit, the legal system, etc., to reduce or limit access for excluded groups to a wide range of economic activities and opportunities while promoting access for privileged groups. That is, an economy that works through segregation is one that makes scarce for some groups of people what is made abundant to other groups.

Suppose, then, we simplify and say in socially stratified economies there are just two basic types of economic destinations and two corresponding qualities of goods people consume in those two destinations. Using economics' standard taxonomy of goods, in one case the goods associated with higher levels of well-being can be called "club

Table 5.2 *Standard taxonomy of goods*

Goods characteristics	Excludable	Nonexcludable
Rivalrous	Private goods	Common pool goods
Nonrivalrous	Club goods	Public goods

goods" while in the other case the goods associated with lower levels of well-being can be called "common pool goods" (*Ibid.*). The standard goods taxonomy, recall, attributes two types of characteristics to goods – whether their consumption is rivalrous and excludable – and then divides the economy into four domains or types of consumption according to the four different ways these characteristics can be combined. The two cases that describe a socially stratified economy that discriminates against some people and privileges others, respectively, refer to the southwest and northeast domains in the standard diagram (Table 5.2).

In mainstream economics, the club goods concept is often used to describe local public goods or public goods provided by political jurisdictions below the state level (Buchanan, 1965). However, it is also used to describe all sorts of private social clubs and other exclusive economic arrangements that employ some system of governance to socially segregate access to the goods. In Table 5.2, this makes those goods excludable like private goods, but unlike private goods it makes their consumption nonrivalrous in that their use by those with access to them does not limit their use other by others with access to them. This effectively creates an economy of abundance for those included in the club. Compared to nonclub goods domains, prices and costs are lower than in nonexclusive settings, creating relatively higher incomes and wealth for their members.

The common pool goods concept originates with the "tragedy of the commons" idea (Hardin, 1968). While it is often associated with developing economies (Ostrom, 1990), it also applies to circumstances in developed economies in which there is no system of social or political governance that regulates the production and consumption of goods, such as labor markets where exploitative practices exist and goods markets where safety issues are ignored. An important dimension of this is how neighborhoods and communities are isolated and cut off from one another – a spatial segregation that describes many US urban areas.

In goods taxonomy terms, the general idea of an unregulated "commons" is thus simply where production and consumption are rivalrous and nonexcludable. People in this worst of all possible circumstances are all on their own – a sort of socially constructed Hobbesian war of all against all. This effectively creates the most extreme economy of scarcity, often idealized in the idea of "free" competition. Compared to the other domains, prices and costs are higher, leading to relatively lower incomes and wealth than in the other domains.

A socially stratified economy, then, when represented as primarily having these two different kinds of economic destinations, operates by sorting people across the club goods and common pool goods locations according to their social group identities. This determines social group income and wealth inequalities and socioeconomic differences in quality of employment, education, housing, and health care. The social system driving these outcomes is one of the intergroup competitions where dominant social groups use their advantages to live lives of abundance while extolling the virtues of competition.[7]

For stratification economics, then, the economy operates on the southwest–northeast diagonal of the goods/economy taxonomy as a self-sustaining system of social inclusion and exclusion where competition is between hierarchically ordered social groups. This diagonal is largely ignored in mainstream economics which emphasizes the southeast–northwest diagonal, and represents the economy as a being in continual contest over the size of the state and extent of the free markets.

c Economic Exclusion and Capability Deficits

Socially stratified, hierarchically organized economies produce another type of capability shortfall – a social structural type – resulting from the different destinations people occupy rather than from the direct effects of stigmatization and discrimination. I term these structural capability shortfalls capability *deficits*. In terms of the two-destination analysis above, when one occupies a common pool-type social location, one's

---

[7] For how the club–common pool destination division operates in the case of cross-national migrants, see Burnazoglu (2021). Similar factors often also operate for within-country rural-to-urban migrants.

opportunities for capability development are on average worse than when one occupies a club-type social location.

I argued above that measurement of capability devaluations depends on the nature of the social role settings in which stigmatization occurs. Social roles determine sets of activities that people need to perform, and this benchmarks the capabilities that may fail to be exercised in those roles when stigmatization substitutes different sets of activities. That is, capability devaluations are tied to the nature of productive activity in a given relational setting. In contrast, the measurement of capability deficits compares different social groups' capability development opportunities. In a two-destination world, what capabilities people on average can pursue is determined by the capabilities that individuals in privileged social groups can pursue, given what an economy's resources permit when abundance is shared.

In the capability literature, capabilities are proxied by functionings, which as observable activities can be measured in a relatively straightforward matter (Sen, 2009, pp. 235ff). But how do we calculate the value of lost functionings to determine the possible functionings people could have achieved were exclusion absent? Of the different methods possible, the most straightforward is simply to measure them by comparing existing levels of wealth inequality between disadvantaged and privileged social groups – a method used recently to estimate reparations needed to redress the effects of slavery and Jim Crow practices in the US (Darity and Mullen, 2020, ch. 13; Darity, Mullen, and Slaughter, 2022; Mason et al., 2022).

The rationale for this approach is that wealth inequality is a consequence of a social system built around social stratification, and thus effectively captures people's accumulated losses. Its measurement is also reasonably straightforward and thus could produce a fairly clear determination of a society's capability/functioning deficits due to social stratification at any point in time.

5 The Interconnection of Stigmatization and Social Exclusion

This section provides a "general theory" of social stratification using a two-level micro-level/macro-level dynamic that explains how stigmatization mechanisms and social exclusion processes are interconnected and how they reinforce one another or break down together. Stratification economics explains how when stigmatization is widespread, expected, and a standard practice, social exclusion is high and economic and social differences between social groups are high. Alternatively, when stigmatization is less common, unexpected, and seen as unacceptable, social exclusion is lower. How is this explained?

When across many societies economic and social differences between social groups are significant and long-lasting, they come to be seen as inevitable and rooted in human nature. Rationalizations of and ideological justifications for their existence then become part of mainstream social science and more importantly are institutionalized and legitimized in legal systems (Harris, 1993; Stewart, 2010). Differences between social groups in economic outcomes come to be seen as "natural" (Darity, 2005). From the point of view of stigmatizers, stigmatization and discrimination are not an objectionable manipulation of people's social identities, but the result of a rational evaluation of their lesser abilities carried out by those who have superior abilities.

However, when in some societies economic and social differences between social groups are less and stigmatization is seen as unacceptable, naturalistic and individualistic explanations of these differences become less plausible and more complex multicausal social science explanations of people's differences are called for. People still differ in their natural abilities, but the effects of those differences on their opportunities are seen to be influenced by society. Social policy then becomes a factor influencing people's opportunities, and social stratification comes to be seen less as inevitable and more as one pathway some societies pursue.

When we see this as a dynamical process, stigmatization and social exclusion can be understood as interacting in either a self-fulfilling or a self-defeating way depending on a society's beliefs, laws and rules, and social norms. This allows us to map out different possible historical pathways under multiple social policy scenarios, producing a range of types of societies from the most apartheid-like to the most democratic (Mason et al., 2022).

I represent this dynamical process using the simple complexity model developed by Herbert Simon (1962) that was discussed in Chapter 1. Simon's view is that a complex system is made up of multiple, relatively independent subsystems whose interaction determines how the overall system they together make up functions, which in turn acts upon and influences how those subsystems function. Each of a system's relatively independent subsystems exhibits an internal

---

Box 5.2   Simon's complex systems model

Complex systems are made up of multiple, relatively independent
  subsystems
Their interaction affects the performance of the entire system they
  make up
This feeds back on how each subsystem internally operates
This changes how these subsystems interact
This again affects the overall performance of the entire system
This goes on and on in a continually evolving dynamic of change

---

activity which affects these subsystems' interaction with each other.
The effects of these subsystems' interaction on the overall system then
feedback upon both these subsystems' internal activities, and this
affects how they interact.

If we describe this in a combined bottom-up/top-down way, a
complex system involves a dynamic relationship where bottom-up
micro-level activities within interacting subsystems affect the entire
macro-level system, and changes in this system then feedback in a
top-down way upon the activities within those subsystems and their
interaction, together producing a continually ongoing two-way
micro-level/macro-level interaction, as in Box 5.2.

We can explain this continually ongoing process in terms of how
micro- and macro-levels interact and interconnect stigmatization and
overall social group inequality. Stigmatization occurs in multiple
domains (employment, housing, education, etc.) – in effect, Simon's
different interacting subsystems. To represent it as the bottom-up part
of this process, let a represent stigmatization by social group identity
occurring in any such domain, and let b represent its effects on social
group inequality at the macro-level.

$$a \rightarrow b \hspace{10em} [1]$$

Mainstream economics and stratification economics share [1] because
they agree that stigmatization, or discrimination for the mainstream,
contributes to social group inequality. However, the mainstream
either ignores or rejects the possibility that change in levels of dis-
crimination/stigmatization over time might change the state of
social group inequality, and the further possibility that changes in
the state of social group inequality across many domains could then
feedback upon and change levels of discrimination/stigmatization in

each or many of them over time. It ignores these possibilities because methodologically it employs a microfoundations reasoning whereby what occurs at the micro-level of the economy involves processes independent of the macro-level, and the representation the macro-level simply aggregates the many activities that occur at the micro-level. It rejects them because more substantively it explains differences between people in terms of their given ("natural") endowments, so that changes in social practices ultimately cannot significantly alter social inequality (also ruling out macro- to micro-feedback effects). Together, this then implies that [1] does not change over time. That is, the mainstream view is that [1] reproduces itself over time in a stable manner, as in [2].

$$a \rightarrow b \rightarrow (a \rightarrow b) \qquad\qquad [2]$$

Thus, not only is b and outcome of discrimination/stigmatization, but so is $a \rightarrow b$, so adding up the effects in [1] and [2] for total effects ($\Rightarrow$) produces [3].

$$a \text{ and } a \rightarrow b \text{ and } a \rightarrow b \rightarrow (a \rightarrow b) \Rightarrow b \text{ and } (a \rightarrow b) \qquad [3]$$

What [3] tells us is discrimination/stigmatization a affects social inequality b but changes in the level of a do not affect b enough to change the $a \rightarrow b$ relationship. What people might do on the micro-level to change social practices cannot influence the macro-level character of inequality in society. This effectively makes the stigmatization–social inequality relationship a static relationship and also self-reinforcing since it promotes a kind of thinking about them that discrimination/stigmatization is only an efficiency concern without wider consequences.

In contrast, stratification economics argues that levels of stigmatization a not only affect social group inequality b but this can also affect and transform the $a \rightarrow b$ relationship, both through how a affects b and through feedback effects of this on $a \rightarrow b$. To capture this, replace [2] by [4] where that relationship becomes $(a \rightarrow b)'$.

$$a \rightarrow b \rightarrow (a \rightarrow b)' \qquad\qquad [4]$$

Relationship [4] drops the independent microfoundations idea in [2] and casts doubt on the "natural" endowment explanation of social inequality. Changes in a, for example, resulting from antidiscrimination laws, not only affect social inequality b, presumably reducing social inequality, but this can also change the relationship between them through feedback effects. This implies we should replace $(a \to b)$ with an $(a \to b)'$. Thus, bottom-up effects interact with top-down effects, in this example, ultimately reducing both a and b. For the overall effects ($\Rightarrow$) of change on both the micro- and macro-levels, [3] now needs to be replaced by [5].

$$a \text{ and } a \to b \text{ and } a \to b \to (a \to b)' \Rightarrow b \text{ and } (a \to b)' \qquad [5]$$

Here, a, the state of stigmatization at any one time, b, the state of social inequality at any one time, and $(a \to b)'$, the state of the stigmatization–social inequality relationship, are interconnected. How they are depends on a society's particular historical pathway.

Might societies' pathways be influenced? This raises the issue of the social policies they adopt. Suppose a society's policies aim at producing a self-defeating dynamic that increasingly reduces both stigmatization and social stratification. Substituting now an $(a \to b)''$ based on this, we can replace $(a \to b)'$ in [5] as follows:

$$a \text{ and } a \to b \text{ and } a \to b \to (a \to b)'' \Rightarrow b \text{ and } (a \to b)'' \qquad [6]$$

Then, we go beyond the idea that different societies are simply on different historical pathways, and imagine we can create policy agendas for transforming those pathways. In stratification economics, these policy agendas need to target both the micro- and macro-levels of society in order to address both stigmatization and social group inequality. The first involves policies that prohibit discrimination to eliminate stigmatization. The second involves policies that establish reparation programs to rectify income and wealth inequalities between social groups. The first targets relationships between individuals and especially concerns their relational social identities, and the second targets relationships between social groups and especially concerns their categorical social identities – the two types of social identities people have as socially embedded individuals. I close, then, with brief remarks about the importance of the concept of social embeddedness and what else it implies about people's capability development.

6 Conclusion: Individuals' Social Embeddedness and Their Capability Development

This chapter's entry point was individuals' strong social embeddedness. This concept makes it possible to introduce social groups into economics in a way that allows us to investigate how social stratification drives the economic process. This not only produces a different causal basis for explaining the dynamics of capitalist economies, but also creates a new agenda for policy, formulated specifically as social policy and alternative to standard welfare/efficiency-based economic approach to policy. In contrast, the mainstream weak social embeddedness concept bars any significant analysis of social stratification, locks in the idea that it is not a policy concern, and leaves policy recommendations to mainstream economists.

In this chapter, my position is that social policies aimed at addressing social stratification ultimately need to be framed in capability terms, specifically in terms of two kinds of capability shortfalls. Capability devaluations and capability deficits call for different kinds of social policies and operate on different levels, but since stigmatization and social exclusion interact so those different types of policies also interact. Preventing stigmatization and discrimination in micro-level relational settings is a means of reducing social stratification at the micro-level of an economy, and reducing social exclusion is a means of reducing it at the macro-level.

This chapter does not discuss the important role legal, institutional, and political systems play and have historically played to structure this interaction. Much valuable research has been done on this subject by researchers in stratification economics, feminist economics, institutional economics, and critical realism that explains the concrete ways in which socially hierarchical societies institutionalize and politically and legally maintain and reinforce this interaction. I leave it to others more knowledgeable on this subject to advance these literatures.

This chapter gave a "general theory" of social stratification using its two-level analysis. But the analysis also takes its generality from its conceptual starting point: the need to abandon the *un*embedded *Homo economicus* utility function individual with its very narrow view of people. That conception acts as the lynchpin of mainstream economics and underlies its single-level view of the economic process that helps secure the self-reinforcing dynamic of social stratification. This chapter's alternative starting point in a conception of individuals as strongly socially embedded not only provides a more realistic account of people's agency and economic behavior, but also shifts our time horizon for social policy. The time horizon of standard theory welfare analysis is very short, since it only aspires to correct modest inefficiencies in an otherwise generally well-functioning market system. Yet when we instead aspire to promote the development of people's capabilities, this includes not only dealing with people's capability shortfalls, but also imagining how their capabilities might be enhanced and expanded in the long run – such as the century ahead. This latter side of human capability development is the subject of the chapter to follow. In it, we imagine not only how people's capabilities might develop over the coming century, but also how this goes hand-in-hand with the goal of replacing socially stratified societies with democratic ones.

6 Roads Not Taken Yet to Be Taken
Enhanced Capabilities

Human beings are thoroughly diverse.

Sen (1992, p. 1)

Public reasoning is clearly an essential feature of objectivity in political and ethical beliefs.

Sen (2009, p. 44)

1 From Capability Shortfalls to Capability Gains ... and from Basic Capabilities to Enhanced Capabilities

In a socially stratified economy, strong social embeddedness works to the disadvantage of stigmatized and socially excluded individuals by limiting their ability to organize themselves as stocks of capabilities and by creating shortfalls in the capabilities they are able to develop. However, should social relationships not be built around discriminatory practices and social exclusion, and should the economy instead be organized around reducing inequality between individuals and between social groups, then people's strong social embeddedness could work to their advantage both by creating new opportunities for how people organize themselves as stocks of capabilities and by generating a new space for possible capability gains.

There is an important difference, then, between improving people's capabilities within socially stratified economies and expanding people's capabilities in more democratic societies. This difference is the central focus of the United Nations Development Programme (UNDP) of human capability development as set out in the recent *Human Development Report 2019*. The *Report* contrasts the immediate, short-run task of promoting people's *basic capabilities* in the world as it is today and the further, long-run task of promoting people's *enhanced capabilities* in the world as it will be by the end of the century.

135

Yet, the UNDP argument is not just that we should extend the horizon for human development. The *Report* also argues that if we fail to think in terms of going "beyond today" when the world is rapidly changing socially and technologically, people developing only their basic capabilities will still leave them vulnerable and possibly worse off in new ways in the future. We thus increasingly need to think in terms of them developing enhanced capabilities.

Capabilities evolve with circumstances as well as with values and with people's changing demands and aspirations. Today, having a set of basic capabilities – those associated with the absence of extreme deprivations – is not enough. Enhanced capabilities are becoming crucial for people to own the "narrative of their lives" (UNDP, 2019, p. 6).

Basic capabilities are essential nutrition, housing, literacy and basic education, safety, work, access to health services, etc. Enhanced capabilities – the capabilities needed to live in a rapidly evolving, increasingly complex world – are access to needed education, mobility, old age security, civil and political rights, access to information, free movement, environmental security, social affiliation, fair treatment, self-respect, etc. (also see Ranis and Stewart et al., 2006). The expression "narrative of their lives" refers to how people understand themselves and their individual or personal identities, in relation to their capabilities – essentially the self-narrative personal identity capability idea advanced in Chapter 4.

The *Report* took the "narrative of their lives" expression from an Angus Deaton interview in which he reflected on his study with Anne Case (Case and Deaton, 2020) regarding "deaths of despair" in contemporary US capitalism (Belluz, 2015). Deaton argued that many white, middle-income men in the US, often thought to have social advantages according to their social position, have lost the narratives of their lives, mirroring and giving a reason behind Case and Deaton's evidence that mortality and morbidity for this social group have significantly deteriorated in recent decades despite decades of economic progress in the US. In capability terms, many people in this otherwise privileged social group perceive they have lost the ability to understand their lives and lost the ability to direct their personal capability development.

Case and Deaton do not use a capability framework, nor does Deaton frame the "narratives of their lives" idea in terms of the idea of a self-narrative personal identity capability as I have. The "narrative of their lives" idea is nonetheless very much like Sen's "reasoning and self-scrutinizing" view of the person in which people are reflexive beings whose individual identities involve continually self-assessing themselves and deciding what goals and values they will act upon.

The UNDP *Report* also associates the loss of having a narrative of one's life with a loss of individual agency, and sees securing people's basic capabilities as both a necessary step toward them acquiring enhanced capabilities and a means of strengthening their individual agency.

Enhanced capabilities bring greater agency along people's lives. Given that some capabilities build over a person's life, achieving a basic set – such as surviving to age 5 or learning to read – provides initial stepping stones to forming enhanced capabilities later in life. (UNDP, *Ibid.*)

The reason people's agency needs to be greater is that the rapidly evolving, increasingly complex world we will live in makes managing the interrelatedness of the capabilities people develop more demanding. It is one thing to work to address the challenges of integrating the need for essential nutrition, housing, literacy and basic education, safety, work, access to health services, etc. It is quite another to address the challenges of integrating the need to access needed education, mobility, old age security, civil and political rights, access to information, free movement, environmental security, social affiliation, fair treatment, self-respect, etc. Developing enhanced capabilities thus not only "bring[s] greater agency along people's lives." It requires that they develop greater agency in regard to their choices and lives.

We saw in Chapter 5 that stigmatization and social exclusion manipulate intersectionality and limit which of their different social identities people can act upon, thus decreasing individual agency. In a democratic society in which people determine which social identities they choose to act upon and which capabilities they seek to develop in the many different sorts of circumstances they face in life, the scope of individual agency is not only greater but also gives new, greater weight to self-direction. This is Mill's idea of being self-directed, though framed in terms of people being made up of capabilities rather than desires. Improving especially people's enhanced capabilities, then, goes hand-in-hand with increasing human freedom where this is not just a matter of removing limitations on people's choices but especially a matter of increasing their choices.

Unfortunately, we now live in a world of increasing social inequality, and the immediate prospects worldwide for promoting both people's basic and enhanced capabilities are not promising. How does the UNDP *Report* see the current situation? The *Report*, then, frames moving from promoting just basic capabilities to increasingly promoting enhanced ones as moving beyond just the 2000 Millennium Development Goals to the new 2012 Sustainable Development Goals. Regarding what success has been achieved of the 2000 Goals, although significant disparities in people's basic capabilities continue to exist across the world, and vulnerability to deprivation and suffering is still widespread, the *Report* provides evidence of "slow convergence" and declining inequality worldwide in people's basic capabilities, for example, with respect to life expectancy at birth and shares of populations with a primary education in many countries. However, regarding the 2012 Goals, not only are there currently significant disparities worldwide in people's enhanced capabilities, but there is also evidence of "rapid divergence" and rising inequality worldwide in people's enhanced capabilities, for example, with respect to life expectancy at age 70 and shares of populations with a tertiary education (UNDP, *Ibid.*, Figure 7). The reasons for this are fairly clear.

The *Report* shows, as have many other studies, that new types of inequalities are emerging throughout the world, and as they accumulate and are institutionally locked in they produce greater social power imbalances between privileged and disadvantaged social groups. What is especially worrisome, the *Report* argues, is that technological and climate change are likely to worsen these imbalances, so that even past progress regarding convergence in basic capabilities may be in jeopardy in the future. What this clearly calls for, therefore, is change in current social and political institutions that on the one hand constrain basic capability development and create capability shortfalls, and that on the other hand close off prospects for the development of people's enhanced capabilities and the possibility of new capability gains.

I argue below that this requires three major changes in economic thinking. First, it means giving up the conventional idea that the economy is only an income generation process and instead reconceptualizing the economy as a capability generation process. Second, it calls for making a commitment to rebuild the economy as a democratic rather than socially stratified economic process. Third, it means rethinking economics' understanding of subjectivity and its relation to identity. Sections 2, 3, and 4 of this chapter take up these three major changes. Section 4 also pulls together the argument of Part II of the book.

2 Reconceptualizing the Economy as a Capability Generation Process

Despite the mainstream belief that the economy is made up of markets, it is also made up of institutions that govern markets. As many institutionalist economists have long argued, institutions underlie and determine the nature and form of economic activity, including the extent to which it relies on market processes (see, e.g., Rutherford, 2010; Ambrosino, Fontana, and Gigante, 2018). Institutions are the outcome of historical processes and can be broadly defined as "humanly devised constraints that structure political, economic and social interaction [that] consist of both informal constraints (sanctions, taboos, customs, traditions, and codes of conduct), and formal rules (constitutions, laws, property rights)" (North, 1991, p. 97). When these informal constraints or norms and formal rules governing social relationships are relatively settled and established, the social relationships they involve acquire the character of "systems of established and prevalent social rules that structure social interaction" (Hodgson, 2006, p. 2).

A socially stratified society is one in which these "prevalent social rules" continually strengthen and sustain social stratification. Reconceptualizing the economy as a process that weakens rather than strengthens social stratification accordingly involves our identifying alternative sets of "prevalent social rules" that would help bring this about. A key first step in doing this, I argue, is to determine *who* any set of rules applies to and what conception of individuals is being employed to which those rules apply.

In mainstream economics, the individuals that "prevalent social rules" apply to are utility-maximizing individuals. While this conception is technically formulated in terms of preference satisfaction, and even though utility maximization is not the same as income maximization, the vast majority of mainstream models treat utility-maximizing individuals as just income maximizers – beings who always prefer more (money) to less – so that utility maximization reduces to income maximization. Thus, the economy as a whole is essentially seen to be an income generation process – one that works well according to pro-market economists or not so well according to many critics of the market, but who generally share this view.

However, as Sen points out, income is only a means people employ to achieve their goals. So, a pursuit of income does not capture what motivates people or therefore what the economy is ultimately all about. To the extent, then, that market institutions are designed to generate income, they may misrepresent what people actually pursue. Sen thus argues that we would do better to shift from "concentrating on the *means* to living to the *actual opportunities* for living" (Sen, 2009, p. 233), since this view is open to the diverse goals that motivate people in contrast to the idea that they are only motivated by utility/money. Thus, the economy should not be explained as an income generation process, even if pursuit of income is a fundamental part of what it involves. The risk of seeing it in these narrow terms is that increasing income is then naturally seen as a sign of economic progress, when this may actually mask worsening well-being, as GDP and inequality rising together in recent years arguably show.[1]

Thus, if we are to focus on genuinely increasing well-being, this requires that we focus on that directly and explain how well the economy functions by that standard. Sen's focus is people's "*actual opportunities* for living," or their capabilities. Rather than an income generation process, the economy ought thus to be understood as a capability generation process – one that works well according to how well institutions, market and nonmarket, are designed and organized to promote this. Seen in these terms, "systems of established and prevalent social rules that structure social interaction" (Hodgson, 2006, p. 2) which continually strengthen social stratification fail in this regard. People suffer capability shortfalls and potential capability gains are unlikely to be realized, because social relationships that work to the advantage of small numbers of socially privileged individuals also reduce most people's opportunities for organizing their capabilities as they would best develop them.

---

[1] See Robeyns (2017) for a comprehensive account of Sen's thinking about capabilities, well-being, and justice and for the distinction between the capability approach and capability theories.

If the first step, then, in reconceptualizing the economy as a process that weakens rather than strengthens social stratification is to change the conception of individuals with which we operate (and in my view, adopt an adaptive individual conception of people as stocks of capabilities), the second step is to set out how institutions need to change to allow the economy to function as a capability generation process. Of course, "changing institutions" is a wide-ranging agenda, likely too large in scale to be susceptible of specific guidelines or strategies. In Section 3, then, I take a different approach, no less challenging but in my view at the very root of the issues here. I argue that "changing institutions" begins with making a commitment to building a democratic society rather than socially stratified one. While many, many others have written about democracy and what it involves, Section 3 examines how to go about this in terms of (i) the relationship between democracy and capabilities, (ii) the task of legitimating democracy, (iii) the nature of collective capabilities, and (iv) the relationship between democracy and pluralism. The goal here is to add further framework to the idea that the economy and its institutions should be seen as a capability generation process.

3 Democracy, Capabilities, and Pluralism

a Democracy and Capabilities

It is fair to say that an important effect of democratic political systems is that they tend to weaken social stratification, where that involves any sort of social organization that systematically orders from better to worse the economic and social opportunities and well-being of groups of people, whatever the basis of those groups. I approach democracy, then, from the same perspective I approached institutions in Section 2. The first step in determining how to proceed in understanding it is to ask *who* are we referring to when we think about democracy and what conception of individuals does democracy involve. Here too, of course, there is a long history of debate, but the outlines of my view should by now be clear and point to where my view falls in that long debate.

When one examines democracy from the perspective of the nature and status of individuals, in modern political theory one often begins with an account of what secures their status as individuals, namely, their rights. Then, a key issue is what do individual rights extend to and cover and what do they not extend to and cover. Thus, in early capitalism of the last several centuries individual rights were generally only seen to extend to and cover some civil and political rights: the right to vote, assemble and organize politically, have access to a free press, speak freely, securely own property, have juries of one's peers, freedom of movement, free religious beliefs, personal privacy, be free of arbitrary arrest, etc. However, in capitalism in the second half of the twentieth century, especially since the United Nations Universal Declaration of Human Rights (UN General Assembly, 1948), individual rights also extend to and cover economic and social rights: the right to adequate nutrition and housing, to health, safety, old age security, education, a decent environment, etc.

This added list of rights is essentially the list of basic and enhanced capabilities above. Thus, individual rights, or human rights, in the United Nations Declaration shift thinking about democracy from an exclusive attention to political freedoms to people's capabilities. There is an important difference, then, between these two types of rights, a difference that corresponds to two visions of contemporary democracy. If civil and political rights essentially protect people from others interfering in their ability to be full legal citizens of a society – presumably, the minimum requirements of a democracy – their having economic and social rights is meant to go farther and advance their abilities beyond the minimum requirements of noninterference to secure their ability to active and equal participation in society. Economic and social rights, that is, promote people's human flourishing as equal members of society, where that depends on not living in systems of social organization that continually creates advantages for some groups of people and disadvantages for other groups, and which sees human flourishing as a condition for full participation in society irrespective of race, gender, religion, etc. In a capability sense, a democratic political system is one which continually weakens social stratification and thereby promotes both people's basic and enhanced capabilities.[2]

The UNDP *Human Development Report 2019*, then, is a call for the second, stronger vision of democracy, particularly in its concern regarding the emergence of new types of inequalities and increasing power

---

[2] The difference between these two types of rights of course also involves the difference between negative and positive conceptions of freedom.

imbalances in the twenty-first century which reflect the effects of technological and climate change, and which reduce the chances for development of people's enhanced capabilities and threaten past gains in basic capabilities. The *Report* frames this challenge around the idea that promoting capability development in the twenty-first century and beyond needs to be understood in terms of 2012 Sustainable Development Goals. The concern the *Report* expresses is that the second, stronger vision of democracy, based on human flourishing and people's active and equal participation in society, will be at risk if human society does not successfully manage technological and climate change.

Consequently, sustainability and democracy in the full sense must go hand-in-hand in the future. Without either, the other is unlikely to be realized. Sustainability also has many interpretations, particularly in light of the complex challenges of climate change, but one clear way to think about it is in traditional economic terms of growth and development. Economic growth in a very general sense refers to continual increases in economic activity and development in a very general sense refers to continual improvements in human well-being. Sustainability, then, concerns how the two interact, whether in a virtuous cycle, each supporting the other, or in a vicious cycle, each limiting the other.

A virtuous cycle operates when human development increases the ability of people to engage productively in the economy, and this creates further opportunities for human development. A vicious cycle operates when a stunted human development reduces that ability to engage productively in the economy, and a less dynamic economy limits and possibly reduces opportunities for human development. Sustainability in this sense has been a concern of economics since classical political economy and especially in postwar development economics. From this perspective, the concern the *Report* expresses is that in the twenty-first century human society is entering upon a vicious stagnation cycle undermining democracy, the environment, and human capability development.

Here, then, is an important reason to explain the economy not solely in GDP accounting terms as an income generation process but rather in capability-based accounting terms. When we conceptualize the economy as an income generation process, we open the door to registering continual economic progress when well-being and people's capabilities are actually deteriorating, as many critics of the GDP framework have shown in one way or another (e.g., Gasper, 2004;

Stiglitz et al., 2010; Fleurbaey and Blanchet, 2013; Coyle, 2014). In contrast, when we conceptualize the economy as a capability generation process, we are able to distinguish and identify reciprocal, mutually supporting chains of causation, on the one hand from economic growth to human development and on the other hand from human development to growth. The specific links between these two interacting chains of causation have been the object of considerable research in the economic development literature, where, for example, there is strong, cross-country evidence that

> there exists a strong positive relationship in both directions and that public expenditure on social services and female education are especially important links determining the strength of the relationship between economic growth and human development, while the investment rate and income distribution are significant links in determining the strength of the relationship between human development and economic growth. (Ranis, Stewart, and Ramirez, 2000)

What public expenditure on social services and female education accomplish is to guarantee that all people have basic capabilities and increasingly enhanced ones. Conceptualizing the economy as a capability generation process thus holds the potential for both creating a virtuous cycle between growth and development and also advancing sustainability and democracy together. Central to this reconceptualization is making a shift from "concentrating on the *means* to living to the *actual opportunities* for living" (Sen, 2009, p. 233), and thus thinking of individuals not as income maximizers, but as beings concerned with organizing themselves as stocks of capabilities to individually address their different values and goals.

Yet if in the twenty-first century this second, stronger vision of democracy and the reconceptualization of the economy it calls for faces the challenge of new types of inequalities and the increasing power imbalances accompanying them, what would "legitimate" the aspiration to create a democratic society built around continually weakening social stratification and promoting human flourishing? I turn to this issue.

b Legitimating Democracy

Political legitimacy in general and democratic legitimacy in particular concern the social justification of political authority where this applies to both the exercise of coercive power and the political obligations this entails (Peter, 2017). On the one hand, if we look at political legitimacy purely descriptively, going back to Max Weber, "the basis of every system of authority, and correspondingly of every kind of willingness to obey, is a belief, a belief by virtue of which persons exercising authority are lent prestige" (Weber, 1964, p. 382). On the other hand, looking at political legitimacy in a normative way, legitimacy depends on whether it is thought justified. Those in positions of power may claim the right to rule and impose obligations on people, but their authority ultimately is a matter of whether people can be thought to consent to it. But what tells us when people have given their consent to a political authority?

In modern social contract theory, John Rawls in his *A Theory of Justice* (1971) used his famous "veil of ignorance" idea to argue that consent of the governed exists when the main principles underlying a system of government are thought fair and impartial in the sense that they are not biased in favor of or against anyone according to their place in society. This ideal, were it realizable, would legitimate a political authority built upon continually weakening social stratification and aspiring to create a democratic society. In his later writings, Rawls interpreted fairness in terms of the idea of "public reason" – an institutions-type view emphasizing concrete social practices (Peter, *Ibid.*, sect. 3.3; Hédoin, 2022). As he explained this, "political power is legitimate only when it is exercised in accordance with a constitution (written or unwritten) the essentials of which all citizens, as reasonable and rational, can endorse in the light of their common human reason" (Rawls 2001, p. 41).[3]

The domain of public reason, then, coincides with all that is involved in the many different processes of political decision-making. In effect, the grounds of legitimacy for democratic political authority are not simply some set of accepted values and beliefs about society – a substantive basis – but the shared commitment people have to those values and beliefs in all the ways in which they interact politically – a procedural basis. What would secure such a basis?

---

[3] In a book manuscript in progress, "Persons, Values and Consent: A Philosophy & Economic Perspective on Social Moral Choice," Cyril Hédoin thus argues that collective choice rules said to exercise legitimate authority are empirically problematic and normatively unjustified unless each person can be said to rationally consent to their endorsement.

One view that perhaps had some plausibility in the past is that it exists when people are relatively similar and alike. Yet in the world we live in, an increasingly cosmopolitan one in which many different kinds of people interact politically and economically, this condition is unlikely to hold. Probably, it really never held in the past either. Thus, in a world in which we say "Human beings are thoroughly diverse" (Sen 1992, p. 1), we need to rely upon rules governing political systems which people accept, despite that those rules sometimes produce outcomes inconsistent with many people's values and beliefs about society, and indeed even if those rules sometimes produce outcomes many people think wrong.

For example, consider the jury system used in court proceedings. Judicial outcomes based on the jury system are the product of what most people in democratic systems regard as fair procedures. Those procedures may certainly be improperly applied, such as when fair representation on juries is blocked, but should they be properly applied, this type of procedural rule is generally taken to be legitimate whatever their outcomes. To take another example, much the same could be said about voting systems. They may produce outcomes many people think wrong, but they are still seen to be legitimate democratic practices. A democratic system, then, is one which is made up of many different procedural rules and methods for adjudicating and balancing the interests of diverse populations of people who are likely to often disagree on substantive grounds about what is fair and just.

We should note, then, that there are not only many types of decision-making practices in democracies today, but it is also likely there will be many such practices in the future we cannot anticipate. Democratic political systems can consequently be characterized as "open political systems" that, given their procedural rather than substantive grounding, allow for constant innovation and evolution regarding how very different kinds of people settle upon rules that govern decision-making practices that they agree upon and find functional to their living together. Democracy as "open political systems," then, has special advantages over other types of political systems in a world of value pluralism, because it draws upon people's capacity to constantly learn how to deal with new decision-making issues (see Peter, 2008).

Recall Sen's understanding of the person is of a being engaged in reasoning and individual self-scrutiny. His view of the society in which such people live is essentially the same. Successful societies are reliant upon public reason, where this involves people being engaged in a shared reasoning and self-scrutiny regarding how they can live together. Sen, then, regards his conception of the person as an objective one, because in his view it is based on the kinds of beings people actually are. They have many goals and values, and consequently cannot but always be engaged in reasoning and self-scrutiny. It follows that for him this conception of successful societies is also objective: "Public reasoning is ... an essential feature of objectivity in political and ethical beliefs" (Sen 2009, p. 44) – and an essential feature of democratic political systems in particular. Thus, his individual reasoning conception of the person and his public reason conception of society are connected and mutually reinforcing (Sen, 2012a, 2012b; Davis, 2012c). Individual self-scrutiny and public reason are two sides of the same coin. Weaken one and you weaken the other. Or strengthen one and you strengthen the other.

Thus, if democracy is to be a political system that continually weakens social stratification, a problem we face is, what is it that motivates people to favor it? Social stratification works like a trap that constantly motivates people to act according to its requirements. How might people come to regard such a system as illegitimate and nondemocratic ones as illegitimate? How are they to feel secure not only in trusting their own ability to engage in reasoning and individual self-scrutiny but more challengingly trust that they should commit themselves to a democratic society whose ability to adjudicate differences can always be questioned?

Sen's answer to these questions, like Rawls', is built around the idea of impartiality, inspired in part by Adam Smith's impartial spectator idea and critique of "parochialism" (Sen, 2009, pp. 44–46, 404–407; 2012b). I understand his view as follows. First, following Smith he attributes to human beings a natural, rational capacity to judge what is fair in virtue of their being able to remove themselves from their own circumstances and see things from the point of view of others. Second, he holds out hope people will indeed exercise this capacity – we might say, at least "in the long run" – and be motivated to make fairness a foundational principle in their interactions with others, even in societies that discourage taking fairness seriously.[4]

---

[4] See Bréban and Gilardone (2020) for a careful evaluation of Sen's use of Smith's impartial spectator idea.

I propose a criterion, then, for determining how long "the long run" is for people that if satisfied would show their willingness to either continue to seek fairness or instead accept unfairness as a way of life. The criterion is an intergenerational one: If people believe that those who follow them in future generations – in the easiest case, their kin and other close relations – would be better off or at least no worse off than themselves, they will be motivated to seek fairness in society. If they believe this will not happen, they may come to accept unfairness as a way of life. The first case legitimates democracy; the second legitimates social stratification.

Thus, just as in the history of political theory there are descriptive and normative conceptions of political legitimacy, so here too there is both a descriptive approach to intergenerational beliefs and a normative one emphasizing justification. Both are difficult to explain because each depends upon making assumptions about people's ability to think about future people who are – even when we focus on the easier case of only kin and close relations – both close to them and yet still largely unknown to them.[5] A further complication is that many also believe technological and climate change will significantly affect future societies. Another complication is that societies in the future may be more cosmopolitan with greater social interaction between people who are quite different in regard to their experiences, values, and goals.

I will not attempt to explain how these different dimensions of people's intergenerational thinking interact – that would involve a more extended discussion than possible here – or hazard predictions regarding how people's future thinking will evolve regarding democratic and socially stratified political systems. We can nonetheless frame the matter in the way the *Human Development Report* frames it with its forward-looking, implicitly intergenerational view of the world. Thus, if our future pathway involves a greater commitment to democratic society, this entails not only maintaining past progress in improving people's basic capabilities, but also entails making future progress in realizing people's enhanced capabilities. Were this indeed to happen, we could reasonably infer that people would come to believe future generations would likely be better off than themselves, and thus be less likely to accept unfairness as a way of life.

---

[5] This is often termed the "nonidentity problem" (Parfit, 1984; see Gutwald et al., 2014).

However, promoting people's enhanced capabilities is more "socially complicated" than promoting their basic capabilities. Combating extreme deprivation, for example, securing basic nutrition and minimum standards of shelter, seems to involve simpler social mechanisms that scale up in much the same way in many societies. By comparison, promoting people's enhanced capabilities, such as is involved in creating safe environments and developing education systems appropriate to a changing world, seems to depend more strongly on how particular societies are organized, and thus less likely replicate easily across different kinds of communities and societies. Thus, while promoting people's basic capabilities seems feasible *within* today's societies despite high levels of inequality, promoting people's enhanced capabilities likely means going *beyond* in some fashion how societies currently function.

Going *beyond* how societies currently function involves establishing new types of social relationships and new institutions with new sets of "prevalent social rules." Where might these new institutions come from? I argue in Section c that follows that one possibility is they will evolve through development of people's collective capabilities understood specifically as a product of new forms of cooperation within society.

c Collective Capabilities, Collective Intentions, and Third Sector Organizations

What collective capabilities are and what their institutional and social importance is has been much debated in the capability movement (Evans, 2002; Stewart and Deneulin, 2002; Stewart, 2005, 2009; Ibrahim, 2006; Deneulin, 2008; Leßmann, 2022). One view is that social groups and other forms of social interaction produce "social goods" that are distinct from and irreducible to individual goods and are especially important to people's capability development (Deneulin, 2008). Sen agrees that collective capabilities and social goods exist, but so also do social bads. For example, in the case of the latter, he regards the capability exercised by Hutu activists to decimate the Tutsis in the Rwandan genocide as a collective capability. In light of the risks of the latter, he prefers to say social interaction generates "socially dependent individual capabilities" and place emphasis on individual capabilities rather than group capabilities (Sen, 2002, p. 85).

There is indeed a particular advantage in treating individual capabilities as foundational and saying they are "socially dependent" in important ways. This not only simplifies our thinking about public reason but also aligns to the nature and history of contemporary democracy. How, it could be asked, do collective capabilities, irreducible to the behavior of individuals but supervenient upon them, fit procedurally into all the practices that make up democracies? Those practices have long been, as it were, individual-centric. Social groups are of course always involved in political processes, but nonetheless the history and ambition of democracies is to make independent individuals their social and normative foundation.

A different concern is that thinking of political systems as structured around social group interests potentially makes competition between social groups the center of our thinking about political systems. Socially stratified societies are organized around social group competition. Increasing the weight given to a group-centric view of society tacitly legitimates political systems being built upon social stratification. Consider, for example, how in many societies traditional ethnic social groups oppress individual women – honor killing, social exclusion, etc. Collective capabilities take precedence over individual capabilities. Emphasizing individual capabilities, albeit socially dependent ones, instead makes the well-being of individuals primary and provides a critical perspective on group behaviors.

An additional problem is that historically the idea of a "social good" has often been subject to abuse. Authoritarian states that reject democracy elevate purported "social goods" to cloak arbitrary exercises of power. The ideology of "the people" is built upon the idea that individuals can be sacrificed for a "higher" purpose. That is, the "social good" is taken to be an alternative to rather than a means of advancing the good of individuals. To preclude this, people's collective capabilities need to be seen as consistent with development of their individual capabilities. How, then, should we explain the nature and source of people's collective capabilities?

Collective capabilities, we can agree, are the product of what people intend to "do together" and not just a by-product of social interaction. Otherwise, almost every human activity would produce collective capabilities. I have argued (Davis, 2003a, 2003b, 2015a) that collective capabilities result from individual people forming collective or shared intentions regarding joint commitments they make to shared activities. These are individual intentions, not "group intentions" – a notion that is metaphorical at best – and are a type of individual intention specifically concerned with what people intend to "do together."[6]

Unfortunately, the concept of intentionality has been ignored in much of the literature on collective capabilities (see Leßmann, *Ibid.*, sect. 2.3.1), perhaps because the concept of intention is often understood individualistically as if individual intentions are always "private" intentions, and must be expressed in first-person *singular* terms – "what *I* intend...." Yet we know that people also commonly express intentions in first-person *plural* terms – "what *we* intend...," when *each* talks about what *we* will do together, as demonstrated by the pervasive usage of first-person plural speech in human language.

First-person singular and first-person plural speech differ in an important way. Whereas an intention expressed in first-person singular speech gives a person considerable freedom regarding their actions, an intention expressed in first-person plural speech can bind the person in a performative way to whatever they use it to refer to and to whomever the "we" applies. In effect, there exists an implicit obligation or responsibility on the part of the person using such language in the presence of another to follow through on the expectations this creates for the other. Of course, a person may fail to do what they say they will do when they include themselves in "we" but this is seen as a failure regarding what they were committed to. This sense of obligation or responsibility, then, socially embeds the person in an activity to which that person and others are jointly committed, whereas in contrast first-person singular speech is only instrumental to bringing about a person's private goals.[7]

Thus, when people repeatedly in similar sets of circumstances talk about what they will do together, this can generate durable forms of cooperation that may evolve into new sets of "prevalent social rules" and new institutions, economic and social, that create new collective capabilities for people – not only in local communities but also for

---

[6] The now classic example in the philosophy literature on collective intentions is taking a walk together (Gilbert, 1990; also see Bratman, 1993). Also see Schmid (2020).

[7] Tuomela (1995) develops an obligation–responsibility interpretation of first-person plural speech in terms of rules and norms, or explicit and implicit ways in which people see themselves as bound by what they intend to do together. I discuss his view in Davis (2003b, p. 134–6).

countries as well. Democracy exists on both levels and flourishes when people think in terms of what "we" can do together. Mainstream economics, of course, is formulated solely in terms of first-person singular intentions, and consequently it is unable to explain circumstances where cooperation involves more than a transitory alignment of people's individual interests. Indeed, there is no "we" in mainstream economics! Thus, not only is its collective choice theory based solely on aggregation algorithms, but it also lacks any way of explaining how socially emergent institutions might evolve out of new forms of long-lasting cooperation.[8]

There are clearly many circumstances, however, in which human beings, for it seems at least a million years or from the Middle Pleistocene era (Foley and Gamble, 2009), have developed long-lasting ways to cooperate with one another, based upon their regular, close association in social groups (Christakis, 2019). Interpreting this cooperation as a way of producing collective capabilities, we may distinguish two forms (Leßmann, 2022): (i) "internally defined collectives" that develop in a bottom-up way through local types of social group associations such as families, acquaintances, friendship, work, experience, neighborhood, etc. (Ibrahim, 2006); and (ii) "externally defined collectives" that develop in a more top-down way out of existing cross-local, large social groups, national and international, such as ethnic and religious groups (Stewart, 2005). The first, reflecting people's close proximity to one another, corresponds to what was referred to in Chapter 5 as their relational social identities, and the second, reflecting more distant connections between people, corresponds to what was referred to there as their categorical social identities.

Returning, then, to the forward-looking, implicitly intergenerational view of the world in the *Human Development Report*, if people increasingly, in effect, "institutionalize" new forms of cooperation generating new collective capabilities, the experience of this could create an optimism among people that future generations could be better off or no worse off than people today. In fact, the recent historical record in this regard is promising. Over roughly the last quarter century, within and across countries, many new forms of cooperation have indeed been "institutionalized" through expansion of third sector

---

[8] The closest idea is perhaps the generally rejected social capital idea (Davis, 2014).

nonprofit, or nonmarket, and nongovernmental (NGO) intermediate, meso-level-type organizations. These organizations promote and embody new collective capabilities. For many, their goal is to promote people's basic capabilities, for example, Médecins Sans Frontières/ Doctors Without Borders, but for many their mission designs are fine-grained enough to also target people's more socially complicated enhanced capabilities, such as the International AIDS Society.

Thus, our future historical pathway may produce a greater commitment to democratic society. If new forms of cooperation produce new institutions that produce new collective capabilities that potentially increase people's enhanced capabilities in particular, people would then have reason to believe that future generations will be better off than people today. I argued above that an "intergenerational optimism" about people's capability development would legitimate democracy. But what form would democracies then take?

d Democracy, Economics, and Pluralism

My claim above was that democratic practices have long been, as it were, individual-centric. Social groups exist in democracies, but procedurally their powers are primarily channeled through and are derivative of the powers and rights of individuals. It also seems important that individuals be seen as the locus of our thinking about political systems, given how social groups in a stratified world do not always promote the well-being of their members.

I also suggested that, with a procedural grounding, democratic systems are "open political systems" that allow for constant innovation and evolution in how often very different kinds of people settle upon and consent to rules that govern the decision-making practices they find functional to living together. This idea of "openness," then, is essentially the concept of pluralism as it is understood in science and economics, where, as Warren Samuels (1997, 1998) explained it, pluralism is the idea that no unique conceptual foundations exist upon which sciences can be constructed and upon which all science would be unified. Samuels, we could say borrowing from political theory, argued for a "proceduralist" view of science, where like how democracies are made up of many decision-making practices, sciences are made up of a diverse array of investigatory practices – different types of theories, methods of investigation, and methodologies. In both cases, these many kinds of practices coexist and evolve in interaction with one another – in effect, an ecosystem conception of both science and politics that recalls Simon's simple complexity model of interacting subsystems and the overall systems they make up.

Different individual approaches within science and economics, then, can be distinguished according to the different ways in which they combine their theories, methods, and methodologies practices. They then essentially organize themselves into what can be called different "schools of thought" whose boundaries are fluid and whose contents change over time (Dow, 2004; Chick and Dow, 2005; see Davis, 2022). Parallel to social groups in society, schools of thought are social groups in science with members whose individual (research) identities are connected to their school's social group (research) identities. Thus, an open systems view of science and economics and an open political systems view of democracy both employ proceduralist conceptions of social organization in which both types of systems take on their overall shape and form in any historical period according to how they "institutionalize" their respective "prevalent social rules" for interaction between groups and between individuals and groups.

Consequently, if open democratic political systems are individual-centric, and the same principles of social organization operate in political systems and in science, the latter are presumably individual-centric as well. But how is science, then, individual-centric when it is organized around schools of thought? Let me, then, answer this question by reviewing my explanation (Davis, 2019b) of how sciences evolve through specialization in research, taking economics as my example, and then use this as a general explanation of how both open democratic political systems and open sciences are individual-centric.

When we think, then, of sciences having different categories of research, we find that those different categories are often classified according to where they fall in those sciences' taxonomies of research. In economics, this is done according to the *Journal of Economic Literature* (JEL) EconLit classification system. In that system, the main fields/categories function like different species *genera* – on the model of the Linnaean natural taxonomy of plants and animals – and the subfields/subcategories under them are like particular kinds of species in a natural taxonomy; for example, E00, Macroeconomics and Monetary Economics: General, is a *genus* of research, and E10, General Aggregative Models: General, is a species of research. However, the JEL code has evolved over time, reflecting change in the kinds of research in economics (Cherrier, 2017), and this tells us we need an explanation of how categories of research evolve in economics A driving factor, I argue, is specialization in research whereby researchers seek to create new knowledge, and to the extent that they do, this can produce new subfields/subcategories/species of research in economics, even whole new fields/categories of research recorded in revisions over time of the JEL system.

Specialization, then, is also central to explanations of natural taxonomies, as in the Darwinian selectionist model. Variation in the characteristics of species individuals acts like specialization, which if "selected" by the environment can produce new species. However, the Darwinian evolutionary model is unhelpful for explaining change in science/economics since there new kinds/species of research are often not the product of parents who are members of a single species. Unlike in the biological world, scientists/economists who create new kinds of research or species liberally draw upon theories, methods, and methodologies from different species, as, for example, when New Classical Macroeconomics microfoundations models went outside of E00 as it was originally understood to draw on subcategories under Microeconomics, D00.

Change and emergence of new ideas, I thus argue, are better explained as being more like evolutionary processes governing technology change. On that model, Brian Arthur (2009) has persuasively argued that

Technology evolution thus appears to proceed in … a combinatorial manner, whereby new technologies unexpectedly combine different, unrelated technology modules, so that new technology species are in effect descended from more than one genus. (Davis, 2019b, p. 284)

Consequently, on a procedural view of science and economics, in which both are made up of collections of different kinds of practices, new species/collections of practices are cobbled together out of different kinds and elements of prior species/collections of practices, often without much regard to the lineage of those prior kinds. Indeed, key to understanding that elusive cognitive ability called "imagination" is being able to cobble together of seemingly unrelated phenomena. What is key, in any case, is whether assemblies of previously unrelated technologies create something useful, since as Arthur says, "technology is a means to fulfill a human purpose" (Arthur 2009, p. 28).

Therefore, evolution of ideas, whether in science or in literature, works quite differently from biological evolution. Its combinatorial basis gives it degrees of freedom that nature does not provide, and makes human creativity a causal factor in historical change. From this perspective, the basis for proceduralism as an understanding of how democratic systems and science are organized lies not only in the advantage of an open systems world in which substantive agreement on foundations for politics and science is often unavailable. A further, deeper basis for an open systems procedural view of the world is the evolutionary nature of the human world, particularly in regard to how individuals opportunistically and ceaselessly innovate with respect to how they interact with one another. Proceduralism, on this view, is then a matter of establishing and relying on rules, and then regularly revising them according to how people's behavior changes.

I suggest that this tells why, despite the importance of social groups in politics and science, both ultimately need to be seen as ultimately individual-centric. That individuals "specialize" in life in the sense of always innovating on how they interact with one another individually and within groups locates agency in social systems in a fundamental way in the behavior of individuals. We certainly do not want to say social groups do not have important impact on how the world works or say that they do not structure individual behavior. We do want to say that people's strong social embeddedness – that people's social group locations and interactions with others modify their behavior – does not eliminate individual autonomy. Sen references this when he asserts that "[h]uman beings are thoroughly diverse" (Sen, 1992, p. 1), and emphasizes that people are beings who can remove themselves from the requirements of groups and reason in a self-scrutinizing way.

This view of individuals then calls for further comment on what their autonomy involves. In economics, individual autonomy is explained in terms of individual subjectivity. I consequently close this chapter with an introduction to what individual subjectivity involves in a capability approach.

4 Reconsidering the Nature of Subjectivity

In mainstream economics, individual subjectivity is explained in terms of private preferences. But what "private" means is never adequately explained. It might be claimed by defenders of the view that explaining what "private" is inconsistent with saying preferences are private, but this confuses saying what a particular person's private preferences are with saying what privacy consists in. Thus, while individual subjectivity is framed by the standard axioms that preferences need to obey for people to make rational choices – transitivity and completeness in particular – these axioms actually tell us nothing about what either privacy or subjectivity is. At the same time, the mainstream insists that having one's "own" preferences is the very source of individuality – circular as it is to say this. Thus, just as economics as the social science most devoted to emphasizing individuality fails to explain it, it also fails as the social science most devoted to emphasizing subjectivity to say anything useful about it (particularly in comparison with what psychologists have done on the subject). The current crisis in rationality theory brought about by the rise of behavioral economics seems to demonstrate this.

I argued above that the economy ought to be seen to be a human capability generation process. The mainstream essentially sees the economy as a preference satisfaction process. Yet while it is obvious that money is only a means that veils what people truly seek, saying the economy is a preference satisfaction process does not say anything about what people seek either, because people's preferences are said to be private and are therefore unknowable. The only thing, then, that ultimately the mainstream says on this score is that people prefer more to less.

However, it is not really correct to say that people's preferences are private and unknowable. What is private and unknowable is why people prefer some things to others. What is not private and unknowable is what the kinds of things people prefer. This is the difference between the *value* people place on things and the *meaning* attached to the things people value. Meanings, as Wittgenstein made clear in his private language argument, are intersubjective and shared. Truly private meanings do not exist, and the idea itself is self-contradictory. Thus, the nature of what people value is not unknowable, while why people value some things and not others perhaps is. The mainstream view of subjectivity in any case collapses this distinction and thus mistakenly infers that everything about what people prefer is private.[9]

Thus, we can often say, if quite generally, what it is that people prefer since this is evident from our knowledge of human behavior in regard to what people are observed to value. One thing they clearly value is improving their ability to do things in life; that is, they seek to improve their capabilities. Further, it seems reasonable to say that why people generally seek to improve their capabilities in one way rather than another is a matter of their individual plans for improving their capabilities. How much people plan their lives certainly varies across people. Yet if asked to explain their choices, they are usually able to produce a narrative about themselves in regard to how they seek to develop their capabilities. How people understand these self-narratives and the self-concepts they involve is understandably private because people are uniquely individual in occupying their particular spatial/temporal/social positions in the world. No one can ultimately be in someone else's shoes. Consequently, they have a private knowledge about themselves others cannot have, this determines how they see themselves, this underlies the narratives they have about themselves, and this determines how they value developing their capabilities in one way or another at any time.

In the capability movement, this interface between developing capabilities and people's understanding of themselves, their self-narratives and thus what individual subjectivity involves, has gone largely uninvestigated. My earlier argument about this was only that people having such narratives involves saying they have a special, reflexive, or meta-level personal identity capability that can be more or less well developed just like any other capability (Davis, 2011; Davis and Wells, 2016). We know children begin to acquire this capability early on, and we can see that people more or less successfully develop it across their lives.

Chris Fuller (2020) has gone farther, using the thinking of the developmental psychologist Carl Rogers, to break down the idea of a person having a personal identity capability into them having a set of

[9] An advantage, of course, of saying that preferences are private is that this legitimates free markets – perhaps the ultimate rationale for the view. Unfortunately, another implication is that it legitimates cruel, malevolent, and other morally unacceptable preferences. The mistaken notion that economics is a purely positive science is at work here.

personal identity capabilities that have different functions in regard to how they understand themselves. I take up this thinking in Chapters 7 and 8, first in Chapter 7 on the normative economics of a capability conception of the person, and second in Chapter 8 on the nature of a socially embedded subjectivity.

Rethinking what individual subjectivity is also puts us in a position to think more carefully about what individual autonomy involves. In a socially embedded individual view of the person, people are strongly socially embedded when their agency is influenced by their social relationships. In a socially stratified economy, this works to the disadvantage of some, creating basic capability shortfalls and closing off possible enhanced capability gains. Taking individual autonomy seriously, then, as opposed to simply assuming free markets automatically deliver it, requires that we think more carefully about how markets should be organized, specifically to reduce the inequalities they currently produce and that foreclose roads not taken yet to be taken. This concern is central in Chapters 7 and 8.

PART III

Value and Subjectivity

The closing part of the book returns to the conceptual foundations of economics and Chapter 1 issue of economics' status as an objective discipline. It focuses on the fundamental concepts of value and human subjectivity, and devotes a chapter to each subject. First, once we give up mainstream positivist value neutrality, we need to explain how values and normativity operate in an economics that is not value-free but is, as I put it, *value-entangled*. Second, when we give up the unembedded *Homo economicus* individual conception with its reduction of value to preference, we need to examine what a socially embedded subjectivity involves, or one that is situated and embodied and distributed in the world, as cognitive science and psychology put it. Should these fundamental questions begin to be addressed in economics, begin to alter what makes it an objective discipline, and change the nature of economics, this would in turn raise additional questions regarding how change in economics might change its structure and research priorities in the future. This is taken up in a discussion of change in economics in Chapter 9.

Drawing on Putnam's famous fact–value entanglement argument, Chapter 7 shows how economics is inescapably value-entangled, and argues that while economics is an inherently value-laden discipline it may still be an objective one. It describes economics' value structure as being anchored by its main normative ideal shared across different approaches, *individual realization* – what most people in the discipline believe is most valuable and good about human society and characteristic of human nature. It compares two competing interpretations of what that ideal involves – one in mainstream economics and one in capability economics – distinguishing them according to the different additional values regarding what well-being involves they adopt to give content to the individual realization ideal. It then evaluates these two approaches according to whether their different value structures are consistent – an analysis I characterize as *value disentanglement*. After this, Chapter 7 turns to a general framework for ethics and economics – or ethics *in* economics – distinguishes four different forms of disciplinary relationships between economics and ethics, and argues that while cross-disciplinarity best describes the current status of economics and ethics, transdisciplinarity represents an aspirational conception of what an objective, value-laden economics ultimately requires.

Chapter 8 takes up what the subjectivity of socially embedded individuals involves. On the externalist view of individual autonomy, subjectivity is an *embodied subjectivity* because institutions and social relationships affect people's choices and actions. To explain this idea, Chapter 8 reviews the situated cognition and the embodied and distributed cognition literatures in cognitive science and psychology to explain the connection between social embeddedness and subjectivity. It then returns to the capability conception of individuals and what individual and personal identity involves. Using a *two-level view of people's capabilities*, it argues that socially embedded individuals develop first-order capabilities regarding specific kinds of things that they can be and do and also second-order self-concept or *self-narrative capabilities* in conjunction with one another, and rely on the latter to evaluate themselves in relation to their capability development. This discussion draws on the thinking of developmental psychologist Carl Rogers. How, and the extent to which, this understanding of individuals allows us to explain them as distinct and re-identifiable individuals closes Chapter 8.

The book's final Chapter 9 on change in economics begins with an examination of the methodological problem of explaining what counts as change, and argues change in economics needs to be explained in terms of *economics' relationships to other disciplines*. It argues that economics' core–periphery structure works to insulate its core from other disciplines' influences upon it, minimizing their influences. This raises the question: Can other disciplines influence economics' core and potentially produce change in economics? To investigate this question, Chapter 9 develops an open–closed systems model of disciplinary boundary crossings, and argues that economics' core is only incompletely closed and consequently its adopting other disciplines' contents can change its interpretation. Using the different forms of relationships between disciplines distinguished in Chapter 7, mainstream economics' relations to other disciplines are argued to currently be interdisciplinarity, but may also be unstable and can break down. When and under what circumstances? Moving from what happens within social science, two sets of *external forces* influencing change in economics – change in *how* research is done and historical changes in social values and social expectations regarding *what* economics is and should be about – are argued likely to increase boundary crossings between economics and other disciplines, undermine the insularity of its core, and move economics toward being a multidisciplinary, more pluralistic discipline. What would then be especially different about economics would be that individuals are seen as socially embedded and an objective economics is seen as a normative, value-entangled science.

7 | Economics as a Normative Discipline
Value Disentanglement in an "Objective" Economics

> I am prepared to ... say that no science of any kind can be divorced from ethical considerations.... Science is a human learning process which arises in certain subcultures in human society and not in others, and a subculture ... is a group ... defined by the acceptance of common values.... This means that even the epistemological content of science, that is, what scientists think they know, has an ethical component.
>
> (Boulding, 1969: p. 2)

1 Positive and Normative in Economics

Mainstream economics draws a hard line between the concepts of positive and normative. By "positive," most mainstream economists mean value-free and without normative content, and by "normative" they mean values that belong to ethics and moral reasoning. Values and normative thinking in this sense should only be brought into economics from outside its scientific practice by policymakers. The choices of policymakers are seen to be independent of what economics as a science produces. It is sometimes allowed that values enter economics in connection with choice of methods of research, but methodological values are held to be without ethical content. A "scientific" economics, then, is a positive and value-free economics.

Yet, mainstream economics itself is clearly built around a concept of freedom – free choice, free markets, etc. – which has significant ethical and normative meaning. Most economic methodologists and philosophers of economics, historians of economics, and heterodox economists recognize economics' value-ladenness and thus reject the idea that economics can be value-free, though there is little agreement among them regarding how and why ethical values enter economics or what the relationship is between ethics and economics. I begin, then, by explaining how I understand the "entanglement" of economics and

165

ethics and how we might "disentangle" them when we reject the idea that economics can be value-free.

The foundation of the mainstream view rests in the idea that science is based on facts and facts are fundamentally different from values – the famous fact–value dichotomy of David Hume (1739). However, philosophers now agree, following W.V.O. Quine's (1953) influential rejection of the analytic–synthetic distinction, that there is no clear way to distinguish facts from conventions about what count as facts, and since conventions reflect values, values inevitably enter into purportedly positive, fact-based theorizing (Walsh 1987; Mongin, 2002, 2006; Putnam, 2003; Crespo and Llach, 2006; Dasgupta, 2009; Sen, 2009; Hands, 2012b; Putnam and Walsh, 2012; Colander and Su, 2015, 2018; Davis 2015b; DeMartino, and McCloskey, 2015; Hausman et al., 2016; Reiss 2017; Małecka. 2021; Badiei and Grivaux, 2022).

The most influential argument in this regard specifically applied to economics is Hilary Putnam's (2002) well-known "value entanglement" view. Many seemingly positive, value-free concepts are what Bernard Williams (1985) called "thick ethical concepts" that mix together evaluative and descriptive meanings. ("Thin ethical concepts" are those that are explicitly evaluative and not mixed together with descriptive meanings.) For Putnam, since these "thick" concepts operate throughout science and economics, this means contrary to Hume that facts and values cannot be sharply separated in economics. It follows that economics should not be seen to be a value-free discipline.

At the same time, in many cases concepts' evaluative meanings are implicit, unclear, disputed, and sometimes relatively benign. Consequently, it is not hard to see that economists strongly attached to the idea of a positive, value-free economics prefer to neglect them. Indeed, adherence to the idea that economics is a value-free science is part of mainstream economists' training and socialization, and so not surprisingly new arguments seem to have emerged in defense of the idea that economics is a value-free science. Most mainstream economists, then, would likely say two things today were they presented with the reasoning in Putnam's argument. First, this does not address their intuition that economics and science are different in some fundamental way from nonscience domains such as the humanities. Second, a value-ladenness view creates a "slippery slope" problem since, if it is allowed that values play a role in economics, one could argue this leads to relativism that undermines economics' status as a science. Putting these points together, we can see how the evolution of mainstream economics creates a new defense of the idea that economics is a value-free positive science – one that builds on the original fact–value distinction and that reflects recent change in methods of research in economics.

Since the 1960s, then, there have been two discernible "turns" or shifts in economic method. First, as many have noted, there was a turn away from natural language argumentation in economics and a turn to mathematical modeling associated especially with recasting economics as an applied science (Backhouse and Cherrier 2017). Second and more recently, there has been what has been called an "empirical turn" in economics coupled with a decline in pure theory research (e.g., Hamermesh 2013; Angrist et al. 2017). Much, then, has been written about what these two turns involve, but despite them the mainstream still aspires to make causal claims about the world and often uses the language of causation in its publications. The caveat "correlation is not causation" remains a cornerstone of mainstream economic method, but it really seems to work more to conceal a third kind of "turn" in the mainstream, one toward a theory agnosticism or unwillingness to take substantive positions regarding theory, which major leading economists commonly did in the past.[1]

Note, then, how these "turns" create a new defense of the idea that economics is a value-free positive science. First, since Putnam's "value entanglement" argument is that values are pervasive in natural language, economics can still be argued to be a value-free positive science because it has cleansed itself of values by removing value-laden "unscientific" natural languages with their "thick" concepts from the discipline by making mathematics its only "scientific" form of expression. Second, its empirical, applied turn allows it to reinterpret economics as a data-driven, evidence-based science, thus implying that theory is essentially just a receptacle and organizing framework for facts. Third, if it has become studiously agnostic about theory, this

---

[1] I suggest this may be motivated by a succession of failings of standard views: the Sonnenschein–Mandel–Debreu results undermining general equilibrium theory, the Cambridge critique of the concept of aggregate capital, the rise of behavioral thinking, experimental results inconsistent with rationality theory, the inability to explain the 2007–2008 financial crisis, the neglect of rising inequality, etc.

places discussions about the nature and status of theory professionally out of bounds.

This new position allows the popular view in the mainstream that values are irredeemably subjective to stand unchallenged and unexamined, tacitly reinforcing the traditional argument that values ought to play no role in economics. Not only, then, does the mainstream's new view of itself set aside Putnam's "value entanglement" argument, but it also sets aside considerable methodological and philosophical debate about the positive and normative in economics (also reinforcing the often expressed idea that methodology and philosophy of economics, and the history of economics, are all irrelevant to the actual practice of economics). In the language of performativity, the mainstream has "performed" itself into being a "positive" science, not through reasoned engagement with the issues Putnam and others have raised, but by defensively isolating itself from them, presumably in the interest of maintaining its purported status as a "science."

However, this twentieth-century positivist conception of science is now widely seen as antiquated and naïve, so that the mainstream's self-isolation from contemporary thinking about the nature of science is more likely to ultimately diminish rather than strengthen its scientific credibility. There are also reasons to think this state of affairs will not continue. Economics' large influence in the world calls for a more enlightened view of its nature as a social science, and increasing connections between social science disciplines may temper economics' positivism. Thus, it is not unreasonable to say that economists may ultimately come to see that the idea of an entirely positive economics is indefensible, and for their own credibility recognize they need to say values play some sort of role in economics.

What, then, might be the way forward? It seems unlikely to be to develop a new conception of "positive" economics and try again to somehow remove values from economics. Given economists' concern with economics being seen as an objective science, a better way forward is to show how a value-laden economics can be an "objective" social science. This implies, as argued in Chapter 1, that we need to reinterpret what objectivity in economics involves, and then show how values can operate in economics in an objective way. I take up this task in this chapter, distinguish two main kinds of values and levels on which they operate in economics, examine their relationship from the perspective of their consistency with one another, and compare the mainstream and capability economic approaches on this basis. An "objective" value-laden approach in economics is then one whose value structure is consistent.

The way I proceed is through what I call "value disentanglement." Different economic approaches are value-entangled when the different values they combine are somehow inconsistent with one another. Disentangling their value structures then involves sorting out their different value commitments, what they depend upon, and determining which values can and which values ought not play roles in those approaches. Putnam was not interested in disentangling facts and values in economics because he apparently believed they could not be disentangled, but if economics is a value-laden science and yet also a credible, objective science, I argue we need to find some way to disentangle different approaches' value structures to show how values work in any given approach and to compare different economic approaches.

Section 2 discusses mainstream economics' value entanglement, identifies the specific value foundation or anchor value I believe the mainstream, and in fact much of economics, orthodox and heterodox employs, and then explains how this foundation value is entangled with a problematic additional mainstream value derived from its particular conception of individuals. It goes on to show how we can disentangle this value structure by setting aside the problematic additional values the mainstream approach employs. This raises the question of what additional values might alternatively be combined with this same foundation value to make economics an objective value-laden science.[2]

Section 3 discusses value entanglement in the capability approach. It argues that it employs the same foundation or anchor value, but not the same problematic additional values the mainstream employs because it operates with a capabilities rather than preferences/utility

---

[2] Within the mainstream, there are of course important differences and similarities between neoclassical and behavioral approaches that specifically depart from it such as the heuristics and biases behavioral economics research program. Many others have discussed how neoclassical and other approaches are related to one another, but I put these differences aside here to focus on the broad individual realization ideal I believe they share. For an excellent recent discussion, see Primrose (2017) who characterizes neoclassical thinking as a hyperrationality view to contrast it with behavioral and other mainstream approaches that employ a broader understanding of rationality. Also see Shaikh, 2016, p. 78.

conception of individuals. I argue, however, that in some cases this value structure is also entangled with another problematic additional value, and thus that we also need to disentangle this particular value structure for the capability approach to be an objective value-laden science.

Section 4 closes the chapter by developing a general framework for ethics and economics, or an ethics *in* economics. It frames this as a matter of relationships between different disciplines and distinguishes four forms of relationships between economics and ethics as different disciplines. It then argues that while the cross-disciplinarity form best describes the current status of the relationship between the two disciplines, multidisciplinarity represents an aspirational conception of what that relationship could become and what an objective value-laden economics ultimately requires.

2 Disentangling Values in Mainstream Economics

a The "Individual Realization" Ideal in Mainstream Economics

Different social sciences, including economics, I argue, are structured around foundation or anchor values that take the form of normative ideals reflecting what most people in those disciplines see as most valuable and good about human society from the perspective of their disciplines. What particular researchers choose to investigate, then, assumes these shared normative ideals, plus additional values about what well-being consists in they also hold that, we might say, constitute their normative "anthropological" priors. In this way, "positive" science is always normatively interested.

I think it is fairly clear, then, what the foundational or anchor normative ideal is in mainstream economics, at least since the early twentieth-century emergence of marginalist neoclassical thinking through to current behavioral economics. It is what I call an "individual realization" ideal, which is that in economic life people ought to be able to realize or fulfil their nature as individuals, if this can be made possible. This ideal, as an ideal, is open-ended, and in the mainstream tradition, it is coupled with an additional value that pertains to the nature of individual well-being, namely, that it consists in people being able to satisfy their preferences/maximize their utilities.

Thus, combining the individual realization ideal and the value that well-being involves preference satisfaction/utility maximization gives us a two-level value structure in mainstream thinking: an ideal and a well-being interpretation of its content.

To be clear, I should emphasize that other approaches in economics either do not employ this ideal or when they do may combine it with alternative well-being values. I return to how different approaches in economics differ below, but here focus on the mainstream understood as the thinking that derives from neoclassical economics. There are three key assumptions that I believe tie this value structure together and provide the basis for economic reasoning in the mainstream:

1) People, anthropologically speaking, are simply "preference satisfiers/utility maximizers."[3]
2) Though clearly people do not always succeed in fully satisfying their preferences/maximizing their utility – thus do not always fully realize their individual nature – they nonetheless always strive to do so.
3) How particular economies are organized and function is what limits or strengthens people's ability to satisfy their preferences/maximize their utility, and thus whether they fully realize their nature.

It could be argued that freedom is the key value and ideal underlying mainstream thinking. Yes, freedom is important, but I take it to only be a popular way of emphasizing individual realization, not as an independent ideal. If it were, it could apply to people in other ways that are not part of mainstream economics, for example, to human rights and the freedom of groups of people, but in the mainstream the concept is used strictly in service of the individual realization ideal. Individuals being able to freely pursue realizing their nature is thus instrumental to their realizing it. Promoting freedom particularly in connection with the third point above accordingly reduces to simply promoting this overall normative view.

---

[3] Often people say that economists see people as self-interested in the sense of only being concerned with themselves. However, many economists today deny this and take the view that preference satisfaction/utility maximization means people are only what I term self-regarding, where that means they act out of their own interest but that this can include the interests of others – thus not self-interested in the sense of being purely selfish and only concerned with themselves.

A central part of mainstream economic reasoning, then, is efficiency analysis, whose rationale, based on the assumptions above, is that we ought to implement what we value, namely, this normative ideal with its preference satisfaction/utility maximization interpretation. That is, what efficiency analysis ultimately says we ought to do is make it possible for people to become what they potentially can be. It consequently derives "ought" from "is" – exactly the opposite of Hume's famous maxim that "ought" cannot be derived from "is." What is the case – that people have a certain nature and strive to realize it – tells us what ought to be the case, namely, that their realizing that nature should always be promoted.

The purportedly "positive" part of efficiency analysis, then, is organized around identifying the circumstances under which actual economies limit people's ability to fully satisfy their preferences /maximize their utility – typically where markets do not function freely, since a supporting belief associated with the long history of liberalism is that free markets are the means of realizing this ideal. The acknowledged "normative" part of efficiency analysis is minimized by its framing in seemingly innocuous Pareto judgment terms to say efficient markets are "better" than inefficient markets – innocuous because presumably no one would say making at least one person better off without making anyone else worse off could ever be doubted or has any significant normative content, though it clearly does.

Not surprisingly, most mainstream economists regard efficiency reasoning as purely a technical tool of analysis. Because of their confusion over the positive and normative, they mistakenly think that no normative ideal is presupposed, that their preference/utility anthropology is purely descriptive, and thus that Pareto efficiency judgments, despite their nature as ought statement prescriptions, are value-free. Thus, though mainstream economics from the ideal it rests on to the form that ideal takes is thoroughly normative, ironically most mainstream economists think it fully positive and value-free! Box 7.1, then, summarizes this normative economic framework.

To disentangle this conception, then, I argue that the content the individual realization ideal takes as preference/utility behavior is inconsistent with holding that ideal, so that the normative structure involved cannot ground an "objective" economics. I focus on two key assumptions the mainstream view of preference/utility behavior employs, which derive from its associated conception of the individual,

---

Box 7.1   The mainstream normative economic framework

normative ideal:
individual realization

well-being content of normative ideal:
individual realization occurs through preference satisfaction/utility
maximization

is–ought economic reasoning:
people strive to realize themselves in this way, so they ought to be
able to freely do so

form of analysis:
Pareto efficiency analysis identifies where they are prevented from
doing so and recommends policies to correct this

---

so that the failure of mainstream economics as an "objective" normative economics is traceable to its problematic individual conception. These two assumptions are:

i. People's preferences are their own preferences and not someone else's preferences.
ii. Satisfying preferences/maximizing utility *per se* never raises issues about what is good or bad for the individual.

Many have criticized these assumptions, but I will instead argue that they show us that preference satisfying/utility maximizing does not increase well-being and is thus inconsistent with the individual realization ideal. I address (i) in connection with the problem of adaptive preferences and (ii) in connection with the problem of "bad" preferences. I then argue that sustaining the individual realization ideal requires we disentangle it from the mainstream preferences/utility anthropology and its attendant view of the individual.

My general method and approach to disentangling value structures, then, is relatively simple in that it takes one key value, for me the value that acts as the foundation value and normative ideal in a science, or as the anchor around which its value structure is organized, and then only argues the need for consistency between that key value and the other values that an approach employs. Consistency in this sense is only a matter of reasoned argument, and people certainly can disagree over when it does and does not hold. Therefore, while there is no "royal road" of a deductive sort to producing credible normative structures for an objective economics, this does not mean we cannot make reasoned progress toward identifying such structures.

b Adaptive Preferences as Own Preferences

The role of assumption (i) is to link the realization ideal to the form it is said to take by ruling out that a person satisfying their preferences/maximizing their utilities might not contribute to their own individual realization but instead to someone else's. The idea is that if a person's preferences are always their own preferences, meaning they are always only agents of themselves, satisfying them primarily benefits them and only incidentally (in a spillover sense) benefits others. Were a person an agent of others, for example, in acting as a representative agent of a social group, it would be the group's preferences that are primarily satisfied and their own only incidentally. The standard view is thus that the spillovers (externalities) concept refers to special cases, not the general case. Generally, satisfying one's preferences is seen to bring about an otherwise unrealized state of the person and must thus promote the person's individual realization.

Yet, the theory offers no explanation of why and when the benefits of people's choices accrue primarily to them and not to others. Why are spillovers not the general case? Even the term prejudges the matter by connoting something rare and unimportant. It certainly seems possible, then, that when a person satisfies their own preferences others can benefit more than they do. Whether this happens seems to be an empirical question, but this is ruled out in the mainstream. Thus, the standard spillover/externalities concept seems *ad hoc* and a good example of theory determining what evidence is accepted.[4]

The rationale for this arguably lies in the theory's internalist view of individual autonomy that derives individual autonomy from the person's private subjectivity (rather than in the externalist view from institutions and social relationships). If preference satisfaction/utility maximization is tied fully to private subjectivity, it would seem it must be associated with a person being a single autonomous individual.

---

[4] Proponents of free markets of course want to exclude this possibility because saying spillovers are the general case would justify intervening in market processes. The argument that externalities are ubiquitous was persuasively made by institutional economist K. William Kapp (1950).

So, the effects of preference satisfaction are, as it were, compartmentalized across individuals. It follows that externalities must be the exception and an uninteresting special case.

However, as noted previously, the idea of a private subjectivity confuses the meaning and the source of preferences. Individuals are indeed the source of their own preferences, including when they are socially influenced. Yet, their meanings, or how what they prefer is described, cannot be private because meanings are by nature shared. Even what something means to a particular individual rests on shared language and discourse. Thus, the internalist individual autonomy idea does not show a person's preferences are only their own preferences, and so when the effects of a person's preferences satisfaction/utility maximization accrue to that person and when they accrue to others depends on the circumstances at hand. That is, when we see the content of preferences possesses shared meanings, where they originate leaves open where the benefits of their satisfaction occur.[5]

Consider in this light, then, the phenomenon of adaptive preferences. Sen (1995) pointed out that often people do not desire things that would appear to improve their well-being because they have been habituated to not desire them or because they have somehow been led to believe it is not for them. For example, as feminist economists and development economists have long argued, in many societies women may prefer traditional lives even though this is ostensibly incompatible with their personal development. In effect, their preferences have been culturally adapted to their social circumstances and the context of their lives (see Nussbaum 2001a, b; Teschl and Comin 2005). They are still their "own" preferences, but they also reflect others' values. How?

Since the meanings of things we prefer are shared, they can reflect shared standards about what is valuable. Those standards come from the societies and cultures we live in. Thus, it may be a woman's "own" preference for how to live her life is incompatible with her personal development because she frames what she prefers in the language of custom. As with Putnam's entanglement concept, how we understand meanings we give to things is entangled with how our language meanings influence the contents of our preferences.

---

[5] For example, if a person preferring some new type of good to more conventional ones influences others in an information–taste cascade to prefer that good as well, the benefits of doing so could accrue primarily to others.

Consequently, it is a mistake to say that (i) people's preferences are always their own preferences and not someone else's preferences. Yes, a person's preferences are their own preferences in the sense that they themselves register what they prefer, but what those preferences involve need not be exclusively their own. Assumption (i) is thus an unsuccessful means of saying that satisfying one's preferences produces higher states of individual well-being and promotes individual realization. I conclude that the preferences/utility form the realization ideal takes in standard theory is inconsistent with that ideal in the sense that the way it is understood does not explain what promotes individual realization.

c The Problem of "Bad" Preferences

The role of assumption (ii) is different. It directly rules out the possibility that a person satisfying their preferences might be inconsistent with promoting their own individual well-being and their realization as individuals. The types of "bad" preference at issue here are those that can result in harm to oneself. (Another type of "bad" preference, sometimes called malevolent preferences, concerns harm to others.) The "bad" preference concept *per se* does not exist in the standard understanding because preferences are not understood in terms of their content, good or bad. Preferences are simply preferrings. To the extent that teaching uses examples of things people prefer, invariably "bad" preferences are ignored. Indeed, making the content of people's preferences a part of the understanding of what a preference is would undermine the idea that economics is a positive science that does not employ values in its explanation of behavior. If the kinds of things, good and bad, affecting themselves and others, that people prefer were to enter into this explanation, this would make values immediately relevant to the analysis of their behavior.

Nonetheless, it is obvious there are many instances of preferences that are harmful to a person: preferences for certain substances (smoking, alcohol, drugs, some foods, etc.), preferences for certain lifestyle behaviors (physical inactivity, excessive risk-taking, ignoring the future, etc.), and preferences for certain socially rejected behaviors (selfishness, breaking laws, violence toward others, etc.). In these cases, it is clear that having such preferences often does not promote individual well-being and thus individual realization. Why is this ignored in economics?

Since the 1930s, preferences have been explained in ordinal utility terms – x is preferred to y. The cardinal utility view – x is preferred to y by some quantitative measure – that utility thinking originated with was set aside at that time on the grounds that quantitative comparisons of different people's utility levels were seen as incompatible with a genuinely subjectivist conception of the individual. Earlier marginalist also aspired to show how individual utility maximization would add up to benefit society as a whole, but the realization that interpersonal comparisons of utility this allowed for could imply that a redistribution of wealth would raise total social utility made the case for narrowing the subjectivist conception of the individual to the idea that a person's subjectivity was entirely private and closed to social inspection. Adam Smith's dream that individualism and the social good were ultimately always in line with one another was thus defended but at the cost of economics falling back on an impoverished conception of the person as an entirely private being.

Thus, since the ordinalist privacy idea constitutes a barrier to any form of scrutiny over the content of people's preferences, there was then no way to judge certain choices as "bad" or somehow unacceptable, for either self-harm reasons or harm-to-others reasons. This was a triumph for the most extreme conception of a *laissez-faire* society. Not even the worst harm-to-others type of preference – racist, sexist, genocidal, molestation of children, torture, cruelty of all kinds, etc., things commonly regarded as socially evil – could be brought into mainstream economics, a very sad doubling down on its claim to be a value-free discipline.

One solution to this problem that some considered is to say people have preferences over their preferences – meta-preferences, second-order preferences, or higher-order preferences that could function so as to counteract "bad" preferences (Frankfurt 1971; Jeffrey 1974; Margolis 1982). This view, while it offers a way of explaining how people might deal with their "bad" preferences, creates a problem for the idea that preferences are value-free preferrings and the private subjectivity doctrine. If people's higher-order preferences originate in their recognition of social values, then their preferences would cease to be purely their own private preferences because they could then reflect social preferences. If such preferences were still somehow their "own" preferences, then people's preferences could be regarded as normative.

However, the higher-order preference idea has not been taken up by mainstream theory, which continues to maintain its specific vision of a positivist preference satisfaction/utility maximization anthropology. Consequently, the "bad" preference problem cannot be solved in the theory, and indeed efforts to accommodate it could put the whole private subjectivity, internalist view of individual autonomy at risk. Thus, the mainstream value that well-being involves preference satisfaction/utility maximization, as that is understood, is inconsistent with the individual realization ideal.

3 Disentangling Values in the Capability Approach

a The "Individual Realization" Ideal When People Are Made Up of Capabilities

It may seem odd to say that the mainstream and capability approaches, which are so different in how they address economic life, share individual realization as a foundation value and agree the normative ideal is that people ought to be able to realize their nature as individuals. Yet, both certainly focus on individuals, albeit with quite different views of what their well-being involves due to their quite different views of what individuals are. Indeed, many capability theorists agree the capability approach rests on an "ethical individualism" (Robeyns 2005). Also, as discussed in the previous chapter, some argue that the capability approach is too individualist (Stewart and Deneulin 2002) and ought to be tempered by greater attention to group or collective capabilities (Stewart 2005, 2009; see Leßmann 2022). Group or collective capabilities, we saw, raise complex questions about the nature of agency that should certainly be addressed, but from a normative economics perspective I take the primary concern in the capability approach still to be explaining how individuals can be better off.

Whereas for mainstream economics, then, the individual realization ideal is coupled with the view that realizing that ideal involves people satisfying their preferences/maximizing their utility, in the capability approach realizing that ideal involves people developing their capabilities. Clearly, this draws on an entirely different view of what people are and what individuality involves. Regarding economic reasoning, in the mainstream since people are identified by their preferences, economics should examine how they can further realize their preferences. In contrast, in the capability approach since people are identified by their capabilities, economics should examine how they can further realize their capabilities. In both cases, anthropological priors – what is taken to be the case about people – provide the basis for policy recommendation – what ought to be the case. Again, the is–ought reasoning they both employ is that since people strive to realize themselves, however they are understood, they ought to be able to freely do so to the extent this can be made possible – is implies ought *contra* to the Humean maxim.

Consider how economic reasoning differs in the two approaches. The mainstream uses Pareto efficiency reasoning to determine what prevents people from further satisfying their preferences/maximizing their utilities. The capability approach, as I argued in Chapters 5 and 6, investigates possible capability improvements in two ways: in terms of remedying capability shortfalls that reflect existing socially stratified economic structures and in terms of capability gains that could result from changing social economic structures to improve capability development. Box 7.2 summarizes this capability approach normative economic framework.

This raises the question of whether there exists a value entanglement problem in the capability approach. I argue in Section b that there is – I characterize it as a paternalism problem – but see it as located at the level of the form of analysis, not at the level of the content of

---

Box 7.2   The capability approach normative economic framework

normative ideal:
individual realization

content of normative ideal:
individual realization occurs through capability development

is–ought economic reasoning:
people strive to realize themselves in this way, so they ought to be able to freely do so if possible

form of analysis:
identify causes of capability shortfalls and potential capability gains and design policies to address them

the normative ideal (where value entanglement is a problem for the mainstream view). As a result, it can be addressed through a disentangling, whereas value disentangling in the mainstream case essentially requires we give up its preferences/utility view of individuals.

b The Paternalism Problem

Given the individual realization ideal and a capability conception of individuals, the capability approach assumes that people ought to be able to freely develop their capabilities as they themselves choose. In effect, people's capability development is a bottom-up type of process because individuals have privileged understanding of their particular circumstances. At the same time, however, we have seen in connection with the adaptive preference problem that bottom-up determination of which capabilities people choose to develop can be contrary to individual well-being. This has led to a debate in the capability movement over whether there ought to be a list of capabilities people generally ought to be able to develop (Nussbaum 2001a, b), or whether this ought to be left open (Sen 2009). That there should be a list might be thought top-down, potentially paternalist, and contrary to the idea that people themselves should determine which capabilities they develop. Yet, the adaptive preference problem also suggests that an entirely bottom-up view of capability development would not always advance people's individual well-being.

I locate this problem at the level of the form of analysis in the capability approach normative economic framework (see Box 7.2), not at the level of the content of the normative ideal (where value entanglement is a problem for the mainstream view). That is, it is not a problem with how the individual realization ideal is coupled with the value that people's well-being resides in their capability development. Rather, it resides in how we go about identifying the causes of capability shortfalls and potential capability gains, and then how we ought to go about designing policies that balance the top-down and bottom-up dimensions in people's capability development. I make two points regarding how we may go about this.

First, there is an extensive history examining what people's capabilities involve that draws on wide-ranging, international, and cross-country evidence regarding the things people value. As summarized in the United Nations Development Programme (UNDP)

Human Development Report 2019, this combines bottom-up input from people across different social circumstances with a top-down analysis that reveals shared, common views pertaining to promoting people's *basic capabilities* in the world as it is today and outlining what people's *enhanced capabilities* will arguably need to be in the future. The argument that there should be a list of capabilities people generally ought to develop has strong support in the evidence regarding the universal appeal of basic capabilities. The argument that people's capability development needs to be more open to their own experiences has strong support in the evidence that people desire to enhance their capabilities as suits their changing experience in a world of new technologies, changing education requirements, and greater geographic and social mobility. The two types of capabilities, moreover, are two sides of the same coin. In principle, then, paternalism need not be a problem, and the challenge lies in how we go about identifying the causes of capability shortfalls and potential capability gains and in then designing policies appropriate to different people's circumstances.[6]

Second, when we say people are made up of capabilities, one centrally crucial capability, particularly when we focus on their individual realization, is the personal identity capability. This is the capability people can develop that concerns their reasoning about and evaluating how all the other capabilities they seek to develop fit their individual circumstances – a self-conception a person has framed in terms of what makes them up operating on two levels. Though people's lives change, and thus the capabilities they believe they need do as well, a personal identity capability, should they increasingly develop it, would enable them to continually better organize their capability development and also communicate more effectively with policymakers. The evidence that communication could deliver would concern not just *what* capabilities people seek to develop but *why* they seek to develop those capabilities. I suggest, then, that maintaining a focus on this unique capability, and encouraging its development in people, can act as an important guide to how societies can promote people's basic and enhanced capabilities.

---

[6] In Chapter 9, I add to the evidence regarding what capabilities people are likely to seek to develop in the future what we have learned about existing and emerging social values across different societies, as captured by the World Values Survey.

Self-narratives and personal testimony are a kind of evidence that is not always well recognized for what they tell about people, but hold a potential to allow individual realization to be seen as both self-directed and socially facilitated.[7]

Thus, while paternalism is an issue for the capability approach, it is not an intractable one, and the value disentangling it calls for can be carried out at the level of its form of analysis. I turn, then, to what the discussion above might tell us about the field of ethics and economics.

4 A Framework for Ethics and Economics in an "Objective" Economics

It seems fair to say that economics' uncomfortable relation to ethics is a long-standing problem (Sen 1987). The mainstream strategy mostly evades the issue through its dismissal of ethics as having any relevance to economics as a science. Yet as Kenneth Boulding (1969) persuasively argued many years ago in his Presidential Address to the American Economic Association, economics is inherently normative and deeply engaged with ethical concepts. This creates high risk for the discipline, since its exclusion of ethics is one foundation of its claim to be an objective science. The way forward, this chapter argues, is for economics to acknowledge its normative foundations and encourage reasonable debate about what they involve. This would lead to a better understanding of the relationship between ethics and economics, or rather when we give up the idea that economics is a value-free discipline would lead to a better understanding of ethics *in* economics.

Note, then, that ethics and economics are also independent domains of investigation. Thus, explaining ethics *in* economics involves explaining not only how economics is normative, but also how economics as a discipline relates to ethics as a discipline. In what follows, to address how ethics and economics relate to one another, I first say more about the approach taken above to motivate the idea that we should take an ethics *in* economics view when we assess the relationship between

---

[7] To explain further what developing a personal identity capability involves, Chapter 8 discusses social psychological research investigating how from childhood through their adult lives people seek to develop distinct "sub"-self-concepts, especially regarding self-image, self-esteem, and the ideal self.

them. Second, to provide a framework for thinking about relationships between disciplines, I introduce a recent one that distinguishes four forms of disciplinary relationships, and then use it to interpret current and possible future relationships between ethics and economics. Third, focusing on that possible future relationship, I return to the issue of how economics can be both a normative and an "objective" discipline, and say why I believe the capability approach, with a capability conception of the individual, provides reasonable basis for explaining how ethics operates *in* economics.

a Economics as a Normative Discipline

My argument in this chapter is that seeing economics as a normative discipline depends on recognizing what its disciplinary anchor ideal is and seeing how, when combined with additional value thinking about what well-being involves, this produces its overall normative structure. The mainstream denial that values operate in economics assumes that if they did they would do so in an arbitrary, even relativistic way. To show values do not operate in an arbitrary way in economics, I argued its anchor ideal not only represents a broad consensus about what most people in economics see as most valuable and good about human society, and that the open-endedness of this ideal as an ideal requires it be coupled with additional values regarding the nature of well-being which come from economists' basic anthropological views about what human nature involves.

Of course, it can be argued that economics is a normative discipline but that values operate within it differently. If we still say they do so in a nonarbitrary way, one way to proceed is to argue economics' anchor ideal is something other than individual realization. My view that it is individual realization rests on seeing this as the product of economics' modern history, especially since the rise of neoclassical marginalism, and on economics' continuing strong concern with individual behavior. One can certainly argue that there are other anchor ideals in the past and today in economics. For example, post-Keynesian and non–microfoundational Keynesian approaches arguably operate with anchor ideals related to promoting the social good, though this invites us to ask what the social good ultimately involves. Classical political economy approaches, Marxian economics, and perhaps stratification economics also can be argued to operate with anchor ideals related to the goal of a just society, though again we should ask what the basis of this is. In my view, current heterodox approaches, in particular, institutionalism in the Veblenian tradition, feminist economics, and social economics, are ultimately anchored by the individual realization ideal, but differ in regard to how they understand well-being and what conceptions of individuals they employ.[8]

Other social science disciplines may operate with other kinds of anchor ideals. Sociology is closer to classical political economy and Marxian economics. Individual psychology is closer to current economics, and social psychology seems to be a cross between sociology and individual psychology. Political philosophy seems quite diverse in the anchor ideals it investigates. John Rawls's influential social contract thinking (1971) is anchored in a conception of social fairness, though his liberal conception of the individual may make the individual realization ideal central (Davis 2012a). Similarly, Avishai Margalit's (1996) idea of a decent society in which people do not humiliate one another makes social decency fundamental, though one can also argue it depends on a dignity conception of the person and thus an individual realization ideal.

I am inclined to argue, then, though will not do so here, that much of the world's emphasis on human rights makes individual realization an ideal at some level in all of economics, social science, and political philosophy. In any case, however one interprets different approaches in economics and different disciplines, and it seems reasonable to say their normative status derives from structured, usually implicit views regarding how values operate within them, where my anchor ideals/well-being values understanding interprets this structure as a means of implementing a range of analytical investigations that assume it. Critical examination of this particular kind of structure, as was undertaken above in Sections 2 and 3 of this chapter, consequently focuses on where that structure is sensitive to particular implementation strategies, especially as concerns what individuals are believed to be.

---

[8] For example, Kantian-inspired approaches, both social economic and institutionalist (White 2011; Ballet et al. 2014; Bromley 2019), characterize people in terms of sets of individual rights and responsibilities, and many feminist economists emphasize individuals' relational nature and the central importance of gender.

Thus, it seems fair to say that when we think about the relationship between ethics and economics we ought to think about it in from the perspective of an ethics *in* economics. What sort of relationship does this involve? After a review next of four different kinds of relationships between disciplines that follow, I argue that its current form is unstable and may end up being replaced by one that more closely integrates the two disciplines.

b Different Relationships between Disciplines and the Status of Economics and Ethics

Though relationships between different disciplines are often discussed under the umbrella term "interdisciplinarity," there are multiple ways in which such relationships have been explained and different names for different types of relationships between disciplines. The classification I adopt was developed by philosopher and historian of science Jordi Cat (2017) who distinguishes four main types of disciplinary relationships.[9]

Interdisciplinary research or collaboration creates a new discipline or project, such as interfield research, often leaving the existence of the original ones intact. *Multidisciplinary* work involves the juxtaposition of the treatments and aims of the different disciplines involved in addressing a common problem. *Crossdisciplinary* work involves borrowing resources from one discipline to serve the aims of a project in another. *Transdisciplinary* work is a synthetic creation that encompasses work from different disciplines. (Cat 2017, sect. 3.3)

Let us interpret his classification according to:

(i) whether the interacting disciplines are significantly affected by their interaction;
(ii) whether their interaction produces new fields between them that draw upon them.

(For simplicity, I discuss only two-discipline relationships in order to focus on economics and ethics, and set aside multiple-discipline relationships – for example, bioengineering combines health science, mathematics, statistical science, and engineering.)

---

[9] Ambrosino et al. (2021) use Cat's framework to explain mainstream economics' different possible relationships to other social science disciplines treating disciplines as analogous to nations. I return to this in Chapter 9.

Thus, for Cat, cross-disciplinarity exists when disciplines borrow resources from one another to serve their respective goals, and no new domain of "interfield research" emerges. Any "borrowing" that goes on is instrumental to the respective disciplines' aims. To capture this instrumentality idea, we could say transfers of concepts and methods from one discipline to another are accommodated to the existing frameworks of the sciences that adopt them – in effect, a "domestication" (my term) of their other-science meanings and uses to fit their new-science locations.

Interdisciplinarity exists where two disciplines still have a high degree of independence from one another, but a "new discipline or project" – or new domain of "interfield research" – begins to emerge to which they each contribute. They may each draw upon it, but the existence of this new field, though an active area of research, has only modest effects on the contributing disciplines.

Multidisciplinarity exists where "common problems" emerge, but "interfield research" has yet to emerge. For Cat, multidisciplinarity exists where different disciplines are working on related issues and there exists a "juxtaposition of the treatments and aims of the different disciplines involved in addressing a common problem." Since they are working on related issues, it follows that developments in either can begin to influence how the other develops, but their work on these issues remains largely confined to the respective disciplines.[10]

Cat's last case, transdisciplinarity, is essentially the opposite of cross-disciplinarity. Transdisciplinarity exists as "a synthetic creation that encompasses work from different disciplines." In this instance, not only do we have active, free-standing fields outside their contributing fields, but they may rival and potentially supplant their respective subfield treatments of its subject matter. The long history of science in

---

[10] A possible future example of a multidisciplinarity is the relationship between the economics' theory of rational choice and individual psychology's heuristics and biases research program. Their "juxtaposition of the treatments and aims of the different disciplines involved in addressing a common problem" arises out of both being concerned with the problem of explaining individual choice behavior. They share "treatments" of that issue in that both explain choice subjectively. At the same time, they both are also influenced by the other: economics by psychology in its need to explain nonrational behavior, and psychology, at least in the heuristics and biases research program, by economics in its framing individual choice as departures from rationality.

which many new disciplines have emerged from old ones can be seen to be the product of transdisciplinarity.[11]

How, then, should we understand economics and ethics? Mark White regards it as a cross-disciplinary field resulting from the postwar history of interaction between economics and ethics (White, 2018; see Davis, 2018c). He recognizes there is active research on economics and ethics today, but argues it is insufficient to constitute an inter-field domain of investigation of any significance. Economics and ethics rather exist in the form of two separate subfields of research, one in economics and one in philosophy. For the mainstream, the economics and ethics subfield operates largely in a way that serves economics' positivist self-image. White accordingly characterizes the mainstream economics and ethics subfield as "accommodationist." Despite the wide variety of conceptual resources ethics and moral philosophy offer, mainstream welfare theory only really draws from utilitarian ethics which it has "domesticated" to fit its ordinalist and positivist interpretation of welfare. Other types of ethical reasoning, for example, deontological ethics and virtue ethics, are ignored.

Research on economics and ethics consequently occurs separately within economics and within philosophy, subfields in each. The two disciplines are so institutionally specialized in academic life that researchers are incentivized to only publish in research outlets in their home disciplines. Thus for mainstream economics, economics and ethics can be referred to as an ethics fully *in* economics, meaning an ethics within the scope of its standard concerns and general posture toward ethics as a whole.

In Chapter 9, I argue that the basis for seeing economics as a whole as an interdisciplinary type of field is that it possesses a core–periphery organization that allows borrowings from other disciplines that little affect the core of economics. This is also a way to understand current economics and ethics. Whereas White sees economics' borrowing from ethics as quite limited, we can also see increased interest in economics in normative ideas, though not that have as yet truly threatened its core ideas, especially as concerns its particular attachment to utility

---

[11] I argued that complexity theory is an example of a transdisciplinary field in Davis (2018c). It is the product of multiple disciplines, and its practitioners, while having different disciplinary origins, increasingly identify with it as an interfield discipline termed "complexity science." Other possible examples are international political economy and cognitive science.

Table 7.1 *Disciplinary relationships and economics and ethics*

	Contributing disciplines affected?	New domain of interfield research?
Cross-disciplinarity	No	No
Interdisciplinarity	No	Yes
Multidisciplinarity	Yes	No
Transdisciplinarity	Yes	Yes

theory. In effect, there now appears to exist a relatively active non-standard ethics *in* economics being pursued in economics' periphery (Caplin and Schotte, 2008; DeMartino and McCloskey, 2015; White, 2019).

Table 7.1 summarizes the four types of disciplinary relationships for economics and ethics according to whether the two fields are significantly affected by their interaction and whether this produces a new domain of interfield research. Cross-disciplinarity and perhaps interdisciplinarity describe the current status of economics and ethics; transdisciplinarity and multidisciplinarity represent conceptions of what the field could become were economics to evolve substantially from its current structure and organization.

c Economics and Ethics as an Ethics in Economics

As argued in Chapter 1, my argument that a value-laden economics can be an "objective" discipline rests on an understanding of objectivity alternative to the positivist mainstream view. Mainstream economics grounds objectivity in facts as if facts are always value-free and values are inherently subjective (like individual preferences). Putnam shows this view is untenable. One implication of this is that we need to reappraise the status of facts in economics. We know, then, that facts are constructed through social–institutional processes, so the status of any particular set of facts depends on how reliable people generally think those processes are. For example, data collection processes in government agencies are often taken to be reliable, and the facts they generate are agreed to provide foundations for science (though of course there will always be debates about how adequate these fact-generating processes are).

The other implication of Putnam's analysis is that we also need to reappraise the status of values. Where we should start, then, is with socially recognized values, that is, with social values. When we go beyond personal values, or those specific to individuals, and focus on social values, or those that are widely shared in society, we can see that, like facts they have an objective status both in virtue of their wide acceptance and in light of how they also become embedded in social–institutional processes. For example, one social value virtually universally recognized is that killing other people is generally morally wrong. This value, then, is also strongly embedded in countries' legal systems which specify a range of circumstances under which people can and ought not be punished for killing other people. Thus, there is little debate over the value that killing other people is generally morally wrong, though there is considerable variety in institutionally detailed determinations of when and when not (e.g., self-defense, preventing harm to others, war, etc.). Thus, like facts, this social value and many others have objective status in most societies.[12]

Using the framework above for explaining values in economics, in whole societies some broad values can consequently be argued to function as anchor values or normative ideals for those societies. These society-level values as ideals are open-ended and general, and their interpretation in any particular society accordingly depends on what additional values are coupled with them. Now, if we look upon this in terms of economics' relations to other disciplines and focus specifically on the relation of ethics to economics, then how economists treat the relationship between ethics and economics would seem to tell us how economics might function as a value-laden "objective" discipline.

White, we saw, bases his critique of mainstream economics' cross-disciplinary posture regarding ethics and economics on its narrow normative profile exclusively rooted in utilitarianism. Were then economics' treatment of ethics to move beyond this posture, it would need at least to make space for other social values in economics, where doing so could provide a platform for more extended discussion of ethics *in* economics. This probably would not lead to a transdisciplinary, ethics and economics interfield. That seems unrealistic as a possible pathway for economics at the present time (and perhaps for ethics as

---

[12] Again, this directs us to the evidence we have about social values worldwide as discussed in Chapter 9 in connection with the World Values Survey.

Table 7.2 *Two possible conceptions of an ethics in economics*

	Other social values incorporated?	Pluralist?
Cross-disciplinary	No	No
Multidisciplinary	Yes	Yes

a field as well). What seems a more realistic alternative is a multidisciplinary understanding of how normative values could play a greater, noninstrumental roles in economics according to their perceived social importance – an investigation that could parallel, in Cat's words, "the treatments and aims of [other] disciplines involved in addressing … common problem[s]." For an economics with a multidisciplinary posture this would be a matter of seeing the relationships between different kinds of values in economics as complementary rather than as substitutive (as in efficiency–equity trade-off thinking). It would also be a matter of pursuing the ethics *in* economics that is intentionally pluralist regarding kinds of values.

Table 7.2 removes the interdisciplinary and transdisciplinary pathways for ethics and economics, both of which assume there is development of an interfield ethics and economics (respectively modest and significant), and compares the cross-disciplinary and multidisciplinary conceptions of an ethics *in* economics, where an interfield ethics and economics do not really exist, as the two possible pathways for the future. My argument in this chapter is that the multidisciplinary pathway would lead to a more pluralist, value-laden economics, and also a more "objective" economics able to operate with a consistent normative structure.

Finally, I close by briefly reviewing why I believe the capability approach, with a capability conception of the individual, provides a stronger basis for explaining how ethics operates *in* economics. What this chapter has argued is that if we accept that much of contemporary economics is organized around the individual realization ideal, then its normative structure should be evaluated according to the further values it employs regarding how individual well-being is understood. Yet, the mainstream understanding of individual well-being based on the standard conception of individuals tells us little about what matters to many people in the world today. What observably matters to them are the many things that people can be seen to want to be and do in life, ranging from basic capabilities such as having adequate nutrition, safe housing, needed education, etc., to all the more complex capabilities people will need to undertake in the evolving world of the next century.

The capability approach, then, not only provides a fuller understanding of what well-being involves, but with a capability conception of the individual it allows us to develop a consistent normative structure for an ethics *in* economics that links economics' individual realization ideal and what well-being involves. If the relationship between ethics and economics is to be multidisciplinary, the openness to incorporating a variety of social values this particular kind of relationship between disciplines involves could allow economics to become a more pluralist, value-laden yet "objective" economics.

I return to the issue of how economics as a whole might change in the future in Chapter 9, but Chapter 8 takes a deeper look at how we might alternatively understand human subjectivity and people's capabilities when they are seen as socially embedded in the world.

8 | Individual Realization?
Rethinking Subjectivity in Economics

What, finally, of the self? Does the extended mind imply an extended self?

Clark and Chalmers, 1998, p. 18

[W]hat can be called "positional objectivity" is about the objectivity of what can be observed from a specified position. We are concerned here with person-invariant but position-relative observations and observability, illustrated by what we are able to see from a given position.

Sen, 2009, p. 157

1 Individual Realization?

This chapter argues that economics' individual realization ideal, which Chapter 7 argued is coupled with values we adopt about the nature of individual well-being, also needs to include an account of what human subjectivity is. If the standard view of subjectivity in mainstream economics is ultimately incoherent, a task economics faces is to produce an alternative account of human subjectivity. This chapter aims to develop such an account and employ it to extend the capability conception of socially embedded individuals in order to then give fuller understanding of what is involved in promoting individual realization in economic and social policy, particularly in connection with the paternalism problem.

The inclination in much (but not all) critical heterodox economic thinking, because of its rejection of neoclassical subjectivism, is to put aside discussion of the nature of subjectivity in economics. Not only does this leave the subject to mainstream thinking, but it also creates a problem for economic and social policies that treat individual realization as a normative goal by ignoring their possible effects on the subjective side of human existence – the domain of life that accrues specifically to the individual. It also leaves incompletely explained how individuals understood in capability terms are distinct and independent, re-identifiable beings when that involves saying they possess and develop a special personal identity capability associated with self-narratives they maintain about themselves. The challenge, then, is to rethink what subjectivity involves, both to escape the inadequate yet influential way it is understood in the mainstream and to more fully explain what people are when seen as socially embedded.

Consider again the role subjectivity plays in mainstream economics. As many have argued, particularly recently behavioral economists, it is dominated by a vision of an abstract, hyperrational, disembodied *Homo economicus*. This is supposed to provide the basis on which individuals can be treated as distinct and independent. That is, it is supposed to guarantee they are by showing what make people autonomous beings – the internalist view of individual autonomy, as I characterized it in Chapter 3.

private subjectivity → individual autonomy ⇒
   individuals are distinct and independent

There is an important condition this logic employs, namely, that markets must function freely – the free market ideal central to mainstream economics. When they do not and when there is interference in markets, for most mainstream economists, at least the most pro-free market ones, people fail to maximize utility, their subjectivity is impaired, individual autonomy is limited, individuals are no longer fully distinct and independent, and they then fail to realize their nature as subjective beings. Efficiency judgments are thus used to describe/prescribe how markets would/should work if policies were to rule out "interferences" in the market process, so that individuals can fully realize their individual nature as autonomous, distinct, and independent utility-maximizing beings. Of course, many mainstream economists have a more mixed view and believe in some instances government intervention improves well-being and enhances individual realization. They nonetheless think free markets generally work well, see interventions in the economy as only modifying how markets work, and thus still employ the internalist view of individual autonomy and understand individual realization in terms of utility maximization.

Yet given its refusal to say anything about the content of preferences, the only explanation of what subjectivity is in the mainstream lies in its axiomatic representation of preferences which tell us nothing about the nature of human subjectivity. These axioms are simply rules that govern the formal interpretation of preferences, the purpose of which is arguably to ensure that individuals' behavior can be interpreted as a response to scarcity and to allow the economy to be modeled in supply-and-demand, equilibrium terms. In any theory, I argued in Chapter 7, the individual realization ideal needs to be coupled with values characterizing the nature of individual well-being – what it is that gets realized. But for the mainstream this is a black box that we saw can include any sort of preferences – good or evil – people may have. Thus, the mainstream treatment of subjectivity really provides no explanation of how preference/utility satisfaction realizes individual well-being.

In contrast, the externalist view of individual autonomy set out in Chapter 3 derives individual autonomy from social relationships, particularly as embodied in social institutions.

social institutions → individual autonomy ⇒
individuals are distinct and independent

Yet when we then couple individual realization with the value that individual well-being is about capability development, whether social institutions promote individual autonomy and people being distinct and independent still depends on what individuals themselves subjectively understand to be involved in their own capability development.

This issue arose in Chapter 7 in connection with the top-down paternalism problem the capability approach confronts when it advocates the redesign of social institutions to promote capability development. Whether people develop their capabilities in ways that strengthen their individual autonomy and whether they are then able to function as distinct and independent individuals depends importantly on what capability development they see as needed for this. I thus argued that a bottom-up determination of what capabilities people individually choose to develop for themselves is in important respects a subjective matter that needs to be understood differently than in mainstream thinking. Without this alternative account, the risk is that it might be assumed by default that people develop their capabilities as utility-maximizing individuals. I regard this as a Trojan horse pathway in the development of the capability approach since reintroducing the utility concept in this way threatens the very meaning of the capability concept.

Thus, this chapter builds out the externalist view of individual autonomy for a capability conception of individuals by advancing an alternative account of human subjectivity. To begin, Section 2 locates the resources for doing this in philosophers and cognitive scientists' understanding of situated cognition (SC) and embodied and distributed cognition (EDC). On this basis, I interpret subjectivity as an "embodied subjectivity" associated with the idea of a person being in a particular position, the meaning of which depends importantly on socially shared cognitive "scaffolding" (Clark, 1997). In normative terms, embodied subjectivity refers us idea of "positional objectivity" (Sen, 2009), which I use as a means of addressing the paternalism problem and as the basis for understanding what capabilities people themselves subjectively believe they ought to develop.[1]

Section 3 links this conception of embodied subjectivity to the capability conception of the individual. On the two-level view of people's capabilities, people develop a second-order personal identity capability in the process of determining which of their first-order capabilities they will pursue (Livet, 2006). Following social psychology research on the self-concept and Carl Rogers' thinking about this (1951, 1959), people's personal identity capabilities are their working self-concepts, the different dimensions of which correspond to multiple, different kinds of narratives or self-narratives they keep about themselves and constantly update as they develop their first-order capabilities. Managing these different self-narratives thus involves people developing different personal, subjective capabilities, which in turn involves them developing sets of habits that they rely on to maintain their personal identities and interact with others (Fuller, 2020). In terms of the externalist view of individual autonomy, these habits then more or less align with societies' institutions and social rules (Spong, 2019).

Indeed, how well people's personal identity habits match up with a society's institutional structures depends importantly on the nature of a society's institutions and economic and social policies themselves. Thus, Section 4 turns to when people fail to self-organize themselves

---

[1] It might be argued that the heuristics and biases program is externalist in its emphasis on context and reference-dependent choice, but as will become clear this falls considerably short of SC and EDC thinking that this chapter examines. The view advanced here also differs from Grayot's intrapersonal processing dual selves view (2019; 2020) in its explicitly externalist approach to intrapersonal processing when cognition is seen as situated and embodied.

as distinct and independent, re-identifiable beings, do not integrate their different self-narratives, fail to develop subjective capabilities for doing so, and fragment into multiple selves. I argue this occurs especially in nondemocratic, hierarchical, socially stratified societies in which in particular, selective stigmatization of people's different identities is institutionalized in ways that induce habit formation built around stigmatizers' goals rather than individuals' own goals. Paternalism in economic and social policy design, though motivated by policymakers' desires to do good, risks reproducing the same result despite its different social basis.

Section 5 returns to economics' individual realization ideal developed and argues that the embodied subjectivity idea this chapter develops provides important foundations for an understanding of well-being needed in an objective value-entangled economics.

This chapter closes the main argument of the book, namely, that the capability individual conception it develops is both descriptively and normatively fundamental to the reorientation of economics as a value-entangled, objective social science. Chapter 9 addresses the issue of the nature of change in economics.

2 Situated Cognition, Embodied and Distributed Cognition, and "Embodied Subjectivity"

The literature on SC and EDC in economics is not large, but there are notable exceptions. One is Vernon Smith. As a proponent of ecological rationality, he differs from Gerd Gigerenzer and his colleagues in the lesser emphasis he places on human psychology and greater emphasis on how particular market institutions structure interaction between individuals (Smith, 2008; see Dekker and Remic, 2019). His experimental work on double-oral-auction markets shows how individuals "off-load" cognitive processing onto institutional structures containing rules and norms that, in Clark's sense, are a type of scaffolding allowing many individuals to apprehend what strategies specifically apply to them and then act on the opportunities their different locations create. On one view, this employs the idea of preferences "extended" beyond the individual (Beck, 2022).

Among philosophers of economics, Don Ross, following Clark and Daniel Dennett (1987), is an advocate of SC-EDC thinking and proponent of an externalist philosophy of mind. His interpretation of neoclassical Samuelsonian economics emphasizes strategic interactions between agents who need not be single individuals with inner psychologies with their own utility functions (Ross, 2005, 2007; see Davis, 2011, pp. 128ff; also see Wilcox, 2008). Agents are collections of individuals such as firms, nations, households, etc., and can also be the sub-personal agents of neurocellular economics. Agency is distributed across "scaffolded" structures made up of markets and networks of interaction. Carsten Hermann-Pillath is also an advocate of SC-EDC thinking. In his monumental *Foundations of Economic Evolution* (2013; also see 2012), human society is distinguished by its capacity to represent the world in systems of signs in many forms – semiosis – a process by which meaning and cognition are physically embodied in the world. The interpretation of signs then constrains and structures human behavior, or rather performs it (also see Herrmann-Pillath and Boldyrev, 2014). And recently, Enrico Petracca and James Grayot (2023) have adopted an embodied cognition approach to "naturalize" rationality, taking the ecological rationality-embodied heuristics thinking of Gigerenzer (e.g., 2021) and others following his approach as the best candidate for doing so.

It should also be noted that in institutionalist thinking in the Veblenian tradition just as individual behavior influences institutions and social structures, so they also influence it. This has been understood in terms of the combined effects of upward and downward causation in social economic systems with the latter functioning as a kind of social structural scaffolding via what Geoffrey Hodgson calls "reconstitutive downward effects" on behavior (see Hodgson, 2011). One way to explain this in terms of SC and EDC is to refer to institutions as "economic cognitive institutions," defined as institutions that allow agents to perform certain cognitive processes in the social world without which some of their cognitive processes would not exist (Petracca and Gallagher, 2020).

However, I focus on the origins of the now quite significant literature in philosophy and cognitive science on SC-EDC to provide foundations for the idea of an "embodied subjectivity" – my expression – for economics. This literature is large and diverse (Shapiro and Spaulding, 2021) so not easy to summarize. Petracca and Grayot (2023) very helpfully distinguish four current forms of embodied cognition, or embodied rationality, ranging from less to more radical views, and review the state of the literature in the field in relation to the philosophical concepts of methodological and ontological naturalism.[2]

Thus, in Sections a and b I give a brief historical review of early developments in the SC and EDC approaches as bear on economics, and emphasize how they explain cognition in terms of human action rather than as a brain process. In the Section c, I argue that embodied subjectivity concerns how people apprehend their particular locations in the world and individually act upon them, and discuss how this goes hand-in-hand with a post-classical concept of objectivity termed "positional objectivity" (Sen, 2009).

a Situated Cognition

SC theory was developed in the late 1970s initially and most influentially by psychologist James Gibson (1977, 1979; cf. Greeno, 1994). Though for Gibson the idea of situatedness had philosophical antecedents in the thinking of William James and American pragmatism, as a psychologist he developed it specifically as a theory of perception in connection with his argument that properties of agents' environments that he labeled "affordances" directly facilitate them performing certain types of actions. His thinking departed from existing thinking about cognition at the time in two important ways.

First, though by the 1970s cognitive science or cognitivism was well established in psychology as an understanding of human reasoning as information processing, Gibson's contribution was to interpret processing in terms of actions individuals performed in concrete environmental settings. Since cognitivism was originally associated with the idea of "the brain as an information-processing device" (Sent, 2004, p. 748), it implicitly employed a dualistic "distinction between the 'mental' and the 'environmental' and the 'Inside' and 'Outside' of human cognition" (Petracca, 2017, p. 30). Gibson's "affordances" idea resisted this by making human cognition inseparable from action (Clancey, 1997) and thus helped to shift cognitivism away from the idea that information processing occurred only in the brain.

---

[2] Whether "human rationality can be *philosophically naturalized*" is a matter of whether it can be "released from the domain of pure speculation and studied in terms of empirically identifiable and measurable processes or structures in the world" (Petracca and Grayot, 2023, p. 4) – a contrast close to one in Chapter 1 between closed and open conceptions of objectivity in economics and science.

Second, in contrast to how much cognitive science thinking at the time understood information processing as a kind of abstract reasoning or symbol manipulation, Gibson argued that our environments' "affordances" were unmediated by mental models or symbolic representations, and rather exhibited a direct, two-way relationship between perception and action. This meant that cognitivism had to take seriously the idea that situatedness or embodiment involved an entirely different conception of information processing, and not simply see information as a kind of abstract entity. Indeed, one view of his thinking is that his "ecological psychology" approach dispenses with mental representations altogether, at least in the study of perception.

Interestingly, Gibson's SC view came in for criticism from Herbert Simon, who had championed the view that cognition is symbolic information processing. Simon's earlier bounded rationality (BR) view shared the idea that cognition needed to be understood in terms of individuals' environments. In his famous scissors metaphor, that was the second blade that accompanied the human processing blade. Yet, he rejected Gibson's idea that environments' "affordances" were unmediated by mental models or symbolic representations. For Simon and his colleagues, "symbolic processing lies at the heart of intelligence," and the "fundamental problem for cognitive modelers is to interleave *internal* and *external* states" (Vera and Simon, 1993, pp. 7–8, 12). Indeed, Simon was deeply involved in investigating artificial intelligence systems and computers when he first developed his BR thinking, and this made symbolic processing central to his understanding (Fiori, 2011). Thus, while accepting the basic idea that cognition is situated (see also Simon, 1992), he and his colleagues characterized and rejected Gibson's view as a "hard form" of situatedness that went too far compared to their own more reasonable "soft form" (Vera and Simon, *Ibid.*, p. 11).

Gibson's defenders saw this critique as a return to traditional dualistic thinking. At issue, was "whether a traditional symbolic information-processing system was able to tackle the newly proposed notions of 'situation' and 'situatedness'" (Petracca, 2017, p. 26). It was not denied that human beings engaged in symbolic processing; rather what was denied was that "symbols are fundamentally involved in *all* cognitive activity," and that "[e]very account of cognitive phenomena consists of a set of operations that construct and modify symbolic structures; that is, *every* cognitive process is a symbolic process" (Greeno and Moore, 1993, p. 50; emphasis added).

Indeed, it was argued, there was a long history, going back to John Dewey and C. S. Pierce, that did not interpret symbols strictly as abstract symbols. Accordingly, if we start by saying that human cognition is situated, it only follows that "a symbol or symbolic expression is a structure – physical or mental – ... is a representation of something," and this then allows us to explain symbols "as something that people do" rather than simply conceptualize (*Ibid.*). Thus, human action and people's interactions with one another – that is, their situatedness broadly understood – are the general cases and abstract symbolic processing a special case.

The SC approach, then, differed from Simon's BR approach in its explicit critique of incipient dualism and in its emphasis on action as the distinguishing feature of situatedness. I turn next to the subsequent extension and development of this idea of situatedness in later embodied and distributed cognition thinking.

b Embodied and Distributed Cognition

EDC is a large collection of different but related research programs in cognitive science and philosophy, and a further development of Gibson's SC approach and critique of dualistic thinking. These programs share the assumption that cognition "in a broad sense" depends on the specific characteristics of the human body understood in both its natural and social environments, and reject the idea standard in much traditional cognitive science that cognition can be understood "in a narrow sense" as primarily brain processing (Wilson and Foglia, 2017). Added, then, to the Gibson's emphasis on the "affordances" that environments provide is the idea that, in virtue of the particular characteristics of the human body and its environments, much of people's cognitive processing is "off-loaded" or embodied in and distributed across specific structures in their environments. That is, those environments can themselves be shown to contain processing structures that co-determine how people process information. For example, human spatial concepts reflect how people's environments are structured around the discrete locations they occupy. The locational nature of their environments thus delivers a type of spatial cognitive processing that people use in how they process such concepts as order and position. The same applies to temporal concepts. Time in the human world is sequential and has a before and after, and this then underlies how people conceptualize their particular ideas of past, present, and future.

The idea that cognition extends across people and their environments, or is embodied in and distributed across them now has many proponents, but perhaps the most influential recently is philosopher and cognitive scientist Andy Clark and his *Being There: Putting Mind, World, and Body Back Together* (1997). Clark sees the world as "scaffolding" our cognition and thus constituting a general cognitive apparatus upon which human cognition occurs. Drawing on the 1930s Soviet psychologist Lev Vygotsky (1986), who observed that students rely on external educational tools such as dictionaries and multiplication tables to process information, Clark pointed to how we rely on everything from paper and pencils to computers to carry out our thinking, and argued that "human reasoners are truly distributed cognitive engines: we call on external resources to perform specific computational tasks, much as a networked computer may call on other networked computers to perform specific jobs" (Clark, 1997, pp. 68–69; also see Clark, 2008).[3]

In a highly cited paper, Clark and David Chalmers then advanced their idea of a "socially extended mind." That people are linked with the world "in a two-way interaction" creates "a *coupled system* that can be seen as a complete cognitive system in its own right" – one in which all "the components in the system play an active causal role, and ... jointly govern behavior in the same sort of way that cognition ... does" (1998, p. 8). As a philosophy of mind, "externalism" was thus offered as an alternative to traditional Cartesian "internalism" that identified mind and cognition solely with some sort of inner, conscious process. Thus, for Clark and Chalmers: "What makes some information count as belief is the role it plays, and there is no reason why the relevant role can be played only inside the body" (*Ibid.*, p. 14). Beliefs exist in the world as well, and the idea that they are intrinsically mental is a vestige of Cartesianism.[4]

---

[3] Think now of smartphones, GPS navigation, and AI machine learning.
[4] Clark later (2018) modified his idea of a socially extended mind, but Gallagher (2013) has replied to Clark and defended the idea.

However, what was perhaps most influential, going back to Clark's *Being There*, its "big idea" and the "one with lasting impact in embodied cognitive science" was "that minds are not for thinking, traditionally conceived, *but for doing*, for getting things done in the world in real time" (Wilson and Foglia, 2017, Sect. 2.3). Action, then, or rather a capacity to act in the world agents inhabit becomes the central focus, countering the idea that cognition is a matter of a knowing that occurs at some remove from the world in people's heads. Like Gibson, Clark saw cognition and action as a single integrated process.

People certainly engage in abstract, symbolic processing, and employ mental models or mental representations of the world, but their capacity to do so, and to act, especially reflects their ability to use language, which should itself be seen as a massively "off-loaded" processing system embodied in whole arrays of institutions, social forms of organization, and historically evolved practices. The social world as a whole, then, connects cognition with individual action and interaction between many individuals, all having capacities of different kinds and various proficiencies to act depending on their individual circumstances and the particular structures their environments possess. Indeed, in EDC thinking cognition is not just embodied in the world but also distributed in a complex way across many different kinds and levels of this continually changing "off-loaded" world.

But if people's mental models or mental representations of the world are channeled through language and other forms of environmental–social scaffolding, what does this tell us about subjectivity and consciousness? As Clark and Chalmers provocatively ask: "What about socially extended cognition? Could my mental states be partly constituted by the states of other thinkers?" Their answer is yes: "We see no reason why not in principle. In an unusually interdependent couple, it is entirely possible that one partner's beliefs will play ... a role for the other" (*Ibid.*, p. 17). Extending this example, social interdependence in its many forms implies people not only share each other's beliefs, but more strongly other's beliefs are often simply their own beliefs.

They thus go on to ask: "What, finally, of the self? Does the extended mind imply an extended self?" Clark and Chalmers again answer yes:

It seems so. Most of us already accept that the self outstrips the boundaries of consciousness; my dispositional beliefs, for example, constitute in some deep sense part of who I am. If so, then these boundaries may also fall beyond the skin. (*Ibid.*, p. 18)

Just then as Cartesian "internalism" identifies mind and cognition solely with some sort of inner, conscious process, so it also identifies the boundaries of the individual and the self with the individual brain and body. Yet when we see cognition as embodied and distributed in the world, we need to see the individual as embodied and distributed in the world as well, or in social terms, as socially embedded in it. What individuals are thus depends upon how they exist in the world and what structures exist in that world.

c Embodied Subjectivity: Being Somewhere as Being in a Position

However, this still does not tell us much about human subjectivity as a domain of human existence that specifically accrues to the individual. EDC thinking, as in Clark and Chalmers' understanding, extends subjectivity and the self into the world, and shows the limitations of Cartesian "internalism." Yet if consciousness and what goes on in the brain alone do not explain cognition, the "*coupled system*" and the "two-way interaction" they describe still require that we say something about what subjectivity is from the point of view of the person. I turn then, to my concept of an embodied subjectivity, associate it with the idea of recognizing being in a position, and based on SC-EDC thinking ascribe it two main features.

First, the subjectivity of embedded individuals concerns how people each recognize or apprehend that they occupy a particular place is in the world – that is, the location or position they find themselves in *per se* and also as compared to others. Following Gibson, people directly perceive how they are situated in the world. If from an SC-EDC perspective, the world is made up of multiple arrays of scaffolded locations, then what accrues specifically to each individual, and one thing that characterizes them subjectively, is their apprehension of how and where they fall or are situated within those multiple arrays of scaffolded locations.

Second, when people apprehend where and how they are located in the world, again following the SC-EDC approaches, this determines their individual opportunities for action in those particular circumstances, and accordingly from a capability perspective which of their capabilities they are likely to draw upon in acting in those circumstances. Having an individual body situated in the world thus brings with it the need for individual action. A person acts in interaction with others but still acts individually, even when doing what others are doing. Systems of embodied cognition, then, not only distribute people across different processing structures, but distribute their actions across those structures as well.

Compare this to the mainstream understanding of subjectivity. With its unembodied "internalist" philosophy of mind anchored by its context independence preference axioms, it lacks any concept of specific or particular location or position a person may occupy, since choice behavior omits reference to what location or position a person is in. This is of course one of the main heuristics and biases behavioral economics critiques of mainstream thinking that instead makes choice reference-dependent. More generally, the mainstream understanding of subjectivity is part and parcel of its "view from nowhere" conception of what objectivity in economics involves discussed in Chapter 1. It also reflects, as Amartya Sen puts it, "the classical conception of objectivity – position independence" (Sen, 2009, p. 157).

Alternatively, then, when we say individuals subjectively always find themselves situated and embodied in concrete circumstances – replacing the idea of position independence with the idea of position dependence – we should say that it is rather this that makes their perception of the world objective – a "view from somewhere." But how? Sen in his *The Idea of Justice* characterizes this post-classical conception of objectivity as "positional objectivity."

[W]hat can be called "positional objectivity" is about the objectivity of what can be observed from a specified position. We are concerned here with person-invariant but position-relative observations and observability, illustrated by what we are able to see from a given position. The subject matter of an objective assessment in the positional sense is something that can be ascertained by any normal person occupying a given observational position. (*Ibid.*, pp. 157–158)

It might seem that "person-invariant" and "position-relative observations and observability" contradict each other, but in SC-EDC terms they do not. A person's "position relativity" seen as an embodied subjectivity is always a view from somewhere or from some specific position, but the apparatus those observations rely upon can make them "person-invariant" observations when it is so structured that it results in "something that can be ascertained by any normal person occupying a given observational position." Antoinette Baujard and Muriel Gilardone thus "define the concept of 'positional view' as a person's judgments concerning alternative states of affairs, where such where such judgments may be considered to be objective relative to the specific context in which she or he stands" (Baujard and Gilardone, 2020, p. 3). This recasts first-person observations as third-person observations despite their first-person expression. It recalls the embodied cognition idea of a socially extended mind, and also how collective intentions theory substitutes first-person plural ("we") shared representations of intentions individuals express for person singular ("I") representations of intentions, as discussed in Chapter 6.

Needless to say, there is much to determine in saying what counts as "normal" in such an apparatus and how it relates to the specific contexts in which people find themselves. It would be a mistake to think that determining this is straightforward and uncontroversial. Debates in science and politics regarding what counts as a "normal person occupying a given observational position" are always ongoing, and they sometimes converge on agreed standards and sometimes do not.[5]

At the least, a person's view from somewhere/some specific position is meaningful and "normal" when it can be successfully communicated to others as a view from somewhere that any informed person in those particular circumstance could understand. This can, I suggest, be explained in terms of the relationship between "person-invariant" accounts or narratives, for example, as expressed in broad economic and social policies, and the accounts or narratives people individually maintain about themselves, or their self-narratives, regarding how such policies affect them.

In a post-classical understanding of objectivity, then, the very generality of "person-invariant" social narratives about the human world rests on their applying to different kinds of people who, despite

---

[5] The long history of the electromagnetic spectrum is an example of how standards for normal observation have developed in science. A parallel history in politics concerns Rawls' (1971) famous "veil of ignorance" idea which is in effect his solution to how "person-invariant" and "position-relative observations and observability" can be combined to generate normal observations regarding the principles of justice. When we focus on the nature of public reasoning as Sen does in his view of justice, his positional objectivity idea can be seen as a proposed replacement for Rawls' veil idea (see Peter, 2012).

being distinguished according to their different "position-relative" circumstances, can still link those narratives to their own individual self-narratives. This may seem paradoxical, but it rests on the proposition that human diversity is foundational to objectivity and objective social science. Indeed as Clark and Chalmers put it, when we think in terms of "socially extended cognition," it is precisely the "two-way interaction" between individuals' scaffolded cognition and the structures doing that scaffolding that explains our science and political systems.

It follows from this that people's own narratives about themselves, or self-narratives, must start with where they find themselves in these broad "person-invariant" social narratives. "Who am I" starts with "Where am I in these broad narratives"? The goal for "person-invariant" economic and social policies understood in this way, it thus seems reasonable to say, is that they be formulated so as to be *inclusive* of the variety of circumstances people face in the different positions they occupy (in order that people can see that they apply to all), but still be formulated so as to be meaningfully *distributed across* differences in people's individual circumstances (in order that they can see they apply fairly to them). When we focus in particular on this latter condition, what an embodied subjectivity view specifically offers us is an improved understanding of people's differences in terms of how they themselves understand them. The source of information for this, Section 3 argues, is a fuller understanding of people's self-narratives and how they function.

3 Self-concepts, Subjective Capabilities, and Habit

a Self-concepts, the Personal Identity Capability, and Self-narratives

The extensive empirical and theoretical psychology literature on the human self-concept provides scientific foundations for the philosophical idea of personal identity. I reviewed this literature in my *Individuals and Identity* book and do not do it again here (Davis, 2011, pp. 177ff). Basically, however, a self-concept involves how people think about themselves as opposed to how they think about things separate from themselves. That is, a self-concept is reflexive; the subject's object is the subject itself. If, then, how people think about things separate from themselves are first-order concepts, how they think about themselves, in association with how they think about other things, are second-order concepts.

In the capability approach, the self-concept can accordingly be seen to be associated with having a second-order capability, or as philosopher Pierre Livet explains, a "capability of reorganizing our paths of choice and the evaluation of our steps of action" (2006, p. 340; cf. Davis, 2011, pp. 179–183). I have characterized this second-order capability as a personal identity capability (Davis, *Ibid.*; see also Crespo, 2020a) that people more or less successfully develop in managing their different first-order capabilities, those things they seek to be able to be and do. In identity terms, the personal identity capability provides the basis, as argued in Chapter 4, on which people can be individuated and reidentified as distinct and independent individuals when one employs a capability conception of individuals. It also anchors, I will argue below, how we understand individual realization and economic and social policies aimed at human capability development.

The social psychology literature, then, characterizes people's self-concepts as "working" self-concepts reflecting how they change over time as people change how they understand themselves in continually organizing and reorganizing their lives. What, then, do people actually "work" with that their self-concepts represent when we understand their subjectivity specifically as situated and embodied? The SC and EDC literature treats human language as a preeminent form of social scaffolding for human cognition. Language, when it is used to characterize the world, involves narratives or accounts of how things fit together, whether in traditional story terms or scientifically in terms of models. An embodied subjectivity, then, links individuals' narratives about the world, including their self-narratives about themselves, with socially shared narratives, according to how they apprehend the relationship of their own narratives to those shared narratives. Our own individual narratives thus both depend on shared narratives and distinguish and relate them to those socially shared ones.

Thus, people's situated and embodied "working" self-concepts are their continually developing self-narratives. Because "working" self-narratives are continually under development, they take the form of capabilities that people develop and exercise more or less successfully, just as people can develop and exercise their first-order capabilities more or less successfully. What, then, does success or lack of it in this regard depend upon? Following social psychology's theory of the self-concept, I argue next that it is a matter of a person developing and integrating a further set of personal, "subjective capabilities" associated with different dimensions of their self-narratives that taken together structure to their overall self-narratives.

b Subjective Capabilities and the Role of Habit

To develop an account of people's subjective capabilities for economics' individual conception, I draw on the thinking of Carl Rogers, the famous social psychologist, perhaps most influential in developing the idea of a self-concept. Rogers' contribution was to distinguish different dimensions of people's self-concepts – he broadly distinguished self-image, self-esteem, and the ideal self – and then investigated how they formed a structure that developed from childhood through adulthood in a process he termed self-actualization (Rogers, 1959).[6] Consistent with the SC and EDC approaches, he emphasized people's interactions with others and their embeddedness in their environments, and regarded the self-concept as always a work in progress. Thus,

> as a result of interaction with the environment and particularly as a result of evaluational interactions with others, the structure of the self is formed – an organised, fluid but consistent pattern of perceptions of characteristics and relationships of the 'I' or the 'me' together with the values attached to these concepts. (Rogers, 1951, p. 498)

Rogers' emphasis on self-actualization clearly employs a kind of capability reasoning – what people can become – and his differentiation of distinct dimensions of people's self-concepts provides us a basis for identifying different subjective capabilities people can be said to have. Rogers' standing in psychology is quite high (see Haggbloom et al., 2002), and the literature using his ideas about self-concepts is extensive, but it can also be given a behavioral interpretation appropriate to our understanding of individual economic agents and economic and social policies when we additionally emphasize habit and habit formation.

---

[6] Self-image is one's conception of oneself, self-esteem is how one values oneself, and ideal self is how one would like oneself to be.

Drawing directly on Rogers, this has been done by economist–philosopher Chris Fuller who distinguishes five different subjective capabilities – C1, C2, C3, C4, and C5 – that people exercise in the face of uncertainty and in light of their sense of personal vulnerability. Importantly, each involves developing a different type of habit whose exercise is key to a person's self-actualization (Fuller, 2020, pp. 238–239).

- C1 is the "capability to generate automatic actions … triggered by situational cues in given environmental contexts," and is central to being able to perform "habitual actions."
- C2 refers to being able to "generate beliefs that can be subsequently triggered by situational cues," or in short, being able "to generate habitual beliefs."
- C3 refers to being able to "use habitual beliefs to inform the planning" a person "needs to do to achieve certain future outcomes."
- C4 "represents the individual's ability to become 'conscious' of 'itself' … and also change its self-concept."
- C5 "is the ability to notice patterns and inconsistencies in the habitual beliefs of other human organisms…" and "the ability to '(cognitively) empathise' with others."

Each of these different types of subjective capabilities and the habits they involve – how to respond automatically to situational cues, form beliefs, decide how to act, be conscious of oneself, and respond empathetically to others – corresponds to a particular kind of self-narrative individuals are able to develop and maintain about themselves. Taken together, these different self-narratives structure how people habitually self-organize their personal identity self-concepts, or self-actualize themselves as Rogers puts it, as individuals distinct from but also connected to others. I say more about this in Section 4.

A habit, then, is a disposition to behave both individually and in one's interaction with others in certain ways (Hodgson, 2004). Habitual behavior stabilizes a person's behavior, reduces personal uncertainty, and helps people achieve their individual goals. Heath Spong, in his explanation of the reflexive individual conception, emphasizes the connection between people's individual habits and socially shared habits, which he argues provide the foundations of societies' institutions (Spong, 2019). Thus, societies' institutional structures have as one important foundation people's self-organizing, self-actualizing habits and capabilities.

Institutions, social rules, and norms accordingly perform a parallel function to people's habits on the larger social scale in that they stabilize social behavior, reduce uncertainty in social relationships, and help achieve social goals. That on a social-level institutions, social rules, and norms do what habits do on the individual level means the two reinforce one another. Individual self-organization and social organization are connected systems that help us see how people are both subjective and socially embedded. Spong shows how this argument has long been made by institutionalist economists in the Veblenian tradition (also see Hodgson, 2003, 2004, 2010; Lawlor, 2006; Fleetwood, 2008), in critical realists' structure–agent analysis (Archer, 1995; Lawson, 1997, 2019; Elder-Vass, 2011), and underlies much Austrian economic thinking about the coordinating function of markets and the coordinate role of individuals' mental models (O'Driscoll and Rizzo, 1996; Kirzner, 1997; Dekker and Kuchar, 2019). It is missing from mainstream economic reasoning with its conception of subjectivity that neither explains habit formation nor sees people as socially embedded.

Putting this all altogether, we have a social ontology that ranges across individuals' subjective capabilities, their first- and second-order capabilities, their individual and socially shared habits, and their accompanying institutions, social rules, coordinating processes, and resulting social structures. As put by Nathaniel Wilcox, we see an interrelationship between the "fission" and "fusion" of individual agency – the former referring to individuals' sub-personal domain and the latter to their suprapersonal domain (Wilcox, 2008, p. 527). But how is this social ontology actually realized in the world? I return to the multiple selves problem and the effects of (selective) social stigmatization as explained earlier.

4 Multiple Selves and Social Stigmatization

a The Multiple Selves Problem Again

The multiple selves problem emerged in mainstream economics with the rise of behavioral economics. As discussed in Chapter 3, it is especially apparent when people exhibit present bias and time-inconsistent behavior, employ quasi-hyperbolic rates of time discount, and effectively break up into different temporal selves who can act like different individuals. Whether there is still a single individual is then seen to be a matter of determining which of these selves is the true self: the initial self, the far-sighted self, the current self, etc. Yet none of the competing theories for deciding this appear to be very persuasive (see Mitrouchev and Buonomo, 2023).

We saw in Chapter 3 that mainstream economics take on multiple selves and what the true self is said to be was developed in connection with its dual selves models with their two-tier treatment of preferences. People have rational and less-than-rational preferences, their rational preferences are their "true" preferences, and their "inner" selves are their true selves. Since there is no obvious reason to say people have "true" preferences and "inner" selves, the issue is then how are these "true" rational preferences elicited, if they exist – a "preferences purification" program (Hausman, 2012) for "an inner rational agent ... trapped inside a psychological shell" (Infante et al., 2015, p. 6). However, the theories of elicitation hinted at have little if any empirical basis, and the inner self idea seems only contrived to maintain traditional rationality and the idea of a single utility-maximizing self.

The understanding of multiple selves in a capability conception of the individual as I have developed it turns on the relationship between individuals' first-order, primary capabilities and their second-order, personal identity self-concept capabilities. First, whether they fragment into multiple selves depends on whether they are able to organize their second-order personal identity self-concept capabilities such that, in particular, they successfully develop and manage what Fuller labels C4, the subjective capability, or "the individual's ability to become 'conscious' of 'itself' ... and also change its self-concept." Second, since the exercise of this capability interacts with his C5 capability, or "the ability to ... 'empathise' with others," the person's development of their C4 capability depends on their development of their C5 capability. Third, people's subjective capability development also depends on what first-order primary capabilities they are able to develop, since what kinds of primary-level activities people engage in influences their personal subjective capability development.

However, in an "externalist" conception of individual autonomy, whether individuals made up of capabilities break up into multiple selves or are distinct and independent single individuals is clearly influenced by what capability development society promotes. In "internalist" dual selves models, whether people are distinct and independent, single individual is a matter of whether different states of individuals can be reconciled putting aside any attention to how society is organized. My view is that this "internalist" states-based framing renders the multiple selves problem unsolvable. It simply becomes an abstract theory puzzle buried in the ambiguities of a purportedly private subjectivity. In contrast, since a capability conception of people is formulated in terms of actions people undertake in developing themselves and their capabilities, resolving the multiple selves problem is a matter of what societies facilitate or not. That is, whether people are re-identifiably distinct and independent single individuals is both a personal and social historical outcome, not something philosophers can bring about.[7]

b Selective Stigmatization and Identity Fragmentation

Consider now how the ways in which societies are structured may influence how people organize their personal identities and whether they fragment into multiple selves. Take the practice of selective stigmatization discussed in Chapter 5. In that analysis, people have multiple selves in the form of multiple social group identities which they seek to organize so as, in their own view, allows them to act as single individuals. For example, for gender and ethnicity as two social identity selves, in one set of circumstances they may think and act from the perspective of their gender, prioritizing it; in another, they may think and act from the perspective of their ethnicity, prioritizing it. Their personal identity self-narratives, then, provide the means by which they determine this and maintain themselves as single individuals.

However, selective stigmatization interferes with this since it favors certain social identities and disfavors others people have according to the interests and priorities of stigmatizers. To the extent that this

[7] For a deeply informed philosophical discussion of the destructive effects on individuals of a world structured to limit individuals' self-realization and reduce their "autonomy and reflection to a ghostly performance" (Pereira, 2019, p. vii), see Gustavo Pereira's examination of how human imagination is damaged when the world exhibits a variety of harmful "social pathologies" Pereira developed his thinking in the "Ethics, Justice and Economy" group at the Uruguay Universidad de la República whose research focus is the idea of "applied anonymous injustice."

causes people to organize their multiple social identities not as they would wish according to their self-narratives but according to how stigmatizers wish them to be organized, they may fragment into sets of multiple social identity selves, undermining their self-narratives regarding the individuals they see themselves as. One case discussed in Chapter 5 on stratification economics is a woman of color whose multiple social identity selves include being a person of color and being a woman. Should her color be stigmatized but not her being a woman, then she is limited in how she manages the relationship between those two identities, and thus in particular how she develops her C4 self-concept capability. Stigmatizers, then, substitute in place of how she might do this and how they want her to manage and organize her different identities. In societies in which social rank depends especially on race and skin color, the aim of stigmatization of skin color is to obscure this practice while at the same time reinforcing it, behind the scenes as it were. Further, since a person's C4 capability is closely connected to her C5 capability, "the ability to … 'empathise' with others," stigmatizers also seek to substitute their preferred empathetic relationships between her different social identities for those she prefers given her understanding of her personal identity.

How people order and act on their different social identities, favoring some of them sometimes and others other times, reflects their ever-evolving self-concepts. Relatedly, shifts in their empathy for different groups of other people they see as like or unlike themselves also reflect their changing views of who they think they are. When we relate people's second-order subjective capabilities to their primary capabilities, one factor influencing these shifts is surely their perceived changing opportunities for developing their primary capabilities, both over their lifetimes and according to their changing social circumstances. This is the domain of a social embedded subjectivity. Thus, if the primary capabilities people are able to develop are limited by others who manipulate their social identity intersectionalities, this manipulates not only their ability to function as distinct and independent individuals but their private subjectivities as well.

Stigmatization, I argued, is one important social mechanism that works to reinforce hierarchical, nondemocratic societies. Hierarchical societies institutionalize stigmatization, and this works to sustain social group stratification. As Fuller and Spong show, capability development involves habit formation and habits connect up with social norms and institutions. An institutionalized stigmatization consequently also institutionalizes social and individual habits, and this locks in both multiple selves self-narratives people may develop about themselves with social stratification.

I turn, then, to what paternalism shares with systems of social stratification.

c The Paternalism Problem Again

Paternalism in social and economic policy is not *per se* a product of some groups of people stigmatizing other groups of people, but can result from policies aimed at improving people's well-being that also limit the autonomy of those they are meant to help. For example, in the case of behavioral economics' libertarian paternalism, choice architects design choice settings that are intended to give people different choice sets, and this essentially substitutes the choice sets policymakers recommend for the choice sets people might have had in the absence of those policies. Proponents of choice architecture design reason that people would prefer the choices these policies make possible were they available. But this is speculative and is generally justified in terms of social benefits rather than what people want. Indeed, one could equally argue that people would prefer the choices their original choice sets make possible, in which case choice architecture redesign limits their autonomy. The problem in sorting this out is that in a world in which people's preferences can be adaptive and they maximize utility whatever their circumstances, the whole issue of autonomy cannot really be coherently discussed.

Libertarian paternalism has been mostly discussed and debated apart from any characterization of the different types of societies in which choice architects might operate, so the whole subject of stigmatization cannot come up. Nonetheless, suppose choice architects operate in socially stratified societies with authoritarian political structures. Then, the policies that end up finding support could well reflect the interests of socially advantaged individuals and stigmatize those to whom they apply. For example, incentivized retirement savings plans reduce national tax burdens that fall especially on high-income individuals. Low-income nonsavers may find recommended saving plans unaffordable, but under such plans could be stigmatized for not being "good savers" all ultimately in the interest of high-income individuals. In identity terms, the effect is again that people's self-narratives are manipulated by others, reducing their individual autonomy.[8]

How, then, does one formulate economic and social policies that aim at improving people's well-being that do not limit the autonomy of those they are meant to help? When policy is normatively motivated by the individual realization ideal, and that ideal is combined with "internalist" utility maximization conception of well-being, individual autonomy is not secured and may well be limited. In a world of adaptive preferences and an agnosticism regarding where preferences come from, there is really no way of ruling this out. In contrast, a capability conception of individuals specifically aims to make people agents of their lives, where this interprets, in Sen's words, "the term 'agent' ... in its older – and 'grander' – sense as someone who acts and brings about change, and whose achievements can be judged in terms of her own values and objectives" (Sen, 1999, p. 19). Economic and social policies, then, ought not to just aim to reduce constraints operating on what people seek to be and do, whatever the sources of those constraints. Their goal should be to put people in greater command of their goals as agents of those goals, and allow them to become more truly the authors of their lives by making development "a participatory and dynamic process" (UNDP 1990, p. 11).

It is this emphasis, then, that provides an important "bottom-up" component for policy formulation to match its "top-down" construction. One should not minimize the challenges involved in identifying and incorporating how people "bottom-up" as agents of their lives understand their goals regarding improving their well-being. Yet, the ambition of making policies more democratic and building them around people's agency is a clear alternative to the standard view of policy built around the utility maximization view of people.

All that the discussion in this section was meant to do, then, was address how the ways in which society is structured affect people's personal identities, and deepen our understanding of individuals made up of capabilities to include an understanding of their subjective capabilities as organized around how they maintain their personal identity self-concepts. The threat to this, overlooked by many, is society-wide,

---

[8] On choice architects' manipulation of people's tastes interfering with their individual autonomy, see Hausman and Welch (2010) and Nagatsu (2015).

institutionalized practices that work to fragment their identities and limit their ability to function as distinct and independent individuals. Thus, the two-level understanding of capabilities and the central importance of the personal identity self-narrative capability are central to the both the capability approach and addressing the problem of multiple selves.

5 The View from Somewhere: Economics as an "Objective" Social Science

This chapter discussed how the individual realization ideal, when combined with a capability understanding of individual well-being, employs an understanding of human subjectivity alternative to the mainstream view. Social psychology tells us that people's subjectivity is cognitively situated and embodied and distributed in the world. On a capability conception of individuals, what people's primary capabilities are for what they can be and do is influenced by what their embodied subjective capabilities are. I argued these subjective capabilities can be seen to be organized around how people maintain their personal identity self-narratives, as shown by the structure Fuller has developed, all in order to, as Rogers puts it, show how people seek to self-actualize themselves as best they can. What primary capabilities people are able to develop, then, needs to be understood in relation to how successfully they self-actualize themselves in this personal identity sense.

"Internalist" accounts of individual autonomy cannot explain individual realization, because they operate with an inadequate conception of well-being whose basis is an unrealistic, artificial conception of human subjectivity. The "externalist" account of individual autonomy advanced here employs a more complex account of individual well-being, because the embodied human subjectivity conception it employs is neither simple nor susceptible to abstract axiomatic regimentation. A further complication is that, because human subjectivity is situated and embodied in the world, individual realization also depends on how well-being is represented in institutions and economic and social policies. Promoting individual realization, economics' anchor ideal, then, needs to coordinate a complex human psychology and institutional policy environments driven by many factors, some related to individual realization but many not.

This calls for a two-sided, both "top-down" and "bottom-up" approach to well-being policy, which in a capability approach integrates the larger aims of human development, associated with people's primary capabilities, and individuals' particular grasp of their own personal development, associated with their conceptions of themselves. The "top-down" part of this has been well laid out in the human development program envisioned in the capability approach and involves, I have argued, two aspects: combatting shortfalls in how people develop their existing potentials for capability development – as discussed in Chapter 5 on social stratification and stigmatization – and pursuing expansions and enhancements of people's capability potentials – as discussed in Chapter 6 on roads yet to be taken. It is the second part of this human development program the current chapter is especially meant to address, or the "bottom-up" part that is generally less familiar, not well examined because of the challenges of explaining human subjectivity, and to which standard economic thinking about subjectivity has been a barrier.

I close this chapter with what the conception of embodied human subjectivity advanced here and a two-sided approach to well-being contributes to our efforts to produce a view from somewhere conception of economics as an "objective" value-entangled economics. Note that the mainstream understanding of subjectivity, the abstract view from "nowhere" conception, leaves us with the conclusion that individual realization basically comes about in some automatic, "natural" way through free markets. Free markets are the standard for what is objective and what policy should promote. In contrast, an understanding of embodied subjectivity, the view from somewhere conception of economics locates its objectivity as a science directly in the individual realization ideal, such as that depends on the relationship between human psychology and institutional policy environments. Whether and in what ways markets should be free accordingly depends on all this, not on a mechanical defaulting to the market process as some sort of objectivity in itself.

The challenge we are left with, however, is to give a deeper account of what people's embodied subjectivity involves, especially to counter the mainstream's black box dismissal of subjectivity. Rogers and others provide foundations for this in their extensive research, empirical and theoretical, into individuals' self-concepts. Objectivity in this instance derives from what we know anthropologically about human beings. Sen provides normative foundations for this with his concept of "positional objectivity" and the idea that position-relative observations can be person-invariant. In connection with economic and social policies, I interpret this to mean that such policies need to be formulated so as to be both *inclusive* of the variety of circumstances people face in the different positions they occupy and still meaningfully *distributed across* differences in their individual circumstances.

Economics is a value-entangled "objective" science, then, in virtue of these foundations. Since they are complex foundations and inevitably subject to debate and dispute, what "objectivity" involves in economics will inevitably be contested. But surely it involves a situated and embodied subjectivity of socially embedded individuals. I turn in the Chapter 9 to how economics may change in the future.

9 | *Change in and Changing Economics*

There is nothing more constant than change.

Heraclitus (535 BC)

The crisis consists precisely in the fact that the old world is dying and the new cannot be born. In this interregnum a great variety of morbid symptoms appear.

Gramsci (1971 [1930]): 276)

1 Change in Economics: The Question of Method

This book has raised many issues regarding how economics might change in the future. Yet the issue of change in economics is hardly a straightforward. This chapter aims to provide a framework for investigating the subject in hope that doing so will allow some insights into the issues raised earlier and more generally regarding how we might think about the future of economics. To do so, it asks what method of investigation is needed for developing a framework of analysis. The method I employ builds on a number of assumptions about economics' recent history.

Change in economics, then, has always been a subject of discussion in economics and political economy. That discussion may have languished in the first post-World War II decades when neoclassicism was ascendent and dominated economics, but the emergence of game theory, more recently behavioral economics, and a variety of other new fields and approaches in economics since the 1980s has reinvigorated interest in the subject so that now there are many views about it. Yet still, systematic investigation of the idea of change in economics seems to have advanced little. Change is clearly always ongoing in any discipline, but when it is said there is or is not change in economics something more significant beyond this is usually intended.

How, then, can this more significant sort of change be identified and explained?

One method employed in making such arguments involves inventorying sets of "new" concepts and theories and comparing them to inventories of "old" concepts and theories. There are two problems with this method. First, what may appear to be "new" theories and concepts may simply be "old" concepts and theories that have been modified or revised. How do we identify genuinely "new" concepts and theories? Second, supposing we could say what is "new" in economics, when are there enough "new" concepts and theories to say there is significant change in it? Fields can certainly have many "new" concepts and theories but still remain largely unchanged.

The underlying problem with the inventory method, I suggest, is that its comparison of "new" and "old" contents depends upon and implicitly makes use of judgments about the state of a field as a whole, but when the starting point is inventories of concepts and theories these judgments are not made explicit and may simply presuppose the interpreter's preferences regarding what is "new" and "old" in it. How, then, might we make judgments about the state of economics as a whole which provide an independent means of judging "new" and "old" contents?

One way of proceeding – a method some historians employ – involves making arguments about the role and place of economics in the world. Thus, economics, and political economy as it was previously understood, clearly had different roles and places in the world in the past than now. What counts as "new" or "old" in economics can then be explained according to how concepts and theories reflect historical changes in institutions and social relationships, particularly as shows up in changes in the scope and nature of social policy thinking. For example, Keynesian economics was "new" compared to what preceded it when it became the basis on which many countries sought to manage aggregate demand. Economics as a whole changed because it played a different role in social policy and was associated with different institutions and social relationships.

However, this method does not capture how economics as a whole may change in more subtle ways that do not materialize in different institutions, social relationships, and policy thinking. A more fine-grained strategy I adopt is to explain change in economics in terms of change in its relations to other disciplines. To the extent that this changes economics' scope, domain of explanation, and definition, I argue it produces "new" contents and theories.[1]

The scope of a discipline is the range of subjects it concerns, its domain is how they are addressed, and its definition that encapsulates its scope and domain is its summary interpretation of that subject matter. Consider, for example, the development in the immediate postwar decades of mathematical form of theorizing in economics, reflecting a change in economics' relation to quantitative sciences. This changed both the scope and domain of economics – what it could be about and how that was addressed – and led many to redefine and reinterpret economics as a mathematical social science that investigated mathematical relationships in economic life.

Nonmathematical, natural language forms of explanation in economics were then often seen as "old" and easily distinguished from its "new" forms. They failed to fall within the scope of a mathematical economics because they could not capture the full reach of economic relationships represented mathematically, and they misrepresented economics' domain because they did not explain the mathematical nature of those relationships. Thus, change in economics arose out of how its relations to other (quantitative) disciplines changed.

Thus, ontologically speaking, what a field is – its disciplinary identity – lies in what distinguishes it from other fields, thereby giving it a distinct epistemological (and ultimately social) character. Economics, in virtue of how it is different in its domain, scope, and definition from other social sciences, investigates dimensions of the world different from those they investigate. We cannot say, then, what kind of knowing is going on in a field independently of how this differs from other fields. Field's identities are consequently established in a comparative manner. This then gets embedded institutionally in how a field's research agenda is materially organized, how researchers reflexively identify themselves regarding what they are doing, how they segregate themselves from other kinds of researchers and forms of investigation, and how they see their social policy/application responsibilities.

Whether there is significant change in economics accordingly depends on whether its relations to other disciplines have changed

---

[1] Here, I use "explanation" in a general sense not implying any one particular account of scientific explanation (covering law, causal, ontic, mechanism, unification, etc.).

Box 9.1   Change in economics

Change in economics is reflected in change in its **scope, definition, and domain**

which is reflected in change in its **relations to other disciplines**

which is reflected in change in its **differences from other disciplines**

which is reflected in changes in its **boundaries with other disciplines**

(which ultimately influences its **institutional role, popular thinking about social relationships, and policy/application responsibilities**).

---

sufficiently to change its definition, scope, and domain of investigation. But how do we capture this? Beginning with a field's scope and domain, we can examine how its differences from other fields change by tracking how their disciplinary boundaries change. If what previously fell primarily within the scope and domain of one discipline is increasingly found in another's, then the boundaries between them have shifted and this may begin to change their respective definitions and identities. Box 9.1 summarizes this overall view of change for economics.

Consider two recent examples of boundary change between economics and other disciplines: the economics imperialism of the Chicago School toward sociology and law and behavioral psychology imperialism toward economics.[2] Note that in both cases, while the imperialist disciplines extended their boundaries regarding what they included in their respective scopes and domains, this did not appear to change their own individual definitions. Most economists still define economics as the science of rational resource allocation, but now also apply this definition to some nonmarket processes. Behavioral psychologists still define their field in terms of how our environments affect individual behavior, but now also apply this to market processes.

Thus, there are both "new" and "old" in both fields, making it possible argument both that they have and have not changed. Whether they ultimately change as disciplines, I argue, depends on whether

---

[2] To be clear, by behavioral psychology I do not mean behaviorism or behaviorist psychology but rather for most economists the heuristics and biases research program. For economics imperialism toward other social sciences, see Fine and Milonakis (2009). For behavioral psychology imperialism toward economics, see Davis (2013a).

their definitions also ultimately change. To deal with this complication, I have used a core–periphery distinction to characterize economics (Davis, 2006, 2008, 2019a), reinterpreting the Lakatosian methodology (hard) core concept, and arguing that change in economics' relations to other fields occurs first on its periphery, and then sometimes, but not always, later in the core of economics where the field's definition is maintained.

Historically, change in the periphery of economics deriving from change in its boundaries has on a number of occasions also produced change in its definition and core. Perhaps, the best example is how nineteenth-century classical political economy was succeeded by twentieth neoclassical century economics when other fields took over the "political" part of political economy, resulting in a narrowing of the economics' domain, and ultimately changing its definition. Political economy can be defined as the science of growth and distribution for entire economies. Economics was subsequently defined as the science of choice for allocative processes occurring within economies. In this case, the core of political economy/economics changed and the field changed at its definitional level.

The more recent behavioral psychology imperialism toward neoclassical economies is interesting. The emergence of behavioral economics in economics' periphery has potentially shifted economics' traditional boundaries inward. If earlier Chicago School economics imperialism might have shifted them outward by claiming choice theory explained nonmarket behavior, psychology imperialism not only seeks to reclaim this ground – such behavior still reflects people's environments – but also seeks to extend this environment influence argument to market behavior. Change in economics' boundaries on its periphery then creates arguments for redefining its core. Should all of economics come to focus on how environments influence choice, the core of economics might then be redefined as no longer concerned with the "pure" theory of choice. But I think the verdict is still out on this because many leading economists still hold the traditional view.[3]

Yet even an analysis of change in economics in terms of changes only in its boundaries seems incomplete. What else might

---

[3] Contrary to the conclusion that "we are all behavioral economists now" (Angner, 2019).

Box 9.2   External forces influencing change in economics

(1) **Disciplinary research practices** in economics:

increasing specialization in research
formal modeling as the preferred form of explanation
the "empirical turn" in economics

(2) **Social expectations** about economics and its policy/application
responsibilities:

the importance of individual identity and social relationships
the importance of values in economics

---

influence change in economics? What other factors act on economics? Discussions of change in economics tied to comparisons of "new" and "old" concepts and theories employ an analysis of change only occurring internally within economics, thus ignoring external forces operating upon it as a discipline that may influence how it changes internally.

To address this latter source of change, I will argue that there are two sets of external forces operating upon economics: (i) in terms of its three kinds of disciplinary research practices and (ii) in terms of two kinds of social expectations about economics and its policy/application responsibilities. When we incorporate these external forces into an analysis of how economics changes internally and in its relations to other disciplines, change is then also a matter of change in economics' individual standing as a science in the world. Box 9.1 is concerned with processes of change in economics internal to it as concerns its boundaries. Box 9.2 complements this by identifying external forces acting upon economics.

My prediction, which I will argue for below, is especially because of these latter external forces, economics will evolve over time into a more pluralistic, less hierarchical, theoretically "flatter" discipline with greater openness and competition between diverse kinds of approaches within economics.

To frame all this in terms of economics' relations to other disciplines, Section 2 first discusses the four different forms of relations between disciplines used in Chapter 7, identifies the form that currently best describes economics, and then investigates whether this form is stable and likely to persist. Second, I turn to the topic of "boundary crossings" to address how theories and contents from one discipline "foreign" to another can nonetheless enter into it. I model boundary crossings using a contemporary classical economics development of open and closed systems thinking, and argue that not only can "foreign" materials readily enter into economics but examine how they may influence it. Third, I argue that were economics' landscape to evolve to become more diverse and pluralistic, this would involve a shift toward multidisciplinarity. A possible consequence would be that economics' imperialist ambition to theorize the unity of all social science in its own image would give way to the ideal of a decentralized, "disunified" social science landscape.

Section 3 discusses the external forces in Box 9.2 influencing economics. First, I discuss how forces operating within it but arising from outside it at the level of its research practices – *how* economics is done – may weaken its theoretical core. I frame this using a non-Darwinian, computational approach to evolutionary change. Second, I discuss what popular expectations about the role and nature of economics – *what* it is and should be about – as reflected in evolving world social values as identified in the World Values Survey (WVS) tell us about possible change in economics. My argument here is that with the increasing weight the WVS shows is being given specifically to emancipative values, people's concern with identity and social relationships may work to bring about change in economics. Third, possibly offsetting these two sets of forces, I briefly review how the oligarchic, hierarchical nature of current economics profession works against change in economics reinforcing its current interdisciplinary nature.

Section 4 returns to the contemporary classical economics open–closed systems analysis to argue that the core of economics is incompletely closed and needs to be completed by thinking from outside it. Regarding the two sets of forces operating upon economics, those at the level of practices affect the core's development, and how they distance the core from theory leaves its closure open to theories and concepts from its periphery and other disciplines. There, social expectations affecting economics as seen in the historical evolution of world social values offer a guide to how the core might evolve that jeopardizes its *Homo economicus* and economics' positivism. Thus, change in economics could come about should what acts externally upon it regarding *what* economics is about were to inform *how* its internal practices are put to use.

2 Forms of Disciplinarity and Boundary Relationships between Economics and Other Fields and Also within Economics

a *Economics' Interdisciplinarity and Its Instability*

The four forms of disciplinary relationships distinguished by Jodi Cat (2017) are cross-disciplinarity, interdisciplinarity, multidisciplinarity, and transdisciplinarity. This typology allows us to characterize disciplines and their interaction in terms of how open or closed they are to one another according to (i) the extent to which they are significantly affected by their interaction and (ii) the extent to which their interaction produces new interfield research that influences them.

Cross-disciplinarity is the most closed case since disciplines borrowing from one other are largely unaffected by this in their own development, and new interfield research disciplines drawing on both do not really develop. Interdisciplinarity is the next most closed form since disciplines are still largely unaffected by their borrowing from one another, and though significant interfield research between them emerges, its ties to its contributing disciplines are weak. Multidisciplinarity and transdisciplinarity are at the other end of the spectrum as the most open since in differing degrees interacting disciplines are significantly affected by their interaction and interfield research begins to rival disciplinary research.[4]

Interdisciplinarity, then, is the case that best characterizes contemporary economics, because its borrowing from other fields can be shown to have influenced its recent development, and on its periphery there are a variety of new approaches that owe much to other fields and have an increasingly interfield research character. To investigate, then, whether this state of affairs is stable, first consider economics' postwar borrowing in three important episodes: its adoption of mathematical forms of explanation in the immediate postwar decades, the emergence of game theory somewhat later, and the more recent adoption of experimentalism. What these three borrowing episodes could show is that economics can borrow freely from other disciplines, but not significantly change what defines it, and thus that it could persist

---

[4] For a deeper examination of these four forms and their differences, see Ambrosino et al. (2021).

as an interdisciplinary type of field. Thus, these episodes constitute one test for the stability of economics' current interdisciplinarity. Note that what these three episodes share is that this borrowing draws especially on other disciplines' methods of explanation and less from their concepts and theories.

In the first case, while there were also transfers of concepts and theories from quantitative sciences, what principally was transferred were quantitative methods of explanation, for example, as used to place general equilibrium theory on a more rigorous basis (Weintraub, 2002), and as also applied to refine microeconomic optimality research. It is widely thought, I believe, that this borrowing strengthened the core of economics. A reason for this is that a borrowing that occurs at the level of method appears to have a largely neutral character, so that adoption of quantitative methods was instrumental to the further development of existing theories. Tools and methods, that is, in themselves often have modest implications for the theories to which they are applied.

While this conception of tools and methods as purely instrumental may be debated, to the extent that tools and methods have this character, their adoption suggests economics' borrowing from other disciplines can have limited impact on its main concepts and theories. Then, it seems, such borrowing would ultimately have little effect on economics' core–periphery divide, since that has not much changed as a result of this borrowing. Indeed, mathematical explanation has now become fairly standard throughout economics. Thus, it could be argued that borrowing from other disciplines strengthens rather than weakens postwar economics' interdisciplinary status.

Now consider the later, more complicated case of borrowing economics engaged in several decades into the postwar period in its adoption of game theory, also from mathematics. This is also widely seen as an adoption of new methods of explanation and so conceivably was also neutral in its effects on dominant thinking in economics. Game theory's assimilation into economics may have challenged its perfect competition conception of markets, but one could argue that as long as game theory employed only noncooperative games, competition as an ideal still characterized economics. This borrowing, then, might also show that economics can draw on other disciplines without significantly changing its main concepts and theories and interdisciplinary character.

Finally, consider the more challenging case of the emergence of experimentalism in economics, also a borrowing of methods rather than concepts and theories from other sciences. While experiments can indeed be used in a neutral sort of way to simply develop new empirical knowledge and applications of existing theories (Santos, 2009; Banerjee and Duflo, 2012; Favereau, 2016), they also potentially create challenges to fundamental assumptions in economics, for example, as seen in the early debates over whether the ultimatum game and inequity aversion show people do not always behave in a self-regarding way (Guala, 2008; Truc and Jullien, 2023). However, many of these debates have been framed in terms of standard rationality assumptions, and nonstandard behavior to the extent that it is admitted is seen only as a departure from it. Thus again, economics' borrowing from other disciplines does not appear to have much changed it.

These three examples make a case for saying economics' borrowing from other disciplines does not really affect its character and interdisciplinary nature. Indeed, they arguably make the opposite case that this borrowing is likely to be done in only an instrumental manner that conforms to economics' core commitments. What, however, should we say about a borrowing that appears to go beyond adopting methods of explanation and involves substantive concepts and theories from other disciplines?

Consider the much-debated case of economics' borrowing from other disciplines, namely, from psychology. On the one hand, when we focus on behavioral psychology and the principle that decision-makers' environments fundamentally influence their choices, we bring in ideas that are more associated with economics' periphery. As many have argued, behavioral economics has been treated as providing a set of choice anomalies – an adjustment in its method of analysis, not a call for rethinking the nature of choice.

On the other hand, that such anomalies derive from how the environment affects choice still raises a fundamental issue regarding the standard choice theory assumption that people always make choices in the same way everywhere irrespective of context. Might this larger issue, in effect smuggled in behind the scenes and working on a different conceptual level than that of method, potentially introduce substantive conceptual matters inconsistent with the core of economics and ultimately challenge its interdisciplinary nature?

To investigate how this could occur, Section b develops a two-level account of disciplinary borrowing using an open and closed systems analysis to explain how a discipline's borrowing from other disciplines can successfully introduce "foreign" contents into it. It describes a mechanism for how disciplinary boundary crossings work, whereby borrowings at the level of method are accompanied by broad conceptual ideas on a second level that can "close" the borrowing discipline's conceptual framework and potentially transform it.

b Disciplinary Boundary Crossings in Open and Closed Systems Terms

Cat's typology does not address how one discipline's contents enter another's. We can assume this readily occurs in multidisciplinary and transdisciplinary interactions because disciplines are less independent and boundaries between them are weak, but in interdisciplinary (and cross-disciplinary) interactions where this is not the case boundary crossings need to be explained. This is particularly the case with broad, substantive concepts and theories since they are especially characteristic of their contributing disciplines and potentially "foreign" in the borrowing ones. On a core–periphery view of economics, this is important since its core principles underlying its definition are broad ideas (e.g., "scarcity" underlying rational allocation).

The open and closed systems analysis I attribute to contemporary classical economics I will argue treats the core of economics (in a classical Ricardian world) as an only relatively or incompletely closed system whose closure is completed by open system concepts and theories drawn from outside it. Applying this to current mainstream economics, I will argue its core is also incompletely closed and is also completed by drawing from open system concepts and theories that lie outside it, whether from economics' periphery or other disciplines.

I attribute this open–closed thinking to contemporary classical economics because it is drawn from Piero Sraffa's rehabilitation of classical Ricardian theory. In 1931, in developing ideas later employed in his *Production of Commodities by Means of Commodities* (1960), Sraffa used an open–closed systems distinction from philosophy of science of the time to argue that the system of equations determining commodity values (the classical core) conceptualized strictly in cost of production terms could not explain the existence of an economic surplus (Sraffa (1931). He consequently reconceptualized his system of equations to include wage and profit components to show that economies generated surpluses divided between workers and capitalists, where this drew on an open system involving the struggle over distribution (Davis, 2012b, 2018c).[5] Thus, an only relatively closed system is closed by incorporating the effects of an open system in and upon it.

Specifically, wages and profits are not determined in the same way the value of material inputs to the production process are. They reflect social struggle and a host of determining factors not reducible to the laws of natural science. Thus, the system of equations for determining commodity values in cost of production terms is only incompletely closed. Further, since social struggle over the distributive shares of the economy's surplus lacks the systematic character of a cost of production determination of commodity values, that struggle can be characterized as a type of open system.[6]

The same analysis, then, can be used to characterize postwar standard general equilibrium theory, the core of postwar mainstream economics. There, rather than a cost of production determination of commodity values, prices are determined according to preferences and resources. Yet, a general equilibrium cannot be established by tallying up knowns and unknowns inherent in that system of prices and an inspection of the equations involved themselves. To show an equilibrium is possible required the application of fixed-point theorems that came from outside the system of price equations, so a general equilibrium price system by itself is an incompletely closed system. Further, since there is considerable debate in mathematics regarding the nature and assumptions underlying fixed-point theorems, this domain itself functions as an open system. In fixed-point theorems, where a fixed point of a function is defined as an element in the function's domain that is mapped onto itself by that function, mathematicians employ

---

[5] This was the understanding Sraffa later developed in his *Production of Commodities by Means of Commodities* (1960), though he did not use the systems framework there.

[6] As Sraffa put it: "When we have defined our 'economic field', there are still outside causes which operate in it; and its effects go beyond the boundary" (Sraffa, 1931, D3/12/7: 161 (3–5); also quoted in Kurz and Salvadori, 2008, p. 268).

a reasoning developed to conceptualize how sets of equations can be taken as unities. This relationship is something that can be applied to any sort of system of equations irrespective of their subject matter, and is consequently an idea external to whatever field in which they are applied.

Returning to economics' overall core–periphery organization, I argue that economics' core is not a fully closed system but rather an incompletely closed one whose closure depends on how it draws from open systems with which it interacts, whether they are from the periphery of economics or other disciplines. Economics' quantitative nature gives the relationships it investigates a systematic, interconnected character that makes it like a closed system analysis. Yet, how these relationships are ultimately conceptualized depends on further assumptions that come from outside that only incompletely closed system of analysis.

In this light, reconsider behavioral economics. Behavioral economics is a research area still mostly located on economics' periphery deriving from behavioral psychology. In standard postwar economics, rational choice theory aspires to be a completely closed analysis of choice, but its independence axioms on which this depends are largely stipulative and motivated by the need to close off choice analysis from context of choice rather than evidence that context does not matter. Thus, economics' choice theory is better seen as an incompletely closed system. Behavioral economics and behavioral psychology, seen as an open system of analysis – open because there are many views of how environments affect choice – provide one way of closing choice theory. Though much of their discussion proceeds on the level of methods of explanation, their rejection of the standard independence axioms and insistence that context of choice matters introduce broad conceptual issues into economics that potentially jeopardize the autonomy of its traditional core.[7]

Thus, while we cannot rule out that change in economics may leave its core unchanged, we also cannot rule out on this closed–open, two-level understanding of disciplinary border crossings that the core principles of economics may change over time, as they have in the

---

[7] Thus, while the asymmetry between gains and losses which was the focus of Kahneman and Tversky (1979) makes one's wealth position a contextual factor, one can equally see one's social position as a contextual factor (Davis, 2011, pp. 33–34).

past, at least in part as a result of economics' interaction with other disciplines. The core–periphery divide in economics might then also erode, and its interdisciplinary nature give way to a more multidisciplinary character. The Section c outlines what economics could then look like.

c A Diverse, Pluralistic, Multidisciplinary Economics

In Cat's taxonomy, multidisciplinarity and transdisciplinarity on the open–closed spectrum are the most open forms of disciplinary interaction. Multidisciplinary interactions significantly affect the interacting disciplines and also produce active interfield research with strong effects on the contributing fields. In transdisciplinary interaction, interacting fields may begin to lose their independent individual identities, and emergent interfield research begins to dominate, sometimes with contributing disciplines being replaced in the long run by new disciplines. For example, it can be argued that economics emerged as a relatively new interfield domain of investigation when its eighteenth-century focus on prices and markets distanced it from earlier narratives of just price and feudal power that had other disciplinary locations. However, I see no evidence that economics will be replaced by new emergent disciplines to which it contributes, so transdisciplinarity is an unlikely scenario. What, then, might economics look like if it were to become a multidisciplinary discipline?

Multidisciplinary disciplines borrow more freely from other disciplines than interdisciplinary and cross-disciplinary ones. Since this characterizes the current periphery of economics, were economics as a whole to become more multidisciplinary it would likely lose its internal core–periphery divide, become more pluralistic and less hierarchical, and exhibit more open competition between different kinds of approaches within economics.[8]

How can we explain this sort of disciplinary structure? To say a discipline is less hierarchical does not mean there are no dominant or especially influential approaches in it, but if there are there is a

---

[8] This, for example, describes sociology as a discipline in which there are many competing approaches with no accepted ranking of their importance (Collins, 1994; Horowitz, 1994; Turner, 1998).

rotation across them over time. This calls for a dynamic representation of change in economics based on how relationships between different kinds of approaches can change. In Simon's (1962) basic complexity model, interaction between different processes has effects on the entire system they make up, which then feedback upon their interaction, a combination of bottom-up and top-down effects. Suppose we characterize those approaches in a discipline dominant at any time as those especially associated with the discipline as a whole and thus as representative of it. Then, as they evolve over time due to this interaction between different approaches, what is seen as representative of the discipline changes as well.

It could still be argued that there is "nothing new" is this sort of process of change if what is "new" only revises and reconfigures what it replaces. However, this view may rest on an understanding of evolution more appropriate to evolutionary processes in the natural world and not those in the social world. In natural systems with evolution understood in a Darwinian way, "new" organisms are only descended from parents who are of the same type. In the human social world when we focus on the evolution of ideas, the ancestry of "new" phenomena is quite different. New ideas can be descended in part from antecedents of the same type when a theory is redeveloped and revised, but can also be descended from unlike antecedents when they result from creative assembly of different idea streams.

One material process driving scientific development is specialization or deeper focus on particular processes within a subject of investigation. Advances in science are then associated in part with how specialization generates discovery of what was previously unrecognized. Discovery is about what is "new" in science. In a non-Darwinian conception of evolution, what is "new" occurs when previously unrecognized, discovered phenomena are seen to be descended from unlike, often unexpected antecedents. Brian Arthur's computational explanation of evolution explains the mechanics of this in terms of how different kinds of technology modules, created independently of one another for different purposes, are combined in unanticipated ways to create altogether new technologies (Arthur, 2009). Over time, as the number of new technologies increases, this increases the base upon which possible new technology modules can be created (Davis 2019b). Thus, a social evolutionary process such as operates in science potentially generates new phenomena, concepts and theories, in an exponential manner. Science is thus biased toward what is "new" rather than what only revises and reconfigures what gets replaced.

A multidisciplinary environment, then, in which change is pervasive is inherently pluralistic, less hierarchical, and possesses many competing approaches. Yet if economics is best described today as an interdisciplinary field, what might cause it to become a multidisciplinary one? Section 3 turns to two kinds of forces operating upon economics.

3 "Change in Economics": Forces Operating upon Economics

Box 9.2 distinguishes two kinds of forces influencing economics. First, specialization in research, formal modeling, and the "empirical turn" involve forces operating throughout science and also upon economics that concern economists' research technologies and *how* economics is done. I characterize them as practices. Second, social expectations about economics and its policy/application responsibilities involve forces operating upon economics that concern *what* economics is about. Of course, economists also have expectations about economics as a science, but my view is they are influenced in significant degree by how society sees economics.

The argument below is that these two kinds of forces will tend to move economics from being an interdisciplinary science to a multidisciplinary one and will tend to reduce hierarchy in economics making it an increasingly pluralistic science. There are also forces influencing economics that work counter to this I discuss briefly at the end of this section.

a Economics' Research Practices: Specialization, Formal Modeling, and the "Empirical Turn"

Above I discussed specialization in evolutionary process terms, but here I focus on it as a practice that influences the way in which research is done and how scientific knowledge develops. It is one of the most fundamental research practices in science and generally seen as a key means by which researchers extend or revise existing knowledge. Will new discoveries confirm or disconfirm accepted beliefs? My view is that in active, growing sciences as specialization increases this tends to weaken the command that existing theories have on a science. Economics in the postwar period has indeed been an active, growing science with continually increasing numbers of people and publications, and research specialization is increasingly characteristic of economics (Davis, 2019b). Thus, we should generally expect the command that existing theories have, whatever their orientation and approach, to weaken. Two properties of specialization support this conclusion.

First, since specialization emphasizes particularity and context, its development lessens the connection of scientific activity to general theory. Specialization involves focusing on individual topics where their specificity is determined by how they are differentiated from each other. In effect, it emphasizes horizontal links to other similar but different kinds of research and de-emphasizes vertical links to theories that motivate it. Theory then becomes secondary in importance in the design and implementation of a research investigation, more of a heuristic guide. Is the phenomenon being investigated truly distinct from like phenomena? Is the contextual setting in which the phenomenon is observed correctly described? Generality, a key concern of theory, becomes a background, less immediate concern.

Second, as specialization advances in a science its overall research landscapes exhibit a greater array of new results. As the volume of new results increases, theory construction becomes more difficult as it becomes less clear how generalization encompasses this greater variety. Not only is scientific activity more removed from theory concerns, but it is less clear how it is even related to theory concerns. Theory may still flourish, but it needs to do so either at a greater remove from much ongoing research as a kind of specialization itself, likely having a more limited and less generalizing nature. The status of particular theories in a science then becomes less obvious, and researchers may consequently lower the priority and time they give to them.[9]

Both of these properties specialization exhibits appear to apply to economics, together lessening the importance of theory in economics.

---

[9] Rodrik (2015), a practitioner with methodological interests, makes this specialization argument in connection with his emphasis on horizontal rather than vertical development of models. New models are differentiated from other similar models, and their relation to underlying theory is secondary if not altogether ignored.

This in turn diminishes the divide between core and periphery. Specialization in economics also seems connected to the other two forces I argue are operating within and upon it in much the same way.

Formal modeling is essentially a more highly specified expression of theory made possible by its mathematical formulation. Narrative-based theorization identifies possible causal relationships between different factors, such as the relationship between income and consumption, but formal models translate factors into variables and describe relationships between them parametrically to determine how income affects consumption. One could argue that the postwar expansion of formal modeling in economics has increased the importance of theory in economics and also strengthened existing theory because models refine theories and because much of the postwar development of models is associated with existing theory. However, I argue the opposite has occurred because this change has shifted economists' priorities away from broad theorizing toward explaining particular causal relationships.

Narrative-based theorization works at a high level of generality in which causal relationships are not sharply defined. In mainstream economics, this involves such claims as incentives matter, prices determine behavior, markets work effectively, etc. Modeling causal relationships involves modifying these claims: They may hold sometimes, in some degree, in some circumstances, etc. What matters scientifically is what specific relationships stand up to empirical testing, not what broad, general claims might motivate economists' intuitions. Indeed, because broad claims operate at a high level of generality, they cannot *per se* be said to be true or false or confirmed or disconfirmed. They essentially occupy an earlier stage of theoretical development and one that also ends up giving way to the more sharply specified causal relationships that replace them.

Theory, of course, still matters in economics, but its character has changed with the rise of formal modeling. If we characterize this shift as one in which applied economics increasingly defines most practitioners' scientific activity (Backhouse and Cherrier, 2017), what particular theoretical motivations underlie economists' research divides them less than disagreements over such things as whether a variable is correctly identified or a parameter properly estimated. What this means is that as formal modeling is adopted across economics irrespective of theoretical orientation, theory motivations divide economists less than disputes over these more concrete issues. Their implications for broad theories consequently become background concerns.

Consider, now, the "empirical turn" in economics. Here, as in the rise of formal modeling in economics, we have a widely recognized change in recent economics research reflected in the falling share of theory research and rising share of empirical research (Hamermesh, 2013; Angrist et al., 2017). While this distinction is not entirely sharp, nonetheless it is fairly clear that empirical research in economics research has increased, and what increasingly characterizes economics as a whole is empirical research. Moreover, it seems unlikely also that this turn might be reversed in the future, since the amount of data available to economists – reflective of a "data explosion" and exponential growth of information across science – is giving additional momentum to empirical research.

Economists can still be distinguished by their different theoretical assumptions, but as with formal modeling their professional standing and credentials increasingly rest on whether their empirical research meets the standards of the profession (Angrist and Pischke, 2010). New theories may be claimed to develop new conceptual relationships compared to previous theories. For example, game theory produced a new understanding of competition compared to prior market theory analysis. However, whether these theories end up being counted as "new" depends on whether there is evidence to support them. Thus, much empirical research aims at contributing to accumulating a body of evidence and rarely is a single empirical result or set of results seen as having "breakthrough" status, whatever its theoretical motivation. The "breakthrough" idea indeed might be a relic of an earlier stage of development in economics.

Specialization, formal modeling, and the empirical turn thus reinforce each other in making the core–periphery divide that characterized economics for the early decades of the postwar period less important going forward. As material practices, they involve change in the technology of economics research. Economics' nature a relatively insular, interdisciplinary field largely precedes the onset of these changes. Its transition to becoming a multidisciplinary field thus reflects less change in ideas and views regarding what economics is about and more how research in it is institutionally organized. I turn now to how social expectations regarding economics operate upon it from outside it.

b Social Expectations Regarding Economics:
The Importance of Social Values

People form expectations about economics based on their belief that economic life affects their lives and well-being, and that it is the scientific responsibility of economics to explain this. By the standard of natural and physical science, they also expect economics to produce objective knowledge, and then bring their values to bear in determining just what this requires. Most economists of course believe values are subjective and should be ignored. This is because they associate them with individual private values and thus fail to recognize how social values are different. Social values are values shared by many people and are objective in much the same way that other facts, demographic and otherwise, about people are objective. The challenge in talking about social values and how they bear on economics lies in how we identify them.

It is a misconception, then, that social values are simply casual opinions about what matters that change from year to year if not from day to day. Social values in fact have been comprehensively surveyed across over 100 countries since 1981 in the World Values Survey (WVS) by a large, global network of social scientists (Inglehart et al., 2014), and exhibit considerable stability and connection to people's different economic circumstances. I rely on the results of these surveys to identify sets of values that motivate large numbers of people, and use this to frame social expectations about economics according to how well it explains what people care about in economic life.

The Inglehart-Welzel World Cultural Map, then, uses multiple survey rounds of the WVS to show there exist two major pairs of ways in which values vary across the countries: (i) traditional values versus secular–rational values and (ii) survival values versus self-expression values (Inglehart and Welzel, 2005). In both cases, these pairs of values are essentially opposite to one another. Traditional values are associated with importance given to religion, family, and political authority, and secular–rational values de-emphasize these. Survival values are associated with existential insecurity and constraints on human autonomy, while self-expression values are associated with tolerance, social equality, and increasing demands for participation in economic and political decision-making.[10]

---

[10] The Inglehart–Welzel main value categories are disaggregated into multiple subsets of values under each of these main divisions, and indicators are

What economic basis, then, do these different sets of values possess? Economic development and the advent of postindustrial, knowledge-based society have generally tended to move countries from both traditional and survival values toward both secular–rational and self-expression values (Inglehart and Welzel, *Ibid.*), though this is not the case for all countries. The US and most of Latin America combine traditional and self-expression values, much of western and northern Europe and Japan combine and secular–rational and self-expression values, former Soviet bloc eastern Europe combines secular–rational and survival values, and many developing countries still combine traditional and survival values.

How, then, does mainstream economics fit the US combination of traditional and self-expression values? The answer is not very well, despite that the postwar development of economics has been strongly associated with US economics. First, traditional values have been generally reinterpreted in secular–rational terms through instrumental rationality explanations of the family (Becker, 1981), religion (Iannaccone, 1998), and political authority (Buchanan and Tullock, 1965) – a departure from their general importance in much of the US. Second, while self-expression values are important in postwar economics since subjective preferences, a form of self-expression, are the foundation of mainstream theory, this view of self-expression is at best a modest version of what many see self-expression values generally mean in the US.

We might think, then, that social expectations about mainstream economics in the US would press for a restoration of emphasis on traditional values. However, it seems highly unlikely that economics will change in the future in this way since instrumental rationality, one of the highest expressions of secular–rational values, is foundational to mainstream economics. Moreover, while traditional values have a strong place in the US, so do secular–rational values, especially in business and government administration.

Things are less clear regarding mainstream economics and self-expression values. A key subset of self-expression values in the WVS framework are what are called "emancipative" values that drive from how people value freedom of choice and equality of opportunity,

constructed to show the degree of attachment people have in the annual WVS to these subsets of values and thus to the overall divisions.

Box 9.3   Emancipative values in the shift from survival to self-expression values

Emancipative values, a key subset of self-expression values, emphasize:
freedom of choice and equality of opportunity, lifestyle liberty, gender equality, personal autonomy, and popular voice

Promote **human empowerment** by strengthening people's capabilities, aspirations, and entitlements, democracy, out-group trust and cosmopolitan orientations toward others

Are motivated by the goal of increasing **individual agency**

---

lifestyle liberty, gender equality, personal autonomy, and popular voice. Among the chief WVS findings across countries regarding emancipative values are that they are seen to (i) underlie broader processes of human empowerment, (ii) concern people's capabilities, aspirations, and desired entitlements, (iii) are associated with a commitment to democracy, and (iv) favor out-group trust and cosmopolitan orientations toward others (Welzel, 2013).

When we link this to the shift worldwide over time from survival values to self-expression values, particularly as has accompanied transitions from industrial to knowledge societies, emancipative values are also associated with increases in people's sense of individual agency and their understanding of what empowers them to do the things they choose to do – their capabilities. Increases in individual agency, then, are seen to be the goal motivating people's higher valuations of emancipative values through self-expression. Box 9.3 summarizes these linkages between emancipative values, human empowerment, and individual agency.

In this light, mainstream economics' conception of self-expression values falls well short of what the WVS evolution toward self-expression values in postindustrial, knowledge-based societies like the US involves. Most of what we see in Box 9.3 is inconsistent with its narrow subjective preferences understanding of self-expression. Indeed, emancipative values, human empowerment, and capabilities do not really fit anywhere in mainstream economics. Further, the mainstream is unlikely to evolve in the direction of this expanded conception of self-expression on account of as what I previously characterized as its commitment to an internalist view of individual autonomy. Autonomy or how individuals are distinct and independent is fundamental to explaining individual agency. Yet, a subjective preference interpretation of self-expression offers no account of increasing freedoms and individual agency. People are free only in that they can form their own preferences, and this fully explains the nature of individual agency. In contrast, emancipative values reflect an externalist view of individual autonomy where how institutions and social arrangements are organized influences the extent to which people can act freely and independently. On this understanding of individual autonomy, increasing human empowerment is always a goal.

Moreover, on an externalist understanding of individual autonomy, people's social relationships and social identities are important. Yet, the idea that people are embedded in such relationships and are social beings is contrary to the mainstream's foundational *Homo economicus* doctrine. Thus, the mainstream's conception of self-expression really cannot be expanded or revised to accommodate emancipative values. This puts the mainstream at odds with the historical development of self-expression values in increasingly postindustrial, knowledge-based economies, and suggests that it will not meet popular expectations about its responsibilities for explaining economic life in the future. It is essentially time-bound by its past commitments and too inflexible to adjust to evolving social values.[11]

c Forces Reinforcing Economics' Interdisciplinary Nature

Though there are these forces operating in and on economics influencing change in it, there also exist forces operating in it tending to reinforce its current character. I associate these with economics' longstanding commitment to being a relatively insular, interdisciplinary science, linked to the belief held by many economists that economics is unique among the social sciences.

Again, an interdisciplinary science draws concepts and theories from other sciences but adapts them to its core ("hard core" in Lakatosian

---

[11] Thus, one way of seeing behavioral economics' challenge to mainstream economics is to say that it reflects an incipient awareness that environmental factors of all kinds influence not only behavior but also individual autonomy. This could encourage economists to adopt an externalist view of individual autonomy where individual freedom and independence are affected by institutions and how the world is organized.

terms) assumptions and principles, thereby securing its identity as an independent science. Most practitioners learn early in their careers that their field has this status, and accordingly learn where the boundaries lie regarding what ought and ought not be investigated. In economics, they may also adopt an economics-centric or economics imperialism view of other social science disciplines, in which they believe the unity of social science rests on other disciplines' adopting economics' principle commitments, in particular its emphasis on rationality (Ambrosino, Cedrini, and Davis, 2021).

One could argue that any field's ability to maintain a set of core assumptions and principles is limited in the long run, whether due to other sciences' own incursions into it or due to its own evolutionary development. However, working against this is economics hierarchical, oligarchic social organization by which the most prestigious individuals and institutions monopolize and direct career and research opportunities (Fourcade et al., 2015; Heckman and Moktan, 2020; Hoover and Svorenčík, 2020). Since these elite individuals and institutions' reputations and standing are closely associated with existing economics, they have much to lose from change in economics. Thus, as long as the field is socially and institutionally organized in this way, forces operating within it tend to preserve past assumptions and principles.

What might we expect of the future? Histories of science and economics show that over time well-entrenched paradigms are nonetheless replaced by new thinking, the transition from classical to neoclassical economics being a clear example. My general argument, then, is that such transitions involve disciplines, temporarily and sometimes in the long run, becoming multidisciplinary and open to many approaches, whether those approaches originate within them or in other disciplines. Above I discussed a contemporary classical economics understanding of openness and the open–closed distinction to discuss boundary crossings. In Section 4, I use this analysis to say how the different forces influencing economics might combine to influence evolution and change in economics.

4 Changing Economics

Sraffa came to regard the system of equations determining commodity values as incompletely closed, because distribution, a comparatively open system needed to close those equations, acted both upon it and within it. In effect, the core of a Ricardian classical economics, its system of equations determining commodity values, was acted upon by what lay outside it on its periphery, the struggle over wages and profits. In terms of mainstream economics core–periphery structure, if its core is only relatively closed, because what lies outside it on its periphery acts upon it and within it, that core is only incompletely closed as well.

Sraffa did not use the terminology of interdisciplinarity and multidisciplinarity, but the idea that interpretation of a core concern in a field depends on what is not part of it is a multidisciplinary idea. If interdisciplinarity is where a field isolates itself independently of what exists outside it, multidisciplinarity is where a field is never fully independent of other approaches and is always dependent on them in ways that close or complete it. This would exist whether a field had a hierarchical core–periphery structure with one or a few dominant approaches, such as economics, or a less hierarchical structure with many comparably influential approaches, such as sociology. In either case, multidisciplinary fields are characterized by boundary crossings between fields and between approaches within them.

Recall the nature of the distinction between two sets of external forces operating within economics and upon economics. The first set – specialization, formal modeling, and the empirical turn – operate at the level of practices in economics, influence *how* economics research is done, and operate within economics. The second set – social expectations operating on economics – influence *what* economics research is about and operate upon economics from outside.

In open–closed system terms, economics' practices, because they determine how economics research is done, leave open what it is about and function as only a relatively closed system. Specialization, formal modeling, and the empirical turn, I argued, have made explaining causal relationships central to economics, make weak commitments to particular theories, and therefore make economics more open to different theoretical approaches. That is, as only relatively closed systems, they are open to completion by different theoretical ideas.

This raises the question of where theoretical ideas come from and how economists determine what subjects they research. When we answer this question in terms of social expectations acting on economists, there were two conflicting answers given above. The first was that broad social expectations about what economics should investigate act on economists and ultimately influence their choices. The second was that what economists work on depends on what elite individuals and institutions do.

It is not difficult to make an argument against the second alternative prevailing in the long run, because in the histories of science and economics over time well-entrenched paradigms are replaced by new thinking. Yet, while it is not easy to make an argument for the first alternative, because explaining social expectations and social values is difficult, the WVS offers a way to proceed on the assumption that values and beliefs on a world scale ultimately will influence economists. In closing, then, I describe how economics might change in the future in light of the social values especially affecting influential US economics.

The WVS shows the growing importance for postindustrial, knowledge-based societies of self-expression and emancipative values and people's concern with their empowerment, capabilities, and individual agency. Their agency, this book has argued, cannot be understood apart from an understanding of individual identity, which taken as socially embedded includes people's social identities and relationships to others. The WVS shows people increasingly see themselves as social beings, not isolated *Homo economicus* beings. On the grounds that people's concern with their identities and social relationships will increase in the future, I take this standard doctrine to be a likely casualty of change in economics. To the extent that people expect economics, like all sciences, to be an objective science and reliable source of knowledge affecting lives, they are likely to see a transformation of its conception of the person as necessary.

The WVS shows what social values operate in societies around the world. As a guide to how social expectations operate on economics, it tells us that people are likely to believe that values pervade economics just as elsewhere in society. This is glaringly inconsistent with economics' claim to be a positive value-free science. In ordinary life, of course, people commonly see values at work in the economy. Thus, it makes sense that the science of the economy contains values as well. The idea that economics is a moral science is unfamiliar to most people, but it nonetheless captures this general belief about the value-laden nature of economic life. I consequently take the standard idea that economics is positive science free of values also likely to be a casualty of change in economics.

That the *Homo economicus* doctrine and economics' self-conception as a positive science have little future may seem improbable to many whose view of the future is framed in backward-looking terms where the past determines present. Yet while there is considerable uncertainty today about how economics is changing, perhaps that reflects that we occupy an interregnum in the history of the discipline when the old world is still dying and the new is yet to be born.

References

Adams, Ernest W. (1975) *The Logic of Conditionals*, Dordrecht and Boston: Reidel.

Addo, Fenaba R. and William A. Darity, Jr. (2021) "Disparate Recoveries: Wealth, Race, and the Working Class after the Great Recession," *Annals of the American Academy of Political and Social Science* 695 (1): 173–192.

Ainslie, George (1992) *Picoeconomics: The Strategic Interaction of Successive Motivational States within the Person*, Cambridge, UK: Cambridge University Press.

Akerlof, George and Rachel Kranton (2000) "Economics and Identity," *Quarterly Journal of Economics* 115 (3): 715–753.

(2002) "Identity and Schooling: Some Lessons for the Economics of Education," *Journal of Economic Literature* 40 (4): 1167–201.

(2005) "Identity and the Economics of Organizations," *Journal of Economic Perspectives* 19 (1): 9–32.

(2010) *Identity Economics: How Identity Shapes Our Work, Wages, and Well-Being*, Princeton, NJ: Princeton University Press.

Allais, Maurice (1953) "Le comportement de l'homme rationnel devant le risque: Critique des postulats et axiomes de l'école Américaine," *Econometrica* 21 (4): 503–546.

Allen, Amy (2016) "Feminist Perspectives on Power," *The Stanford Encyclopedia of Philosophy* (Fall Edition), Edward N. Zalta, ed., https://plato.stanford.edu/archives/fall2016/entries/feminist-power/

Ali, Omer, William A. Darity, Jr., Avra Janz and Marta Sánchez (2021) "The Association between Wealthy Inequality and Socioeconomic Outcomes," *American Economic Review* 111 (May): 211–215.

Ambrosino, Angela, Mario Cedrini and John B. Davis (2021) "The Unity of Science and Disunity of Economics," *Cambridge Journal of Economics* 45 (4): 631–654.

Ambrosino, Angela, Magda Fontana and Anna Azzurra Gigante (2018) "Shifting Boundaries. In Economics: The Institutional Cognitive Strand and the Future of Institutional Economics," *Journal of Economic Surveys* 32 (3): 761–791.

Andersen, Hans Christian (1837) "Kejserens nye Klæder," in *Fairy Tales Told for Children*, translated as "The Emperor's New Clothes," *The Complete Andersen* (1949), translated by Jean Hersholt, New York; 1949.

Andre, Peter and Armin Falk (2021) "What's Worth Knowing? Economists' Opinions about Economics," CRC TR 224 Discussion Paper Series crctr224_2021_308, University of Bonn and University of Mannheim, Germany.

Angner, Eric (2012) *A Course in Behavioral Economics*, London: Palgrave Macmillan.

(2018) "What Are Preferences?" *Philosophy of Science* 85: 660–681.

(2019) "We're All Behavioral Economists Now," *Journal of Economic Methodology* 26 (3): 195–207.

Angrist, Joshua and Jörn-Steffen Pischke (2010) "The Credibility Revolution in Economics: How Better Research Design Is Taking the Con out of Econometrics," *Journal of Economic Perspectives* 24 (2): 3–30.

Angrist, Joshua, Pierre Azoulay, Glenn Ellison, Ryan Hill and Susan Feng Lu (2017) "Economic Research Evolves: Fields and Styles," *American Economic Review: Papers & Proceedings* 107 (5): 293–297.

Annet, Anthony (2018) "Modern Economics Should Return to Its Roots," Finance and Development 55/1, IMF; 54–56. www.imf.org/external/pubs/ft/fandd/2018/03/pdf/point2.pdf; accessed 31 March 2021.

Archer, Margaret (1995) *Realist Social Theory: A Morphogenetic Approach*, London: Routledge.

Arestis, Philip, Aurelie Charles and Giuseppe Fontana (2014) "Identity Economics Meets Financialisation: Gender, Race, and Occupational Stratification in the US Labour Market," *Cambridge Journal of Economics* 38 (6): 1471–1491.

Aristotle (1984) "De Interpretatione," in *The Complete Works of Aristotle*, Princeton, NJ: Princeton University Press, Chapter 9.

Arthur, Brian (2009) *The Nature of Technology: What It Is and How It Evolves*, New York: Free Press.

(2015) *Complexity and the Economy*, New York: Oxford University Press.

(2021) "Foundations of Complexity Economics," *Nature Reviews Physics* 3 (February): 136–145.

Bacharach, Michael (2006) *Beyond Individual Choice: Teams and Frames in Game Theory*, N. Gold and R. Sugden, eds., Princeton: Princeton University Press.

Backhouse, Roger and Béatrice Cherrier (2017) "The Age of the Applied Economist: The Transformation of Economics Since the 1970s," *History of Political Economy* 49 (Supplement): 1–33.

Backhouse, Roger and Béatrice Cherrier, eds. (2017) *The Transformation of Economics Since the 1970s*, Durham and London: Duke University Press.

Badiei, Sina and Agnès Grivaux, eds. (2022) *The Positive and the Normative in Economic Thought*, London: Routledge.

Ballet, Jérôme, Damien Bazin, Jean-Luc Dubois and François-Régis Mahieu (2014) *Freedom, Responsibility and Economics of the Person*, London: Routledge.

Banerjee, Abhijit V. (1992) "A Simple Model of Herd Behaviour," *Quarterly Journal of Economics* 107 (3): 797–817.

Banerjee, Abhijit and Esther Duflo (2012) *Poor Economics*, New York: Public Affairs.

Barker, Drucilla and Susan Feiner (2004). *Liberating Economics: Feminist Perspectives on Families, Work, and Globalization,* Ann Arbor, MI: University of Michigan Press.

Baujard, Antoinette and Muriel Gilardone (2020) "Reconciling Agency and Impartiality: Positional Views as the Cornerstone of Sen's Idea of Justice," Economics Working Paper from Condorcet Center for Political Economy at CREM-CNRS, 2020–03-ccr, Condorcet Center for Political Economy.

Baumeister, Roy and Kathleen Vohs (2007) "Realistic Group Conflict Theory," *Encyclopedia of Social Psychology* 2: 725–726.

Beck, Lukas (2022) "Why We Need to Talk About Preferences: Economic Experiments and the Where-Question," *Erkenntnis*. https://doi.org/10.1007/s10670-022-00590-2

Becker, Gary (1957) *The Economics of Discrimination*, Chicago, University of Chicago Press.

(1981) *A Treatise on the Family*, Cambridge, MA: Harvard University Press; enlarged edition, 1991.

Bellamy, Edward (1889) *Looking Backward: 2000–1887*, Boston: Houghton Mifflin and Co.

Belluz, Julia (2015) "Nobel Winner Angus Deaton Talks about the Surprising Study on White Mortality He Just Co-Authored," *Vox* 7 November.

Bénabou, Roland and Jean Tirole (2002) "Self-Confidence and Personal Motivation," *Quarterly Journal of Economics* 117(3): 871–915.

(2003) "Self-Knowledge and Self-Regulation: An Economic Approach," in I. Brocas and J. Carrillo, eds., *The Psychology of Economic Decisions: Volume 1: Rationality and Well-Being*, Oxford: Oxford University Press: 137–167.

(2004) "Willpower and Personal Rules," *Journal of Political Economy* 12 (4): 848–86.

Berg, Nathan and Gerd Gigerenzer (2010) "As-If Behavioral Economics: Neoclassical Economics in Disguise?" *History of Economic Ideas* 18 (1): 133–166.

Bernheim, B. Douglas (2008) "Behavioral Welfare Economics," *NBER Working Paper Series*, no. 14622 (December).

(2016) "The Good, the Bad, and the Ugly: A Unified Approach to Behavioral Welfare Economics," *Benefit Cost Analysis* 7: 12–68.

Bernheim, B. Douglas and Antonio Rangel (2007) "Toward Choice-Theoretic Foundations for Behavioral Welfare Economics," *American Economic Review* 97 (2): 464–470.

Bernheim, B. Douglas and Antonio Rangel (2008) "Choice-Theoretic Foundations for Behavioral Welfare Economics," in A. Caplin & A. Schotter, eds., *The Foundations of Positive and Normative Economics*, Oxford: Oxford University Press, 155–192.

(2009) "Beyond Revealed Preference: Choice-Theoretic Foundations for Behavioral Welfare Economics," *Quarterly Journal of Economics* 124 (1): 51–104.

Bernheim, B. Douglas and Dmitry Taubinsky (2018) "Behavioral Public Economics," in B. D. Bernheim, B. Douglas, S. DellaVigna and D. Laibson, eds., *Handbook of Behavioral Economics – Foundations and Applications* 1, 1st edition, Amsterdam: North-Holland: 381–516.

Bertalanffy, Ludwig von (1968) *General Systems Theory: Foundations, Development, Applications*, New York: George Braziller.

Bikhchandani, Sushil, David Hirschleifer and Ivo Welch (1998) "Learning from the Behavior of Others: Conformity, Fads, and Informational Cascades," *Journal of Economic Perspectives* 12 (3): 151–70.

Binmore, Ken (2009) *Rational Decisions*, Princeton, NJ: Princeton University Press.

Blumer, Herbert (1958) "Race Prejudice as a Sense of Group Position," *Pacific Sociological Review* 1 (1): 3–7.

Bögenhold, Dieter (2021) "Economics in the Social Science Spectrum: Evolution and Overlap with Different Academic Areas," *Atlanta Economics Journal* 49: 335–347.

Boland, Lawrence (1981) "On the Futility of Criticizing the Neo-classical Maximization Hypothesis," *American Economic Review* 71 (5): 1031–36.

Bolander, Thomas (2107) "Self-Reference," *The Stanford Encyclopedia of Philosophy*, Fall edition, E. N. Zalta, ed., https://plato.stanford.edu/archives/fall2017/entries/self-reference//

Boldyrev, Ivan and Ushakov, Alexey (2016) "Adjusting the Model to Fit the World: Constructive Mechanisms in Postwar General Equilibrium Theory," *Journal of Economic Methodology* 23(1): 38–56.

Boulding, Kenneth E. (1969) "Economics as a Moral Science," *American Economic Review* 59 (1): 1–12.

Boumans, Marcel (1999) "Built-in Justification," in M. Mary and M. Morrison, eds., *Models as Mediators*, Cambridge: Cambridge University Press: 66–96.

    (2001) "Measure for Measure: How Economists Model the World into Numbers," *Social Research* 68 (2): 427–453.

Boumans, Marcel and Catherine Herfeld (2022) "Progress in Economics," in Y. Shan, ed., *New Philosophical Perspectives on Scientific Progress*, London: Routledge: 224–244.

Boumans, Marcel and Catherine Herfeld (2023) "Progress in Economics," in Yafeng Shan, ed., *New Philosophical Perspectives on Scientific Progress*, London: Routledge.

Bratman, Michael (1993) "Shared Intention," *Ethics* 104 (1): 97–113.

Bréban, Laurie and Muriel Gilardone (2020) "A Missing Touch of Adam Smith in Amartya Sen's Account of Public Reasoning: The Man Within for the Man Without," *Cambridge Journal of Economics* 44 (2): 257–283.

Brewer, Marilyn (2001) "The Many Faces of Social Identity: Implications for Political Psychology," *Political Psychology* 22: 115–125.

Brewer, Marilyn and Wendy Gardner (1996) "Who Is This 'We'? Levels of Collective Identity and Self-Representations," *Journal of Personal and Social Psychology* 71 (1): 83–93.

Brisset, Nicolas (2016) "Economics Is Not Always Performative: Some Limits for Performativity," *Journal of Economics Methodology* 23 (2): 160–184.

Brocas, Isabelle and Juan Carrillo (2014) "Dual-Process Theories of Decision-Making," *Journal of Economic Psychology* 41: 45–54.

Bromley, Daniel W. (2019) *Possessive Individualism: A Crisis of Capitalism*, New York: Oxford.

Brubaker, Rogers and Frederick Cooper (2000) "Beyond 'Identity'," *Theory and Society* 29: 1–47.

Buchanan, James (1965) "An Economic Theory of Clubs," *Economica* 32 (125): 1–14.

Buchanan, James and Gordon Tullock (1965) *The Calculus of Consent: Logical Foundations of Constitutional Democracy*, Ann Arbor: University of Michigan Press.

Bureau of Labor Statistics (2016) "Women's Earning 83 Percent of Men's, But Vary by Occupation," www.bls.gov/opub/ted/2016/womens-earnings-83-percent-of-mens-but-vary-by-occupation.htm, January 15 (accessed 19 May 2019).

Burnazoglu, Merve (2021) "An Identity-Based Matching Theory Approach to Integration," *Forum for Social Economics* 50 (1): 108–123.

Buss, Sarah and Andrea Westlund (2008) "Personal Autonomy", The Stanford Encyclopedia of Philosophy (Spring Edition), E. N. Zalta (ed.), https://plato.stanford.edu/archives/spr2018/entries/personal-autonomy/

Byrne, Ruth (2016) "Counterfactual Thought," *Annual Review of Psychology* 67 (1): 135–157.

(2005) *The Rational Imagination: How People Create Alternatives to Reality*, Cambridge, MA: MIT Press.

(2007) "Precis of The Rational Imagination: How People Create Alternatives to Reality," *Behavioral and Brain Sciences* 30: 439–480.

Callon, Michel (1998) "The Embeddedness of Economic Markets in Economics," in M. Callon, ed., *The Laws of the Markets*, Oxford: Blackwell: 1–57.

Camerer, Colin, Samuel Issacharoff, George Loewenstein, O'Donoghue, Ted. and Matthew Rabin (2003) "Regulation for Conservatives: Behavioral Economics and the Case for 'Asymmetric Paternalism'," *University of Pennsylvania Law Review*, 151 (3), 1211–45.

Candlish, Stewart. and George Wrisley (2014) "Private Language," *The Stanford Encyclopedia of Philosophy*, E. N. Zalta, ed., https://plato .stanford.edu/archives/fall2014/entries/private-language/

Caplin, Andrew and Andrew Schotte, eds. (2008) *The Foundations of Positive and Normative Economics: A Handbook*, Oxford: Oxford University Press.

Case, Anne and Angus Deaton (2020) *Deaths of Despair and the Future of American Capitalism*, Princeton, NJ: Princeton University Press.

Cat, Jordi (2017) "The Unity of Science," in E. N. Zalta, ed, *The Stanford Encyclopedia of Philosophy* (Fall Edition), https://plato.stanford.edu/ archives/fall2017/entries/scientific-unity/.

Chelwa, Grieve, Darrick Hamilton and James Stewart (2022) "Stratification Economics: Core Constructs and Policy Implications," *Journal of Economic Literature* 60 (2): 377–399.

Chen, Shu-Heng and Shu G. Wang (2011) "Emergent Complexity in Agent-Based Computational Economics," *Journal of Economic Surveys* 25 (3): 527–546.

Cherrier, Beatrice (2017) "Classifying Economics: A History of the JEL Codes," *Journal of Economic Literature* 55 (2): 545–579.

Chetty, Raj, David Grusky, Maximilian Hell, Nathaniel Hendren, Robert Manduca and Jimmy Narang (2017) "The Fading American Dream: Trends in Absolute Income Mobility Since 1940," *Science* 356 (6336): 398–406.

Chetty, Raj, Nathaniel Hendren, Maggie Jones and Sonya Porter (2018) "Race and Economic Opportunity in the United States: An Intergenerational Perspective," National Bureau of Economic Research Working Paper No. 24441 (March).

Chen, Shu-Heng (2012) "Varieties of Agent-Based Computational Economics: A Historical and an Interdisciplinary Perspective," *Journal of Economic Dynamics and Control* 36 (1): 1–25.

(2016) *Agent-Based Computational Economics: How the Idea Originated and Where It Is Going*, London: Routledge.

Chester, Lynne and Robert McMaster (2023) "Understanding Social Stratification: The Case of Energy Injustice," *Forum for Social Economics*, DOI: 10.1080/07360932.2023.2191294

Chick, Victoria and Sheila Dow (2005) "The Meaning of Open Systems," *Journal of Economic Methodology* 12 (3): 363–381.

Christakis, Nicholas (2019) *Blueprint: The Evolutionary Origins of A Good Society*, New York: Little Brown Spark.

Clancey, William (1997) *Situated Cognition: On Human Knowledge and Computer Representations*, New York: Cambridge University Press.

Clark, Andy (1997) *Being There: Putting Brain, Body, and World Together Again*, Cambridge: MA: MIT Press.

(2018) *Supersizing the Mind: Embodiment, Action, and Cognitive Extension*, New York: Oxford University Press.

Clark, Andy and David Chalmers (1998) "The Extended Mind," *Analysis* 58 (1): 7–19.

Clifford, James and George E. Marcus, eds. (1986) *Writing Culture: The Poetics and Politics of Ethnography*, School of American Research Advanced Seminar, Berkeley, CA: University of California Press.

Coase, Ronald (1937) "The Nature of the Firm," *Economica* 4 (16): 386–405.

(1988) *The Firm, the Market, and the Law*, Chicago: University of Chicago Press.

Colander, David, Richard Holt, and Barkley Rosser (2004) "The Changing Face of Mainstream Economics," *Review of Political Economy* 16 (4): 485–499.

Colander, David, Richard Holt and Barkley Rosser, Jr. (2006) "The Changing Face of Mainstream Economics," *Review of Political Economy* 16 (4): 485–499.

Colander, David and Roland Kupers (2014) *Complexity and the Art of Public Policy*, Princeton, NJ: Princeton University Press.

Colander, David and Huei-Chun Su (2015) "Making Sense of Economists' Positive-Normative Distinction," *Journal of Economic Methodology* 22 (2): 157–170.

Colander, David and Huei-Chun Su (2018) *How Economics Should be Done. Essays on the Art and Craft of Economics,* Cheltenham: Edward Elgar.

Collins, Randall (1994) *Four Sociological Traditions*, Oxford University Press.

Coyle, Diane (2014) *GDP: A Brief but Affectionate History*. Princeton, NJ: Princeton University Press.

Crenshaw, Kimberle (1991) "Demarginalizing the Intersection of Race and Sex: A Black Feminist Critique of Antidiscrimination Doctrine, Feminist Theory, and Antiracist Politics," in K. T. Barlett and R. Kennedy, eds., *Feminist Legal Theory: Readings in Law and Gender*, Boulder, CO: Westview Press: 139–168.

Crespo, Ricardo (2020a) "Identity: Individual and Social, and a Theory of a 'Polymorphic' but Unique Identity," in W. Dolfsma, D. W. Hands and R. McMaster, eds., *History, Methodology and Identity for the 21st Century*, London: Routledge: 51–66.

(2020b) *The Nature and Method of Economic Sciences: Evidence, Causality, and Ends*, London: Routledge.

Crespo, Ricardo and Juan José Llach (2006) "Conceptions of Human Beings Implicit in Economics and in The Practice of Economic Policy," in E. Malinvaud and M. Glendon, eds., *Conceptualization of the Person in Social Sciences*, Vatican City: The Pontifical Academy of Sciences, Acta 11, Vatican City: 447–97.

Darity, William A. Jr., (2005) "Stratification Economics: The Role of Intergroup Inequality," *Journal of Economics and Finance* 29 (2): 144–153.

(2009) "Stratification Economics: Context Versus Culture and the Reparations Controversy," *Kansas Law Review* 57: 795–811.

(2022) "Position and Possessions: SE and Intergroup Inequality," *Journal of Economic Literature* 60 (2): 1–27.

Darity, William A. Jr., Darrick Hamilton and James B. Stewart (2015) "A Tour de Force in Understanding Intergroup Inequality: An Introduction to Stratification Economics," *The Review of Black Political Economy*, 42 (1–2): 1–6.

Darity, William A. Jr., Darrick Hamilton, Patrick Mason, Gregory Price, Alberto Davila, Marie Mora and Sue Stockley (2017) "Stratification economics: A General Theory of Intergroup In-equality," in A. Flynn, S. Homberg, D. Warren and F. Wong, eds., *The Hidden Rules of Race*, Cambridge: Cambridge University Press: pp. 35–51.

Darity, William A. Jr., Darrick Hamilton, Mark Paul, Alan Aja, Anne Price, Antonio Moore and Caterina Chiopris (2018) "What We Get Wrong About Closing the Racial Wealth Gap," Durham, NC: Samuel DuBois Cook Center on Social Equity and Oakland, CA: Insight Center for Community Economic Development (April).

Darity, William A. Jr. and A. Kirsten Mullen (2020) *From Here to Equality: Reparations for Black Americans in the Twenty-First Century*, Chapel Hill, NC: University of North Carolina Press.

Darity, William A. Jr., A. Kirsten Mullen and Marvin Slaughter (2022) "The Cumulative Costs of Racism and the Bill for Black Reparations," *Journal of Economic Perspectives* 36 (2): 99–122.

Darity, William A. Jr., Patrick L. Mason and James B. Stewart (2006) "The Economics of Identity: The Origin and Persistence of Racial Identity Norms," *Journal of Economic Behavior and Organization* 60 (3): 283–305.

Dasgupta, Partha (2009) "Facts and Values in Modern Economics," in H. Kincaid and D. Ross, eds., *The Oxford Handbook of Philosophy of Economics*, Oxford: Oxford University Press: 580–640

Davis, John B. (1988) "Looking Backward: Looking Forward," *Forum for Social Economics* 17 (2): 13–22.

Davis, John B. (2003a) "Collective intentionality, complex economic behavior, and valuation," *Protosociology* 18–19:163–183.

(2003b) *The Theory of the Individual in Economics: Identity and Value*, London: Routledge.

(2006) "The Turn in Economics: Neoclassical Dominance to Mainstream Pluralism?" *Journal of Institutional Economics* 2 (1): pp. 1–20.

(2007a) "Akerlof and Kranton on Identity in Economics: Inverting the Analysis," *Cambridge Journal of Economics* 31 (3): 349–362.

(2007b) "Identity and Commitment: Sen's Fourth Aspect of the Self," in F. Peter and B. Schmid, eds., *Rationality and Commitment*, Oxford: Oxford University Press, 2007: 313–335.

(2008) "The Turn in Recent Economics and Return of Orthodoxy," *Cambridge Journal of Economics* 32 (3): 349–366.

(2009a) "The Capabilities Conception of the Individual," *Review of Social Economy* 67 (December 2009): 413–429.

(2009b) *The Theory of the Individual in Economics: Identity and Value*, London: Routledge.

(2011) *Individuals and Identity in Economics*, Cambridge: Cambridge University Press.

(2012a) "Rawlsian individuals: Justice, experiments, and complexity," *Journal of Economic Issues* 46 (3): 729–743.

(2012b) "The Change in Sraffa's Philosophical Thinking," *Cambridge Journal of Economics* 36 (6): 1342–1356.

(2012c) "The Idea of Public Reasoning," *Journal of Economic Methodology* 19 (2): 169–172.

(2013a) "Economics Imperialism under the Impact of Psychology: The Case of Behavioral Development Economics," *Economia* 3 (1): 119–138, https://doi.org/10.4000/oeconomia.638

(2013b) "Soros's Reflexivity Concept in a Complex World: Cauchy Distributions, Rational Expectations, and Rational Addiction," *Journal of Economic Methodology* 20 (4): 368–376.

(2014) "Social Capital and Social Identity: Trust and Conflict," in A. Christoforou and J. B. Davis, eds., *Social Capital: Social Values, Power, and Social Identity*, London: Routledge, 2014: 98–112.

(2015a) "Agency and the Process Aspect of Capability Development: Individual Capabilities, Collective Capabilities, and Collective Intentions," *Filosofía de la Economía* 4: 5–24.

(2015b) "Economists' Odd Stand on the Positive-Normative Distinction: A Behavioral Economics View," in G. DeMartino and D. McCloskey, eds., *Oxford University Press Handbook on Professional Economic Ethics: Views from the Economics Profession and Beyond*, Oxford: Oxford University Press.

(2015c) "Stratification Economics and Identity Economics," *Cambridge Journal of Economics* 39 (5): 1215–1229.

(2017a) "Hodgson, Cumulative Causation, and Reflexive Economic Agents," in F. Gagliardi and D. Gindis, eds., *Institutions and the Evolution of Capitalism, Essays in Honour of Geoffrey M. Hodgson*, Cheltenham: Edward Elgar: 78–91

(2017b) "Is Mainstream Economics a Science Bubble?" *Review of Political Economy* 29: 4: 523–538.

(2018a) "Agent-Based Modeling's Open Methodology Approach: Simulation, Reflexivity, and Abduction," *Oeconomia* 8–4 (2018): 509–529.

(2018b) "Behavioral Economics and the Positive-Normative Distinction: Sunstein's *Choosing Not to Choose* and Behavioral Economics Imperialism," *Revue Éthique et Économique* 15 (1): 1–15.

(2018c) "Comment on White on the Relationship Between Economics and Ethics," *Annals of the Fondazione Luigi Einaudi* 52 (2): 57–68.

(2018d) "Extending Behavioral Economics' Methodological Critique of Rational Choice Theory to Include Counterfactual Reasoning," *Journal of Behavioral Economics and Policy* 2 (2): 5–9.

(2018e) "Sraffa on the Open Vs. 'Closed Systems' Distinction and Causality," *Research in the History of Economic Thought and Methodology* 35B: 153–170.

(2019a) "Economics and Economic Methodology in a Core-Periphery World," *Brazilian Journal of Political Economy* 39 (3): 408–426.

(2019b) "Specialization, Fragmentation, and Pluralism in Economics," *The European Journal of the History of Economic Thought* 26 (2): 271–293.

(2019c) "Stratification Economics as an Economics of Exclusion," *Journal of Economics, Race, and Policy* 2 (3): 163–172.

(2020a) "Belief Reversals as Phase Transitions and Economic Fragility: A Complexity Theory of Financial Cycles with Reflexive Agents," *Review of Evolutionary Political Economy* 1 (1): 67–84.

(2020b) "Change and Continuity in Economic Methodology and Philosophy of Economics," *Revue de Philosophie Économique/Review of Economic Philosophy* 21(2): 187–210.

(2021) "Deepening and Widening Social Identity Analysis in Economics," *Erasmus Journal of Economics and Philosophy* 14 (2): 87–98.

(2022) "A General Theory of Social Economic Stratification: Stigmatization, Exclusion, and Capability Shortfalls," *Review of Evolutionary Political Economy* 3: 3 (2022): 493–513.

(2023a) "Sheila Dow's Open Systems Methodology," in I. Negru and P. Hawkins, eds., *Economic Methodology, History and Pluralism*, London: Routledge: 31–47.

(2023b) "What are Reflexive Economic Agents? Position-Adjustment, SLAM, and Self-Organization," P. Chen, W. Elsner and A. Pyka, eds., *Handbook of Complexity Economics*, London: Routledge.

Davis, John B. and Matthias Klaes (2003) "Reflexivity: Curse or Cure?" *Journal of Economic Methodology* 10 (3): 329–352.

Davis, John B. and Robert McMaster (2017) *Health Care Economics*, London: Routledge.

Davis, John B. and Theodore Koutsobinas (2021) "Counterfactual Thinking and Attribute Substitution in Economic Behavior," *Review of Behavioral Economics* 8 (1): 1–23.

Davis, John B. and Tom Wells (2016) "Transformation without Paternalism," *Journal of Human Development and Capabilities* 17: 3: 360–376.

Dekker, Erwin and Blaž Remic (2019) "Two Types of Ecological Rationality: or How to Best Combine Psychology and Economics," *Journal of Economic Methodology* 26 (4): 291–306.

Dekker, Erwin and Pavel Kuchar (2019) "Lachmann and Shackle: On the Joint Production of Interpretation Instruments," *Research in the History of Economic Thought and Methodology* 37B, 25–42.

DeMartino, George and Deirdre McCloskey (2015) *Oxford University Press Handbook on Professional Economic Ethics: Views from the Economics Profession and Beyond*, Oxford: Oxford University Press.

Deneulin, Severine (2008) "Beyond Individual Freedom and Agency: Structures of Living Together," in F. Comim, M. Qizilbash and S. Alkire, eds., *The Capability Approach: Concepts, Measures and Applications*, Cambridge, MA: Cambridge University Press: 105–24.

Dennett, Daniel (1987) *The Intentional Stance*, Cambridge, MA: MIT Press.

Denzin, Norman (1970) "Strategies of Multiple Triangulation," in N., Denzin, ed., *The Research Act in Sociology: A Theoretical Introduction to Sociological Method*, New York: McGraw-Hill: 297–313.

Dequech, David (2007–2008) "Neoclassical, Mainstream, Orthodox, and Heterodox Economics, *Journal of Post Keynesian Economics* 30 (2): 279–302.

De Vroey, Michel and Luca Pensieroso (2021) "Grounded in Methodology, Certified by Journals: The Rise and Evolution of a Mainstream in Economics," LIDAM Discussion Papers IRES 2021015, Université catholique de Louvain, Institut de Recherches Economiques et Sociales (IRES).

Dold, Malte F. and Christian Schubert (2018) "Toward a Behavioral Foundation of Normative Economics," *Review of Behavioral Economics* 5 (3–4): 221–241.

Dostoyevsky, Fyodor (1918) "Notes from Underground," in Constance Garnett, ed., *White Nights and Other Stories*, trans. Constance Garnett, London: Heinemann.

Dow, Sheila (2004) "Structured Pluralism," *Journal of Economic Methodology* 11 (3): 275–90.

(2015) "Addressing Uncertainty in Economics and the Economy," *Cambridge Journal of Economics* 39 (1): 33–47.

(2021) "Economic Methodology, The Philosophy of Economics and the Economy: Another Turn?" *Journal of Economic Methodology* 28 (1): 46–53.

Downward, Paul and Andrew Mearman (2007) "Retroduction as Mixed-Methods Triangulation in Economic Research: Reorienting Economics into Social Science," *Cambridge Journal of Economics* 31 (1): 77–99.

Drakopoulos, Stavros A. (2022) "The Conceptual Resilience of the Atomistic Individual in Mainstream Economic Rationality," *Review of Political Economy*, DOI: 10.1080/09538259.2022.2144721

(2023) "Value Judgements, Positivism and Utility Comparisons in Economics," *Journal of Business Ethics*, https://doi.org/10.1007/s10551-023-05395-z

Dutt, Amitava (2017) "Heterodox Theories of Economic Growth and Income Distribution: A Partial Survey," *Journal of Economic Surveys* 31 (5): 1240–1271.

Elder-Vass, Dave (2011) "Top-down Causation and Social Structures," *Interface Focus* 6 (2): 82–90.

Emery, Nina, Ned Markosian and Meghan Sullivan (2020) "Time," The Stanford Encyclopedia of Philosophy (Winter Edition), E. N. Zalta (ed.), https://plato.stanford.edu/archives/win2020/entries/time/; accessed 14 February 2021.

Engelen, Bart (2017)"A New Definition of and Role for Preferences in Positive Economics," *Journal of Economic Methodology* 24 (3): 254–273.

Engelmann, Dirk and Martin Strobel (2004) "Inequality Aversion, Efficiency, and Maximin Preferences in Simple Distribution Experiments," *American Economic Review* 94 (4): 857–869.

Erasmo, Valentina (2021) "Rights, Capabilities and Recognition: An Alternative Reading of Amartya Sen and Paul Ricoeur's 'Dialogue'," *Critical Hermeneutics* 5(2): DOI 10.13125/CH/4673

(2022) "Amartya Sen's Earlier Conception of Economic Agents through the Origins and Development of his Capability Approach (1970–1993)," PhD Thesis Summary, *Erasmus Journal for Philosophy and Economics* 15 (1): 184–193, https://doi.org/10.23941/ejpe.v15i1.596

Evans, Peter (2002) "Collective capabilities, Culture and Amartya Sen's Development as Freedom," *Studies in Comparative International Development*, 37 (2): 54–60.

Favereau, Judith (2016) "On the Analogy Between Field Experiments in Economics and Clinical Trials in Medicine," *Journal of Economic Methodology* 23 (2): 203–222, DOI: 10.1080/1350178X.2016.1157202

Feduzi, Alberto, Phil Faulkner, Jochen Runde, Laure Cabantous and Christopher Loch (2022) "Heuristic Methods for Updating Small World Representations in Strategic Situations of Knightian Uncertainty," *Academy of Management Review* 47 (3): 402–424.

Fehr, Ernst and Fischbacher, U. (2002) "Why Social Preferences Matter: The Impact of Non-Selfish Motives on Competition, Cooperation and Incentives," *The Economic Journal* 112 (478), C1–C33.

Fine, Ben and Dimitris Milonakis (2009) *From Economics Imperialism to Freakonomics: The Shifting Boundaries between Economics and Other Social Sciences*, London: Routledge.

de Finetti, Bruno (1937) "La Prevision: Ses lois logique, Ses Sources Subjectives," *Annales de l'Institut Henri Poincare* 7:1–68.

Fiori, Stefano (2011) "Forms of Bounded Rationality: The Reception and Redefinition of Herbert A. Simon's Perspective," *Review of Political Economy* 23 (4): 587–612.

Fleetwood, Steve (2008) "Structure, Institution, Agency, Habit, and Reflexive Deliberation," *Journal of Institutional Economics* 4 (2): 183–203.

(2021) "A Definition of Habit for Socio-Economics," *Review of Social Economy* 79 (2): 131–165.

Fleming, Peter and André Spicer (2007) *Contesting the Corporation: Struggle, Power and Resistance*, Cambridge: Cambridge University Press.

Fleurbaey, Marc and Didier Blanchet (2013) *Beyond GDP: Measuring Welfare and Assessing Sustainability*, Oxford: Oxford University Press, https://doi.org/10.1093/acprof:oso/9780199767199.001.0001

Foley, Robert and Clive Gamble (2009) "The Ecology of Social Transitions in Human Evolution," *Philosophical Transaction of the Royal Society B (Biological Sciences)* 364: 3267–3279.

Fourcade, Marion, Etienne Ollion and Yann Algan (2015) "The Superiority of Economists," *The Journal of Economic Perspectives* 29 (1): 89–113.

Frankfurt, Harry (1971) "Freedom of the Will and the Concept of a Person," *Journal of Philosophy* 68 (1): 5–20.

Frederick, Shane, George Loewenstein and Ted O'Donoghue (2002) "Time Discounting and Time Preference: A Critical Review," *Journal of Economic Literature* 40 (2): 351–401.

Fuller, Chris (2013) "Reflexivity, Relative Autonomy, and the Embedded Individual in Economics," *Journal of Institutional Economics* 9 (1): 109–129.

Fuller, Chris (2020) "Uncertainty, Insecurity, Individual Relative Autonomy and the Emancipatory Potential of Galbraithian Economics," *Cambridge Journal of Economics* 44 (1): 229–246.

Gale, Richard, ed. (1967) *The Philosophy of Time*, Garden City, NY: Anchor Doubleday: 65–85.

Gallagher, Shaun (2013) "The Socially Extended Mind," *Cognitive Systems Research* 25–26: 4–12.

Gasper, Des (2004) *The Ethics of Development. From Economism to Human Development*, Edinburgh: Edinburgh University Press.

Georgescu-Roegen, Nicholas (1971) *The Entropy Law and Economic Process*, Cambridge: Cambridge University Press.

Gibson, James (1977) "The Theory of Affordances," in R. Shaw and J. Bransford, eds., *Perceiving, Acting, and Knowing*, Hillsdale, NJ: Erlbaum: 67–82.

Gibson, James (1979) *The Ecological Approach to Visual Perception*, Boston: Houghton Mifflin.

Giedeman, Daniel (2018) "Introduction to the Special Issue: The Effects of the 2007–2009 Financial Crisis and the Great Recession Across Racial and Ethnics Groups," *Journal of Economics, Race, and Policy* 1 (2–3): 45–46.

Gigerenzer, Gerd (2008) "Why Heuristics Work," *Perspectives on Psychological Science* 3 (1): 20–29.

(2019) "Axiomatic rationality and ecological rationality," *Synthese* 198 (4): 3547–3564.

(2021) "Embodied Heuristics," *Frontiers in Psychology* 12: article 711289.

Gigerenzer, Gerd, Peter Todd and the ABC Research Group (1999) *Simple Heuristics That Make Us Smart*, Oxford: Oxford University Press.

Gigerenzer, Gerd and Reinhard Selten, eds. (2001) *Bounded Rationality: The Adaptive Toolbox*, Cambridge, MA: MIT Press.

Gilbert, Margaret (1990) "Walking Together: A Paradigmatic Social Phenomenon," *Midwest Studies in Philosophy*, vol. 15: 1–14.

Gilboa, Itzhak and David Schmeidler (2001) *A Theory of Case-Based Decisions*, Cambridge: Cambridge University Press.

Gilboa, Itzhak, Postlewaite Andrew, David Schmeidler (2009) "Is it always rational to satisfy Savage's axioms?" *Economics and Philosophy* 25: 285–296.

Giocoli, Nicola (2003) *Modeling Rational Agents. From Interwar Economics to Early Modern Game Theory*, Cheltenham: Edward Elgar.

Giovanola, Benedetta (2009) "Re-Thinking the Anthropological and Ethical Foundation of Economics and Business: Human Richness and Capabilities Enhancement," *Journal of Business Ethics* 88 (3): 431–444; DOI 10.1007/s10551-009-0126-9

Goffman, Erving (1963) *Stigma: Notes on the Management of a Spoiled Identity*, New York, Prentice-Hall.

Gold, Natalie and Robert Sugden (2007) "Theories of Agency," in F. Peter and H. Bernhard Schmid, eds., *Rationality and Commitment*, Oxford: Oxford University Press: 280–312.

Gramsci, Antonio (1971 [1930]) *Selections from the Prison Notebooks of Antonio Gramsci*, ed. and trans. Quintin Hoare and Geoffrey Nowell-Smith, London: Lawrence & Wishart.

Granovetter, Mark (1985) "Economic Action and Social Structure: The problem of Embeddedness," *The American Journal of Sociology* 91 (3): 481–510.

Grayot, James (2019) "From Selves to Systems: On the Interpersonal and Intraneural Dynamics of Decision Making," *Journal of Economic Methodology* 26 (3): 208–227.

Grayot, James (2020) "Dual Process Theories in Behavioral Economics and Neuroeconomics: A Critical Review," *Review of Philosophy and Psychology* 11 (1): 105–136.

Greeno, James (1994) "Gibson's Affordances." *Psychological Review* 101(2): 336–342.

Greeno, James and Joyce Moore (1993) "Situativity and Symbols: Response to Vera and Simon," *Cognitive Science* 17 (1): 49–59.

Greski, Leonard (2009) "Business Capability Modeling: Theory & Practice," *Architecture and Governance Magazine* 5 (7): 1–4.

Grunberg, Emile and Franco Modigliani (1954) "The Predictability of Social Events," *Journal of Political Economy* 62: 465–478.

Grüne-Yanoff, Till, Caterina Marchionni and Markus Feufel (2018) "Toward a Framework for Selecting Behavioural Policies: How to

Choose Between Boosts and Nudges," *Economics and Philosophy* 34 (2): 243–266.

Grüne-Yanoff, Till and Ralph Hertwig (2016) "Nudge Versus Boost: How Coherent are Policy and Theory?" *Minds and Machines,* 26(1–2): 149–183.

Guala, Francesco (2008) "Paradigmatic Experiments: The Ultimatum Game from Testing to Measurement Device," *Philosophy of Science* 75 (5): 658–669, https://doi.org/10.1086/594512

(2012) "Are Preferences for Real," in A. Lehtinen and P. Yilkoski, eds., *Economics for Real,* London: Routledge.

(2019) "Preferences: Neither Behavioral nor Mental," *Economics and Philosophy* 35 (3): 383–401.

Gul, Faruk and Wolfgang Pesendorfer (2008) "The Case for Mindless Economics," in A. Caplin and A. Scotter, eds., *The Foundations of Positive and Normative Economics*: A Handbook, New York, Oxford University Press: 3–39.

Gutwald, Rebecca, Ortrud Leßmann, Torsten Masson and Felix Rauschmayer (2014) "A Capability Approach to Intergenerational Justice? Examining the Potential of Amartya Sen's Ethics with Regard to Intergenerational Justice," *Journal of Human Development and Capabilities* 15 (4): 355–368.

Haggbloom, Steven J., Renee Warnick, Renee, Jason E. Warnick, Vinessa K. Jones, Gary L. Yarbrough, Tenea M. Russell, Chris M. Borecky, Reagan McGahhey, John L. Powell (2002) "The 100 Most Eminent Psychologists of the 20th Century," *Review of General Psychology* 6 (2): 139–152.

Hamermesh, Daniel (2013) "Six Decades of Top Economics Publishing: Who and How?" *Journal of Economic Literature* 51(1): 162–172.

Hands, D. Wade (1990) "Grunberg and Modigliani, Public Predictions and the New Classical Macroeconomics," *Research in the History of Economic Thought and Methodology* 7: 207–223.

(2001) *Reflection without Rules: Economic Methodology and Contemporary Science Theory,* Cambridge: Cambridge University Press.

(2008) "Introspection, Revealed Preference, and Neoclassical Economics: A Critical Response to Don Ross on the Robbins-Samuelson Argument Pattern," *Journal of the History of Economic Thought* 30 (4): 453–478.

(2012a) "Normative Rational Choice Theory: Past, Present, and Future," *Voprosy Economiki,* N.P. Redaktsiya zhurnala "Voprosy Economiki", vol. 10.

(2012b) "The Positive–Normative Dichotomy and Economics," in U. Mäki, ed., *Philosophy of Economics,* Amsterdam: Elsevier: 219–239.

(2014) "Paul Samuelson and Revealed Preference Theory," *History of Political Economy* 46 (1): 85–116.

(2020) "Libertarian Paternalism: Taking Econs Seriously," *International Review of Economics* 67 (4): 419–441.

Hansson, Sven Ove and Till Grüne-Yanoff (2022) "Preferences," The Stanford Encyclopedia of Philosophy (Spring Edition), Edward N. Zalta (ed.), https://plato.stanford.edu/archives/spr2022/entries/preferences/.

Hardin, Garrett (1968) "The Tragedy of the Commons," *Science* 162 (3859): 1243–1248.

Harris, Cheryl. (1993) "Whiteness as Property," *Harvard Law Review* 106 (8) (June):1709–1791.

Harrison, Glenn W. (1980) "The Stock-Flow Distinction: A Suggested Interpretation," *Journal of Macroeconomics* 2 (2): 111–125.

Haslam, Alex (2018) "War and Peace and Summer Camp," *Nature* 556 (17 Apr.): 306–307.

Hatfield, Gary (2021) "Sense Data," The Stanford Encyclopedia of Philosophy, Fall edition, E. N. Zalta, ed., https://plato.stanford.edu/archives/fall2021/entries/sense-data/.

Hausman, Daniel (2012) *Preference, Value, Choice, and Welfare*, New York: Cambridge University Press.

(2023) "Hands on Nudging," in J. B. Davis, B. Caldwell, U. Mäki and E-M. Sent, eds., *Wade Hands as an Historian and Philosopher of Economics*, London: Routledge.

Hausman, Daniel and Brynn Welch (2010) "Debate: To Nudge or Not to Nudge," *Journal of Political Philosophy* 18 (1): 123–136.

Hausman, Daniel, Michael McPherson, Debra Satz (2016) *Economic Analysis, Moral Philosophy, and Public Policy*, 3rd ed., Cambridge: Cambridge University Press.

Heckman, James and Sidharth Moktam (2020) "Publishing and Promotion in Economics: The Tyranny of the Top Five," *Journal of Economic Literature* 58 (2): 419–470.

Hédoin, Cyril (2022) "Persons, Values and Consent: A Philosophy & Economic Perspective on Social Moral Choice," book manuscript.

Herrmann-Pillath, Carsten (2012) "Institutions, Distributed Cognition and Agency: Rule-Following as Performative Action," *Journal of Economic Methodology* 19 (1): 21–42, DOI: 10.1080/1350178X.2012.661066

(2013) *Foundations of Economic Evolution: A Treatise on the Natural Philosophy of Economics,* Cheltenham: Edward Elgar.

Herrmann-Pillath, Carsten and Ivan Boldyrev (2014) *Hegel, Institutions and Economics: Performing the Social*. London: Routledge.

Hertwig, Ralph and Till Grüne-Yanoff (2017) "Nudging and Boosting: Steering or Empowering Good Decisions," *Perspectives on Psychological Science* 12 (6): 973–986.

Heukelom, Floris (2015) "A History of the Allais Paradox," *British Journal for the History of Science* 48 (1): 147–169.

Hintikka, Jaakko (1973) *Logic, Language-Games, and Information*, Oxford, Clarendon Press.

Hodgson, Geoffrey (2003) "The Hidden Persuaders: Institutions and Individuals in Economic Theory," *Cambridge Journal of Economics* 27 (2): 159–175.

(2004) "Reclaiming Habit for Non-Mainstream Economics," *Journal of economic psychology* 25 (5): 651–660.

(2006) "What are Institutions?" *Journal of Economic Issues* 40 (1): 1–25.

(2010) "Choice, Habit and Evolution," *Journal of evolutionary economics* 20 (1): 1–18.

(2011) "Downward causation: some second thoughts," www.geoffrey-hodgson.info/downward-causation.htm (accessed 30 October 2020).

(2012) "On the Limits of Rational Choice Theory," *Economic Thought* 1 (1): 94–108.

Hommes, Cars (2013) *Behavioral Rationality and Heterogeneous Expectations in Complex Economic Systems*, Cambridge: Cambridge University Press.

Hoover, Kevin D. (2012) "Microfoundational Programs," in P. G. Duarte and G. T. Lima, eds., *Microfoundations Reconsidered: The Relationship of Micro and Macroeconomics in Historical Perspective*, Cheltenham: Edward Elgar: 19–61.

Hoover, Kevin D. and Andrej Svorenčík (2023) "Who Runs the AEA?" *Journal of Economic Literature*, 61 (3): 1127–71.

Horowitz, Irving (1994) *The decomposition of sociology*, Oxford University Press Human Development Capabilities Programme (2019) *Human Development Report 2019*, New York, NY: United Nations.

Hume, David (1739) *A Treatise of Human Nature*, edited by L. A. Selby-Bigge, 2nd ed. revised by P. H. Nidditch, 1978, Oxford: Clarendon Press.

Hurwicz, Leonid and Stanley Reiter (2006) *Designing Economic Mechanisms*, Cambridge: Cambridge University Press.

Iannaccone, Laurence R. (1998) "Introduction to the Economics of Religion," *Journal of Economic Literature* 36 (3): 1465–1495.

Ibrahim, Solava (2006) "From Individual to Collective Capabilities: The Capability Approach as a Conceptual Framework for Self-Help," *Journal of Human Development* 7 (3): 397–416.

Infante, Gerardo, Guilhem Lecouteux and Robert Sugden (2016) "Preference Purification and the Inner Rational Agent: A Critique of the Conventional Wisdom of Behavioural Welfare Economics," *Journal of Economic Methodology* 23 (1): 1–25.

Inglehart, R., C. Haerpfer, A. Moreno, C. Welzel, K. Kizilova, J. Diez-Medrano, M. Lagos, P. Norris, E. Ponarin and B. Puranen et al., eds. (2014) World Values Survey: All Rounds – Country-Pooled Datafile Version: www.worldvaluessurvey.org/WVSDoctumentation WVL.jsp. Madrid: JD Systems Institute.

Inglehart, Ronald and Christian Welzel (2005) *Modernization, Cultural Change and Democracy: The Human Development Sequence*, New York: Cambridge University Press.

Jacobson, Sheldon H, Shane N. Hall and James R. Swisher (2006) "Discrete-Event Simulation of Health Care Systems," *International Series in Operations Research & Management Science* in R. W. Hall, ed., *Patient Flow: Reducing Delay in Healthcare Delivery*, New York: Springer: 211–252.

Jeffrey, Richard (1974) "Preference Among Preferences," *Journal of Philosophy* 71 (13): 377–391.

Jo, Tae-Hee, Lynne Chester and Carlo D'Ippoliti, eds. (2017) *The Routledge Handbook of Heterodox Economics: Theorizing, Analyzing, and Transforming Capitalism*, London and New York: Routledge.

Kahneman, Daniel (1996) "Comment," in K. Arrow, E. Colombatto, M. Perlman and C. Schmidt, eds., *The Rational Foundations of Economic Behavior*, Basingstoke: Macmillan: 251–254.

(2003). "Maps of Bounded Rationality: Psychology for Behavioral Economics," *American Economic Review* 93 (5): 1449–1475.

Kahneman, Daniel and Amos Tversky (1979) "Prospect Theory: An Analysis of Decision under Risk," *Econometrica* 47 (2): 263–292.

(1982) "The Simulation Heuristic," in D. Kahneman, P. Slovic and A. Tversky, eds., *Judgment Under Uncertainty: Heuristics and Biases*, New York: Cambridge University Press: 201–208.

Kahneman, Daniel and Carol Varey (1990) "Propensities and Counterfactuals: The Loser that Almost Won," *Journal of Personality and Social Psychology* 59(6), 1101–1110.

Kahneman, Daniel and Robert Sugden (2005) "Experience Utility as a Standard of Policy Evaluation," *Environmental and Resource Economics* 32 (1): 161–181.

Kaplan, Greg and Giovanni Violante (2018) "Microeconomic Heterogeneity and Macroeconomic Shocks," *Journal of Economic Perspectives* 32 (3): 167–194.

Kapp, K. William (1950) *The Social Costs of Private Enterprise*, Cambridge, MA: Harvard University Press.

Kao, Ying-Fang and K. Vela Velupillai (2015) "Behavioural Economics: Classical and Modern," *European Journal of the History of Economic Thought* 22: 223–271.

Kierkegaard, Søren (1843) *Journalen* JJ:167 *Søren Kierkegaards Skrifter*, vol. 18, Søren Kierkegaard Research Center, Copenhagen, 1997.

Kirzner, Israel (1997) "Entrepreneurial Discovery and the Competitive Market Process: An Austrian Approach," *Journal of Economic Literature* 35 (4): 60–85.

Keynes, John M. (1921) *A Treatise on Probability*, London: Macmillan.

(1936) *The General Theory of Employment, Interest and Money*, London: Macmillan.

Kirman, Alan (1992) "Whom or what does the Representative Individual Represent?" *Journal of Economic Perspectives* 6 (2): 117–136.

(2011) *Complex Economics: Individual and Collective Rationality*, London: Routledge.

Knight, Frank (1921) *Risk, Uncertainty, and Profit*, Boston: Houghton Mifflin.

Koppl, Roger and J. Barkley Rosser, Jr. (2002) "All That I Have to Say Has Already Crossed Your Mind," *Metroeconomica* 53: 339–360.

Kripke, Saul (1980) *Naming and Necessity*, Cambridge, Mass.: Harvard University Press.

Kuhn, Thomas (1962; 1970) *The Structure of Scientific Revolutions*, Chicago: University of Chicago Press.

Kuorikoski, Jaakko, Aki Lehtinen and Caterina Marchionni (2010) "Economic Modelling as Robustness Analysis," *British Journal for the Philosophy of Science* 61 (3): 541–567.

Kurz, Heinz and Neri Salvadori (2008) "Representing the Production and Circulation of Commodities: on Sraffa's Objectivism," in Heinz Kurz L. Pasinetti and Salvadori, eds., *Piero Sraffa: The Man and the Scholar*, London: Routledge: 249–77.

Laibson, David (1997) "Golden Eggs and Hyperbolic Discounting," *Quarterly Journal of Economics* 112 (2): 443–478.

Lakatos, Imre (1970) "Falsification and the Methodology of Scientific Research Programmes," in I. Lakatos and A. Musgrave, eds., *Criticism and the Growth of Knowledge*, Cambridge: Cambridge University Press: 91–196.

Landsberger, Henry (1958) *Hawthorne Revisited*, Ithaca, NY: Cornell University.

Larrouy and Lecouteux (2018) "Mindreading and Endogenous Belief in Games," *Journal of Economic Methodology* 24 (3): 318–343.

Lawlor, Michael (2006) "William James's Psychological Pragmatism: Habit, Belief and Purposive Human Behaviour," *Cambridge Journal of Economics* 30 (3): 321–345.

Lawson, Tony (1997) *Economics and Reality*, London: Routledge.

(2003) *Reorienting Economics*, London: Routledge.

(2019) *The Nature of Social Reality: Issues in Social Ontology*, London and New York: Routledge.

(2023) "Categorisation, Criticism and Pluralism in context," in I. Negru and P. Hawkins, eds., *Economic Methodology, History and Pluralism*, London: Routledge: 48–60.

(2006) "The Nature of Heterodox Economics," *Cambridge Journal of Economics* 30 (4): 483–505.

Lee, Fred S. (2009) *A History of Heterodox Economics: Challenging the Mainstream in the Twentieth Century*, London: Routledge.

Lee, Kyu Sang (2016) "Mechanism Designers in Alliance: A portrayal of a Scholarly Network in Support of Experimental Economics," *History of Political Economy* 48 (2): 191–223.

Lehmann-Waffenschmidt, Marco (1990) "Predictability of Economic Processes and the Morgenstern Paradox, *Schweizerische Zeitschrift für Volkswirtschaft und Statistik*, Heft 2: 147–160.

Lehtinen, Aki and Jaakko Kuorikoski (2007) "Computing the Perfect Model: Why Do Economists Shun Simulation?" *Philosophy of Science* 74 (July): 304–329.

Leßmann, Ortrud (2022) "Collectivity and the Capability Approach: Survey and Discussion," *Review of Social Economy* 80 (4): 461–490.

Lewis, David (1973) *Counterfactuals*, Cambridge, MA: Harvard University Press.

(1986) *On The Plurality of Worlds*, Oxford: Blackwell.

Livet, Pierre (2006) "Identities, Capabilities, and Revisions," *Journal of Economic Methodology* 13 (3): 327–348.

Longino, Helen (1990) *Science as Social Knowledge: Values and Objectivity in Scientific Inquiry*, Princeton University Press.

Lucas, Robert E. (1976) "Econometric Policy Evaluation: A Critique," in K. Brunner and A. H. Meltzer, eds., *The Phillips Curve and Labor Markets*, Vol. 1 of Carnegie-Rochester Conference Series on Public Policy, Amsterdam: North-Holland: 19–46.

(2011) "Ethics, Economic Policy and the Understanding of Economic Development," in Pontifical Council for Justice and Peace, ed., *Social and Ethical Aspects of Economics: A Colloquium in the Vatican*, Pontifical Council for Justice and Peace (ed.), Vatican City: Vatican Council: 105–139.

Lukes, Steven (2005) *Power: A Radical View*, 2nd Ed., London: Palgrave.

Lykke, Nina (2010) *Feminist Studies: A Guide to Intersectional Theory, Methodology and Writing*, London: Routledge.

MacKenzie, Donald (2007) "Is Economics Performative? Option Theory and the Construction of Derivatives Markets," in D. MacKenzie, F. Muniesa and L. Siu, eds., *Do Economists Make Markets? On the*

Performativity of Economics, Princeton: Princeton University Press: 54–86.

Mäki, Uskali (2013) "Performativity: Saving Austin from Mackenzie," in *EPSA11 Perspectives and Foundational Problems in Philosophy of Science,* V. Krakostas and D. Dieks, eds., Dordrecht: Springer: 443–453).

Małecka, Magdalena (2021) "Values in Economics: A Recent Revival with a Twist," *Journal of Economic Methodology* 28 (1): 88–97. DOI: 10.1080/1350178X.2020.1868776

Marchionni, Caterina and Petri Ylikoski (2013) "Generative Explanation and Individualism in Agent-Based Simulation," *Philosophy of the Social Sciences* 43 (3): 323–340.

Margalit, Avishai (1996) *The Decent Society,* Cambridge, MA: Harvard University Press.

Margolis, Howard (1982) *Selfishness, Altruism, and Rationality,* New York: Cambridge University Press.

Martins, Nuno Ornelas (2022) "Social positioning and the pursuit of power," *Cambridge Journal of Economics* 46 (2): 275–292.

Mason, Patrick, James Stewart and William A. Darity, Jr. (2022) "Collective wealth and Group Identity: Insights from Stratification Economics," *Review of Evolutionary Political Economy* 3 (3): 463–491.

Mayhew, Anne (1998) "On the Difficulty of Evolutionary Analysis," *Cambridge Journal of Economics* 22 (4): 449–461.

McCulloch, Heather (2017) "Closing the Women's Wealth Gap: What It Is, Why It Matters, and What Can be Done About It," Closing the Women's Wealth Gap Initiative.

McKernan, Signe-Mary, Caroline Ratcliffe, C. Eugene Steuerle, Sisi Zhang (2013) "Less Than Equal: Racial Disparities in Wealth Accumulation," Washington D.C.: Urban Institute.

McQuillin, Ben and Robert Sugden (2012) "Reconciling normative and behavioural economics: the problems to be solved," *Social Choice and Welfare* 38 (4): 553–567.

McTaggart, J. M. Ellis (1908) The Unreality of Time. Mind, New Series, Vol. 17, No. 68, pp. 457–474.

McTaggart, J. M. Ellis (1927) *The Nature of Existence,* vol. II, Cambridge: Cambridge University Press: Bk. V, Ch. 33; also in Gale (1967): 86–97.

Mearman, Andrew (2011) "Who do Heterodox Economists think they are?" *American Journal of Economics and Sociology* 70: 480–510.

Merton, Robert K. (1936) "The Unanticipated Consequences of Purposive Social Action," *American Sociological Review* 1 (6): 894–904.

(1949) *Social Theory and Social Structure,* New York: Free Press.

Michaelson, Eliot and Marga Reimer (2022) "Reference," The Stanford Encyclopedia of Philosophy, *Summer* Edition, Edward N. Zalta, ed., https://plato.stanford.edu/archives/sum2022/entries/reference/

Mill, John Stuart (1859) *On Liberty*, London: John Parker and Son.

Mitrouchev, Ivan and Valerio Buonomo (2023) "Identity, Ethics and Behavioural Welfare Economics," *Economics and Philosophy*, 1–27.

Mongin, Philippe (2002) "Is There Progress in Normative Economics?" in S. Boehm, C. Gehrke, H. Kurz and R. Sturn, eds., *Is There Progress In Economics? Knowledge, Truth and the History Economic Thought*, London, Routledge: 145–170.

(2006) "A Concept of Progress for Normative Economics," *Economics and Philosophy* 22 (1): 19–54.

(2019) "The Allais Paradox: What it became, What it really was, and What it now Suggests to us," *Economics and Philosophy* 35 (3): 423–459.

Morgan, Mary (2012) *The World in the Model: How Economists Work and Think*, Cambridge: Cambridge University Press.

Morgenstern, Oskar (1928) *Wirtschaftsprognose. Eine Untersuchun ihrer Voraussetzungen und Möglichkeiten*, Wien: Springer Verlag.

Moscati, Ivan (2016) "How Economists Came to Accept Expected Utility Theory: The Case of Samuelson and Savage," *Journal of Economic Perspectives* 30 (2): 291–236.

(2018) *Measuring Utility: From the Marginal Revolution to Behavioral Economics*, Oxford: Oxford University Press.

Myers, Samuel L. and Won Fy Lee (2018) "Racial Disparities, Homeownership, and Mortgage Lending in the Post-Great Recession Period: The Case of the Minneapolis-St. Paul Metropolitan Area," *Journal of Economics, Race, and Policy* 1 (2–3): 47–59.

Nagatsu, Michiru (2015) "Social Nudges: Their Mechanisms and Justification," *Review of Philosophy and Psychology* 6 (3): 481–494.

Nagel, Thomas (1986) *The View from Nowhere*, Oxford: Oxford University Press.

von Neumann, John and Oskar Morgenstern (1944) *Theory of Games and Economic Behavior*, Princeton, NJ: Princeton University Press. 2nd ed., 1947; 3rd ed., 1953.

Noël, Reginald (2018) "Race, Economics, and Social Status," U.S. Bureau of Labor Statistics, Washington, D.C.; www.bls.gov/spotlight/2018/race-economics-and-social-status/pdf/race-economics-and-social-status.pdf (accessed 19 May 2019).

North, Douglass (1991) "Institutions," *Journal of Economic Perspectives* 5 (1): 97–112.

Nussbaum, Martha (2001a) "Adaptive Preferences and Women's Options," *Economics and Philosophy* 17 (1): 67–88.

(2001b) *Women and Human Development: The Capabilities Approach*, Cambridge: Cambridge University Press.

Obeng-Odoom, Franklin (2020) *Property, Institutions, and Social Stratification in Africa*, Cambridge: Cambridge University Press.

O'Driscoll, Gerald and Mario Rizzo (1996) *The Economics of Time and Ignorance*, London: Routledge.

OECD (2015-10-15) "Making Open Science a Reality," *OECD Science, Technology and Industry Policy Papers*, No. 25, OECD Publishing, Paris. https://dx.doi.org/10.1787/5jrs2f963zs1-en; accessed 20 April 2021.

Ostrom, Elinor (1990) *Governing the Commons: The Evolution of Institutions for Collective Action*, Cambridge: Cambridge University Press.

Palmer, R. G., W. Brian Arthur, John Holland and Blake LeBaron (1999) "An Artificial Stock Market," *Artif Life Robotics* 3: 27–31.

Parfit, Derek (1984) *Reasons and Persons*, Oxford: Oxford University Press.

Peirce, Charles S. (1931–1958). *Collected Papers of Charles Sanders Peirce* (Vols. 1–8), H. Charles, P. Weiss, & A. Burks, eds., Cambridge, MA: The Belknap Press of Harvard University Press.

Pereira, Gustavo (2019) *Imposed Rationality and Besieged Imagination: Practical Life and Social Pathologies*, Springer.

Peter, Fabienne (2017) "Political Legitimacy," *The Stanford Encyclopedia of Philosophy*, ed. E. N. Zalta, https://plato.stanford.edu/archives/sum2017/entries/legitimacy/; accessed 15 July 2020.

(2008) *Democratic Legitimacy*, New York: Routledge.

(2012) "Sen's Idea of Justice and the locus of normative reasoning," *Journal of Economic Methodology* 19 (2): 165–167.

Peterson, Janice and Margaret Lewis (1999). *The Elgar Companion to Feminist Economics*. Cheltenham, UK Northampton, MA: Edward Elgar.

Petracca, Enrico (2017) "A Cognition Paradigm Clash: Simon, *Situated Cognition* and the Interpretation of Bounded Rationality," *Journal of Economic Methodology* 24 (1): 20–40.

Petracca, Enrico and Grayot, James (2023) "How can embodied cognition naturalize bounded rationality?" *Synthese* 201 (115), https://doi.org/10.1007/s11229-023-04124-3

Piketty, Thomas and Saez, Emmanuel (2003) "Income Inequality in the United States, 1913-1998," *The Quarterly Journal of Economics* 118 (1): pp. 1–39.

Petracca, Enrico and Shaun Gallagher (2020) "Economic Cognitive Institutions," *Journal of Institutional Economics* 16 (6): 747–765.

Plato (1941) *The Republic of Plato*, trans. with introduction and notes by F. M. Cornford, Oxford: Oxford University Press.

Platow, Michael J. and John A. Hunter (2012) "Intergroup Relations and Conflict: Revisiting Sherif's Boys' Camp Studies," *Social Psychology: Revisiting the Classic Studies*, J R. Smith and S. Alexander Haslam, eds, Thousand Oaks, CA: Sage.

Polanyi, Karl (1944) *The Great Transformation*, Boston: Beacon Press.

Polanyi, Michael (1958) *Personal Knowledge: Towards a Post-Critical Philosophy*, Chicago: University of Chicago Press.

Popper, Karl (1959; 1934) *The Logic of Scientific Discovery*, translation of Logik der Forschung. London: Hutchinson.

Postmes, Tom and Nyla Branscombe, eds. (2010) *Rediscovering Social Identity: Key Readings*, New York: Psychology Press.

Primrose, David (2017) "The Subjectification of *Homo Economicus* in Behavioural Economics," *Journal of Australian Political Economy* 80: 88–128.

Primrose, David, Frank Stilwell and Tim Thornton, eds. (2022) *Elgar Handbook of Alternative Theories of Political Economy*, Cheltenham: Edward Elgar.

Putnam, Hilary (2002) *The Collapse of the Fact/Value Dichotomy and Other Essays*, Cambridge, MA: Harvard University Press.

(2003) "For Ethics and Economics without the Dichotomies," *Review of Political Economy* 15 (3): 395–412.

Putnam, Hilary and Vivian Walsh (2012) *The End of Value-Free Economics,* London: Routledge.

Quine, Willard van Orman (1953) "Two Dogmas of Empiricism," in W.V.O Quine, ed., *From a Logical Point of View*, Cambridge, MA: Harvard University Press: 20–46.

Ramsey, Frank (1926) "Truth and Probability," in F. P. Ramsey (1931) *Foundations of Mathematics and other Logical Essays*, ed., R. B. Braithwaite, New York: Harcourt Brace: 156–198.

Ranis, Gustav, Frances Stewart and Alejandro Ramirez (2000) "Economic Growth and Human Development," *World Development* 28 (2): 197–219.

Ranis, Gustav, Frances Stewart and Emma Samman (2006) "Human development: beyond the Human Development Index," *Journal of Human Development* 7 (3):323–358.

Rawls, John (1971) *A Theory of Justice*, Cambridge: Belknap Press.

(2001) *Justice as Fairness: A Restatement*, Cambridge: Harvard University Press.

Reichenbach, Hans (1938) *Experience and Prediction. An Analysis of the Foundations and the Structure of Knowledge*, Chicago: University of Chicago Press.

Reiss, Julian (2017) "Fact-Value Entanglement in Positive Economics," *Journal of Economic Methodology* 24 (2): 134–149.

Reiss, Julian and Jan Sprenger (2020) "Scientific Objectivity," The Stanford Encyclopedia of Philosophy (Winter Edition), Edward N. Zalta (ed.), https://plato.stanford.edu/archives/win2020/entries/scientific-object ivity/; accessed 15 April 2021.

Reynolds, Katherine, John Turner, S. Alexander Haslam (2003) "Social Identity and Self-Categorization Theories' Contribution to Understanding Identification, Salience and Diversity in Teams and Organizations," in J. Polzer, eds., *Identity Issues in Groups (Research on Managing Groups and Teams, Volume 5)*, Bingley, UK: Emerald Publishing: 279–304.

Robeyns, Ingrid (2005) "The capability approach: A theoretical survey," *Journal of Human Development* 6 (1): 93–117.

(2017) *Wellbeing, Freedom and Social Justice: The Capability Approach Re-Examined*, Cambridge, UK: Open Book Publishers, https://dx.doi .org/10.11647/OBP.0130

Rodrik, Dani (2015) *Economics Rules: The Rights and Wrongs of the Dismal Science*, New York: W. W. Norton.

Roese, Neal and Mike Morrison (2009) "The Psychology of Counterfactual Thinking," *Historical Social Research* 64 (2): 16–26.

Rogers, Carl (1951) *Client Centered Therapy, London: Constable.*

(1959) "A Theory of Therapy, Personality, and Interpersonal Relationships as Developed in The Client-Centered Framework," in S. Koch, ed., *Psychology: A Story of a Science*, Vol. 3, New York: McGraw-Hill: 184–256.

Ross, Don (2005) *Economic Theory and Cognitive Science: Microexplanation*, Cambridge, MA: MIT Press.

(2006) "The Economic and Evolutionary Basis of Selves," *Cognitive Systems Research* 7: 246–258.

(2007) "*H. Sapiens* as Ecologically Special: What Does Language Contribute?" *Language Sciences* 95 (5): 710–731.

(2010) "The Economic Agent: Not Human, But Important," in U. Maki, ed., *Elsevier Handbook of Philosophy of Science, V. 13: Economics*, Elsevier: 627–667.

(2022) "Economics is converging with sociology but not with psychology," *Journal of Economic Methodology*

Rosser, J. Barkley Jr. (2021) *Foundations and Applications of Complexity Economics*, London: Springer Nature.

Roth, Alvin E., Tayfun Sönmez M. Utku Ünver (2004) "Kidney Exchange," *Quarterly Journal of Economics* 119 (2): 457–488.

Ryle, Gilbert (1945) "Knowing How and Knowing That," *Proceedings of the Aristotelian Society* New Series 46 (1945–1946): 1–16.

Rutherford, Malcolm (2010) *Institutions in Economics: The Old and the New Institutionalism*, Cambridge: Cambridge University Press.

Saez, Emmanuel (2021) "Public Economics and Inequality: Uncovering our Social Nature," *American Economic Review* 111: 1–26.

Saez, Emmanuel and Gabriel Zucman (2014) "Wealth Inequality in the United States Since 1913: Evidence from Capitalized Income Tax Data," *Quarterly Journal of Economics* 131 (2): 519–578.

Samuels, Warren J. (1997) "The Case for Methodological Pluralism," in A. Salanti and E. Screpanti, eds., *Pluralism in Economics: Theory, History and Methodology*, Cheltenham: Elgar: Edward Elgar: 67–79.

(1998) "Methodological Pluralism," in J. B. Davis, D.W. Hands and U. Mäki, eds., *The Handbook of Economic Methodology*, Cheltenham: Elgar:

Samuelson, Paul (1937) "A Note on Measurement of Utility," *The Review of Economic Studies* 21: 1–9.

(1938) "A note on the pure theory of consumers' behaviour," *Economica, new series* 5 (17): 61–71.

Samuelson, Paul A. and W. D. Nordhaus (2001) *Economics*, 17th Edition, McGraw-Hill, New York.

Santos, Ana C. (2009) "Behavioral experiments: how and what can we learn about human behavior," *Journal of Economic Methodology* 16 (1): 71–88, DOI: 10.1080/13501780802684278

Savage, Leonard (1954) *The Foundations of Statistics*, New York: Wiley.

Schechtman, Marya (1996). *The constitution of selves*. Cornell University Press.

Schickore, Jutta (2018) "Scientific Discovery," The Stanford Encyclopedia of Philosophy (Summer Edition), Edward N. Zalta (ed.), https://plato.stanford.edu/archives/sum2018/entries/scientific-discovery/; accessed 20 April 2021.

(2020) "Mess in Science and Wicked Problems," *Perspectives on Science* 28 (4): 482–504.

Schmid, Hans Bernhard (2020) "Groups Speaking for Themselves: Articulating First-Person Plural Authority," *Language and Communication* 70: 38–45.

Schofield, Janet Ward (2010) "Realistic Group Conflict Theory," in J. Levine and M. Hogg, eds., *Encyclopedia of Group Processes and Intergroup Relations*, Los Angeles: Sage: 681–683.

Sen, Amartya (1985) "Goals, Commitment, and Identity," *Journal of Law, Economics, and Organization* 1 (2): 341–355.

(1987) *On Ethics and Economics*, Oxford: Basil Blackwell.

(1992) *Inequality Reexamined*, Cambridge, MA: Harvard University Press.

(1995) "Gender Inequality and Theories of Justice," in M. Nussbaum and J. Glover, eds., *Women, Culture, and Development*, Oxford: Clarendon Press: 259–273.

(1999) *Development as Freedom*, New York: Anchor.

(2002) *Rationality and Freedom*, Cambridge, MA: Belknap Press of Harvard University.

(2009) *The Idea of Justice*, Cambridge, MA: Belknap Press.

(2012a) "A Reply to Robeyns, Peter and Davis," *Journal of Economic Methodology* 19 (2): 173–176.

(2012b) "Values and Justice," *Journal of Economic Methodology* 19 (2): 101–108.

Sent, Esther-Mirjam (2004) "Behavioral Economics: How Psychology Made its (limited) way back into Economics," *History of Political Economy* 36 (4): 735–760.

Shaikh, Anwar (2016) *Capitalism: Competition, Conflict, Crises*, New York: Oxford University Press.

Shapiro, Lawrence and Shannon Spaulding (2021) "Embodied Cognition," The Stanford Encyclopedia of Philosophy (Winter 2021 Edition), Edward N. Zalta (ed.), https://plato.stanford.edu/archives/win2021/entries/embodied-cognition/ (accessed 13 February 2022).

Sherif, Muzafer (1956) "Experiments in Group Conflict," *Scientific American* 195: 54–58.

Sherif, Muzafer, O. J. Harvey, B. Jack White, William R. Hood and Carolyn W. Sherif (1954/1961) *Intergroup Conflict and Cooperation: The Robbers Cave Experiment*, Norman: University of Oklahoma Book Exchange.

Simon, Herbert (1954) "Bandwagon and Underdog Effects and the Possibility of Election Predictions," *Public Opinion Quarterly* 18: 245–253.

(1955) "A Behavioral Model of Rational Choice," *Quarterly Journal of Economics* 69: 99–118.

(1956) "Rational Choice and the Structure of the Environment," *Psychological Review* 63 (2): 129–138.

(1962) "The Architecture of Complexity," *Proceedings of the American Philosophical Society* 106 (6): 467–482.

(1983) *Reason in Human Affairs*, Stanford: Stanford University Press.

(1990) "Invariants of Human Behavior," *Annual Review of Psychology*, 41: 1–19.

(1992) "What is an 'Explanation' of Behavior?" *Psychological Science* 3 (3): 150–161.

Smith, Vernon (2005) "Behavioral Economics Research and the Foundations of Economics," *Journal of Socio-Economics* 34 (2): 135–150.

(2008) *Rationality in Economics: Constructivist and Ecological Forms*, Cambridge: Cambridge University Press.

Soros, George (2013) "Fallibility, Reflexivity, and the Human Uncertainty Principle," *Journal of Economic Methodology* 20 (4): 309–329.

Speaks, Jeff (2021) "Theories of Meaning," The Stanford Encyclopedia of Philosophy (Spring Edition), Edward N. Zalta, ed., https://plato.stanford.edu/archives/spr2021/entries/meaning/

Spong, Heath (2019) "Individuality and Habits in Institutional Economics," *Journal of Institutional Economics* 15 (5): 791–809.

Sraffa, Piero (1931) "Surplus Product," D3/12/7, August, Wren Library, Trinity College, Cambridge UK.

Sraffa, Piero (1960) *Production of Commodities by Means of Commodities*, Cambridge: Cambridge University Press.

Stalnaker, Robert (1968) "A Theory of Conditionals," in N. Rescher, ed., *Studies in Logical Theory* (American Philosophical Quarterly Monograph Series: Volume 2), Oxford: Blackwell, pp. 98–112.

(1976) "Possible Worlds," *Noûs* 10 (1): 65–75.

(1987) *Inquiry*, Boston: Bradford Books, MIT Press.

Starr, Martha (2014) "Qualitative and Mixed-Methods Research in Economics: Surprising Growth, Promising Future," *Journal of Economic Surveys* 28 (2): 238–264.

Starr, William (2019) "Counterfactuals," *The Stanford Encyclopedia of Philosophy* (Spring), E. N. Zalta, ed., https://plato.stanford.edu/archives/spr2019/counterfactuals/

Steele, Claude, Steven Spencer and Joshua Aronson (2002) "Contending with Group Image: The Psychology of Stereotype and Social Identity Threat," *Advances in Experimental Psychology* 34: 379–440.

Stewart, Frances (2005) "Groups and capabilities," *Journal of Human Development* 6 (2): 185–204.

(2009) "Horizontal Inequality: Two Types of Trap," *Journal of Human Development and Capabilities* 10 (3): 315–340.

Stewart, Frances and Severine Deneulin (2002) "Amartya Sen's Contribution to Development Thinking," *Studies in Comparative International Development* 37 (2): 61–70.

Stewart, James (1995) "Toward Broader Involvement of Black Economists in Discussions of Race and Public Policy: A Plea for a Reconceptualization of Race and Power in Economic Theory, NEA Presidential Address, 1994," *The Review of Black Political Economy* 23 (3), 13–36.

(2008) "Stratification Economics," *International Encyclopedia of the Social Sciences*, Farmington Hills: Cengage.

(2010) "Racial Identity Production Dynamics and Persisting Wealth Differentials: Integrating Neo-Institutionalist Perspectives into Stratification Economics," *The Review of Black Political Economy* 37 (3): 217–222.

Stiglitz, Joseph E., Amartya Sen and Jean-Paul Fitoussi (2010) *Mismeasuring Our Lives: Why GDP Doesn't Add up*, New York: The New Press.

Stowe, Harriet Beecher (1852) *Uncle Tom's Cabin*, 2 vols., John P. Jewett and Company.

Sugden, Robert (1991) "Rational Choice: A Survey of Contributions from Economics and Philosophy," *Economic Journal* 101 (4): 751–785.

(2000) "Team Preferences," *Economics and Philosophy* 16 (2): 175–204.

(2003) "The Logic of Team Reasoning," *Philosophical Explorations* 6 (3): 165–181

(2015) "Looking for a psychology for the Inner Rational Agent," *Social Theory and Practice* 41 (4): 579–598.

(2018) *The Community of Advantage: A Behavioural Economist's Defence of the Market*. Oxford: Oxford University Press.

Sunstein, Cass (2015) *Choosing Not to Choose: Understanding the Value of Choice*, New York: Oxford University Press.

Szymborska, Hanna (2022) "The Evolution of Gender Wealth Inequality in the United States in a Changing Institutional Context," *Feminist Economics* 28 (2): 32–63.

Tajfel, Henri and John Turner (1979) "An Integrative Theory of Intergroup Conflict," in W. Austin and S. Worchel, eds., *The Social Psychology of Intergroup Relations*, Monterey, CA: Brooks-Cole: 33–40.

(1986) "The Social Identity Theory of Intergroup Behaviour," in S. Worchel & W. G. Austin, eds., *Psychology of Intergroup Relations*, Chicago, IL: Nelson-Hall: 7–24.

Taleb, Nassim Nicholas (2007), *The Black Swan: The Impact of the Highly Improbable*, New York, Random House.

Teschl, Miriam and Flavio Comin (2005) "Adaptive Preferences and Capabilities: Some Preliminary Conceptual Explorations," *Review of Social Economy* 63 (2): 229–247.

Tesfatsion, Leigh (2002) "Agent-Based Computational Economics: Growing Economies from the Bottom Up," *Artificial Life* 8: 55–82.

(2006) "Agent-Based Computational Economics: A Constructive Approach to Economic Theory," in L. Tesfatsion & K. L. Judd, eds.,

Handbook of Computational Economics, Volume 2: Agent-Based Computational Economics, Elsevier: 831–880.

Thaler, Richard (2000) "From *Homo Economicus* to *Homo Sapiens*," *Journal of Economic Perspectives* 14 (1): 133–141.

(2016) "Behavioral Economics: Past, Present, and Future," *American Economic Review* 106 (7): 1577–1600.

Thaler, Richard and Cass Sunstein (2003) "Libertarian Paternalism," *American Economic Review* 93 (2): 175–179.

(2008) *Nudge: Improving Decisions about Health, Wealth, and Happiness*, New Haven: Yale University Press.

Thoits, Peggy and Lauren Virshup (1997) "Me's and We's: Forms and Functions of Social Identities," in R. Ashmore and L. Jussim, eds., *Self and Identity: Fundamental Issues*, Oxford: Oxford University Press: 106–133.

Tohmé, Fernando and Ricardo Crespo (2013) "Abduction in Economics: A Conceptual Framework and Model," *Synthese* 190 (18): 4215–4237.

Truc, Alexandre (2022) "Interdisciplinary Influences in Behavioral Economics: A Bibliometric Analysis of Cross-Disciplinary Citations," *Journal of Economic Methodology* 29 (3): 217–251.

Truc, Alexandre and Dorian Jullien (2023) "A controversy about modeling practices: the case of inequity aversion," *Journal of Economic Methodology*, DOI: 10.1080/1350178X.2023.2180153

Tuomela, Raimo (1995) *The Importance of Us: A Philosophical Study of Basic Social Norms*, Stanford, CA: Stanford University Press.

Turner, J. C. (1999). "Current Issues in Research on Social Identity and Self-Categorization Theories," in N. Ellemers, R. Spears, & B. Doosje, eds., Social *Identity: Context, Commitment, Content* (pp. 6–34) Oxford, UK: Blackwell.

Turner, Jonathan (1998) *The Structure of Sociological Theory*, Belmont, CA: Wadsworth Publishing.

UNDP (1990) "Human Development Report 1990: Concept and Measurement of Human Development," United Nations Development Programme (UNDP), https://hdr.undp.org/en/reports/global/hdr1990, (accessed 22 November 2020).

UNDP (2019) "Human Development Report 2019: Beyond income, beyond averages today: Inequalities in human development in the 21st century," United Nations Development Programme (UNDP), https://hdr.undp.org/content/human-development-report-2019.

UNESCO [61719] (2021) "UNESCO Recommendation on Open Science," SC-PCB-SPP/2021/OS/UROS; https://unesdoc.unesco.org/ark:/48223/pf0000379949.locale=en; accessed 21 January 2021.

United Nations (1948) "Universal Declaration of Human Rights," United Nations, 217 (III) A, Paris: UN General Assembly; www.un.org/en/universal-declaration-human-rights/ (accessed 15 July 2020).

Vellupillai, K. Vela (2010) *Computable Foundations for Economics*, London: Routledge.

Vera, Alonso and Herbert Simon (1993) "Situated Actions: A Symbolic Interpretation," *Cognitive Science* 17 (1): 7–48.

Vulkan, Nir, Alvin E. Roth and Zvika Neeman, eds. (2013) *The Handbook of Market Design*, Oxford: Oxford University Press.

Vygotsky, Lev (1986).*Thought and Language*, A. Kozulin, trans., Cambridge: MIT Press; originally published 1934.

Walsh, Vivian (1987) "Philosophy and Economics," in J. Eatwell, M. Milgate and P. Newman, eds., *The New Palgrave: A Dictionary of Economics*, vol. 3, London: Macmillan: 861–869.

Wasserman, Stanley and Katherine Faust (1994) *Social Network Analysis: Methods and Applications*, Cambridge: Cambridge University Press.

Weber, Max (1964) *The Theory of Social and Economic Organization*, T. Parsons (ed.), New York: Free Press.

Weeden, Kim A., Youngjoo Cha and Mauricio Bucca (2016) "Long Work Hours, Part-Time Work, and Trends in the Gender Gap in Pay, the Motherhood Wage Penalty, and the Fatherhood Wage Premium," *RSF: The Russell Sage Foundation Journal of the Social Sciences* 2 (4): 71–102.

Weintraub, Roy (2002) *How Economics Became a Mathematical Science*, Durham, NC: Duke University Press.

Welzel, Christian (2013) *Freedom Rising: Human Empowerment and the Quest for Emancipation*, New York: Cambridge University Press.

White, Mark (2011). *Kantian Ethics and Economics: Autonomy, Dignity, and Character*. Stanford, CA: Stanford University Press.

(2018) "On the Relationship Between Economics and Ethics," *Annals of the Fondazione Luigi Einaudi* 52 (2): 45–56.

White, Mark, ed. (2019) *Oxford Handbook on Ethics and Economics*, Oxford: Oxford University Press.

Wilcox, Nathaniel (2008) "Against Simplicity and Cognitive Individualism," *Economics and Philosophy* 24 (3): 523–532.

Williams, Bernard (1985) *Ethics and the Limits of Philosophy*, London: Collins.

Wilson, Robert A. and Lucia Foglia (2017) "Embodied Cognition," The Stanford Encyclopedia of Philosophy (Spring 2017 Edition), Edward N. Zalta (ed., https://plato.stanford.edu/archives/spr2017/entries/embodied-cognition/; accessed 1 October 2020.

Wittgenstein, Ludwig (1953) *Philosophical Investigations*, translated by G. E. M. Anscombe, Oxford: Blackwell, 3rd edition, 1967.

(1974) *On Certainty*, edited by G. E. M. Anscombe and G. H. von Wright, translated by Denis Paul and G.E.M. Anscombe, Oxford: Blackwell.

Woodward, James (2003) *Making Things Happen: A Theory of Causal Explanation*, Oxford: Oxford University Press.

Ylikoski, Petri (2014) "Agent-Based Simulation and Sociological Understanding," *Perspectives on Science* 22 (3): 318–335.

Zappia, Carlo (2018) "Rationality Under Uncertainty: Classic and Current Criticisms of the Bayesian Viewpoint," *European Journal of the History of Economic Thought* 25 (6): 1387–1419.

Index

ability concepts
  capacities, contrasted with, 88–89
  Sen, Amartya, 96–97
  Sugden, Robert, 96
action (doing), 201–202
adaptive adjustment behavior, 86–87
adaptive individuals
  concept, 30–32
  stock–flow reasoning and, 90–91
  time and, 86–90
adaptive reflexive individuals, 51–52,
  104–107
adjustment behavior feedback
  patterns, 86–87, 93–96
affordances, 198–200
agency
  autonomy and, 240–241
  defined, 106
  loss of individual, 137–138
  social embeddedness and,
    112–113, 156, 159,
    244–245
  social policy built around, 215
  stigmatized individuals
    and, 121
agents, group interests as, 137–138,
  196–197
Akerlof, George, 31–34, 32n1,
  40–41, 54
Allais, Maurice, 31, 32, 48–52, 54
anchor ideals, 183–184, 216
Anscombe, Elizabeth, 10, 10n5
Aristotle, 11, 13, 22, 89n4
Arrow, Kenneth, 7–8
Arthur, Brian, 155–156, 233–234
autonomy, individual
  externalist views of, 31, 62–77,
    109–110, 241n11
  internalist views of, 31, 60–61
  overview, 55

Bacharach, Michael, 50–51, 55–56,
  67–69
Baujard, Antoinette, 205
Bayesian decision theory, 50, 51n13,
  77, 83
behavioral psychology, 65n5, 222n2,
  228–229
Behavioral Welfare Economics, 53–60,
  241n11
*Being There: Putting Mind, World,
  and Body Back Together* (Clark),
  201–202
belief reversals, 25n16
Bénabou, Roland, 56, 63–66
Bernheim, Douglas, 53–55,
  57–59
Binmore, Kenneth, 50
Black–Scholes–Merton option pricing
  model, 75–77
Boulding, Kenneth, 182
Boumans, Marcel, 92–93
boundaries, 154, 202–203,
  221–226, 229–232. *See also*
  interdisciplinary research
Buonomo, Valerio, 107
Byrne, Ruth, 102

Callon, Michel, 75
capability. *See also* ability concepts;
  intentionality, collective
  abilities, contrasted with 88–89
  adjustment behavior and,
    103–104
  basic, 136
  collective, 149–153
  deficits, 111, 127–128, 133
  devaluations, 80–81, 111,
    120–123, 133
  economics, 161
  maintenance, 103–104

capability (cont.)
  personal identity and, 106–107,
    158–159, 207. *See also*
    subjectivity
capability development
  counterfactual thinking and,
    103–104
  democracy and, 142n2, 153
  enhanced, 135–136
  habit formation and, 213–214
  Human Development Report
    (United Nations, 2019) and,
    142–143
  individual realization ideal and, 179
  paternalism problem and, 180–182
  reflexive adaptive individuals,
    identity of and, 104–107
  social embeddedness and,
    132–134, 162
  social stratification and, 62, 79–80,
    108, 111, 113–114, 116n2,
    119n6, 136–137, 142n2
  stigmatization, selective, 114,
    120–121
  stratified economies and, 135
  subjective, 211
  utility maximization and, 194
capability shortfalls
  benchmarking, 122
  capability gains and, 179
  individual autonomy and, 159
  policy design and, 180–181, 217
  selective stigmatization and,
    111, 121
  social power imbalances and, 79,
    87–88, 138, 140–141
cascade theory, 40
Case, Anne, 136–137
Cat, Jordi, 185–187, 190, 229
categorical social identity
  collective capabilities and, 152
  defined, 115–116
  overview, 115–117
causality/causal process
  counterfactual reasoning and, 101,
    101n17
  economic method, shifts in and,
    167, 243
  feedback mechanism and, 93–96
  modeling, formal and, 236–237, 243

proceduralism and, 156
social science explanations
  of, 129
Chalmers, David, 61, 201–203, 206
choice architects
  libertarian paternalism and, 69–71
  paternalism problem and, 214
  small and large worlds and, 84,
    95n13
  social and economic embeddedness
    of, 76
choice behavior, 29–30, 83–87.
  See also context-dependent
    preferences
  adaptive individual concept and,
    29–30, 88–104, 84n1
  independence axioms and, 31–32
  individual, 31–32, 186n10
  mechanism design and, 75
  rational versus psychologically-
    based, 58–60
Clark, Andy, 61, 201–203, 201n4, 206
Classical Ricardian theory, 229–230
closed science economics. *See also*
  open science economics
  methodological analysis and, 19–20
  methods of investigation and, 20–21
  principle practices of, 15–16
Coase, Ronald, 36–38, 41–42,
    43n10, 68
cognitivism, 198–200
collective capabilities, 150–152
comparative statics reasoning, 12–13
complexity modeling, 16–18, 16n10,
    19n12, 25n16, 187n11
computational complexity economics,
    93–95
conflict, 22–23, 57, 114, 116,
    119–120. *See also* realistic conflict
    theory
connectedness, 105–106
context-dependent preferences
  context independence and, 58–60
  embeddedness and, 2
  Homo economicus doctrine and,
    29–30, 54–55
  independence axioms and, 63
  individual fragmentation and, 77
  reflexive adjustment ability
    and, 86

socially shared meanings and, 47
stock–flow, state description/process
   description of, 77
contingents, future, 11
counterfactual reasoning, 87, 98–101,
   98n14, 101n17
counterfactual thinking, 98–99,
   98n14, 101–104, 103n18
counterfactuals, close
   counterfactual thinking and, 98
   imagined possibilities and, 102, 104
   non-"close counterfactuals" and,
      102–103
counterperformativity, 75–76
Cretan liar paradox, 35–36, 36n5
crossdisciplinary, defined, 185–187

Deaton, Angus, 136–137
Debreu, Gerard, 7–8
decision rules, adjustments in, 17–18,
   18n11
decoy effect, 45, 65n5
default rules, 71–72, 72n8
democracy
   fairness and, 147–149
   legitimization of, 144–146, 145n3
   in modern political theory, 141–142
   open systems procedural view of,
      154–156
Dewey, John, 200
DSGE (dynamic stochastic general
   equilibrium) model, 39
"dual selves" view of individuals
   Behavioral Welfare Economics and,
      56–60
   individual reconstruction strategies
      and, 54–55, 58n3, 60
   utility maximization and, 211
dynamic stochastic general equilibrium
   model (DSGE), 39

ecological rationality-embodied
   heuristics, 197
economic activity
   as capability generation process,
      140, 143–144
   democratic societal structure and,
      140–141
   as income generation process,
      138–140, 143–144

institutional base for, 139
misconceptions about, 5–6
reconceptualization of, 140–141,
   143–144
socially embedded subjectivity
   and, 161
economic cognitive institutions, 197
economic methods, 167–168
economics. *See also* utility
   maximization; value
   disentanglement; value
   entanglement
anchor ideals in, 183–184, 216
capabilities approach to, 179–180
change in as discipline, 162–163,
   219–224, 232–234
efficiency analysis and, 171–172
empirical research in, 237
ethics in, 187–191
failings of, 167n1
forces influencing change in,
   224–225, 234, 241–243
formal modeling in, 236–237
individual realization ideal in, 161,
   170–174, 177–179, 183–184,
   192–196
instrumental rationality, 239
just society and, 183–184
as normative discipline, 165–166,
   170–174, 183–185
objective value-laden approach to,
   168–169, 216–218
paternalism in capability
   development and, 180–182
positive, 165, 168
post-Keynesian, 183
preference/utility behavior in,
   172–174
self-expression values and, 239–241
self-interest and, 6
specialization in, 234–236
theory versus modeling in, 236–237
value-free, 166–167
as value-laden discipline, 30–31,
   161–162, 165–167, 169–170,
   189, 190
values in play in, 183
EDC (embodied and distributed
   cognition), 194–198,
   195n1, 200

efficiency analysis, 171–172, 193
emancipative values, 239–241
embeddedness. *See also* social embeddedness
  economic, 76
  economic agents and, 18
embodied and distributed cognition (EDC), 194–198, 200
embodied subjectivity, 197–198, 207–208
epistemology, 28
equilibrium
  adjustment model, 12
  context-dependent preferences and, 55
  dynamic stochastic general equilibrium model (DSGE), 39
  general theory of, 230–231
  indeterminacy, contrasted with, 8–10
essentialism
  abstract, 9–10
  as fundamental error, 22
EUT (expected utility theory), 48–51
exclusion
  economic, 127–128
  social, 133
  by social group identity, 111, 128–132
expected utility theory (EUT), 48–51
experimentalism, 226–228
experimentation, 8, 196, 227–228
externalities, 122, 174–175, 174n4

fairness, 147–149
fallacious inferences, affirming the consequent, 34–35
fatalism, 1, 5, 10–13, 11n7
feedback relationships, 17–18. *See also* reflexivity; time
Finetti, Bruno de, 49
Foundations of Statistics, The (Savage), 48
free market rationale, 158n9
freedom. *See* human freedom
Frege, Gottlob, 7–8
Frisch, Ragnar, 7–8
Fuller, Chris, 158–159, 208–209, 211
functionings, 128

Gallagher, Shaun, 197, 201n4
game theory
  "Holmes–Moriarty" problem, 35–36
  interdisciplinary research and, 227
  market competition and, 237
  as stimulus to change in economics, 219
  "variable frame" theory, 50–51, 51n13
Gibson, James, 198–201, 203
Gigerenzer, Gerd, 196
Gilardone, Muriel, 205
Gödel, Kurt, 7–8
Gödel incompleteness problems, 35–36
Grayot, James, 195n1, 197
group formation, 113

habitual behavior, 97–98, 209–210
harm principle (Mill), 69–72, 70n6
HDI (Human Development Index), 103
Hermann-Pillath, Carsten, 197
heuristic and biases behavioral economics research program, 29–30, 83–84, 169n2, 186n10, 195n1, 222n2
hierarchical social role settings, 114, 116n2
Hodgson, Geoffrey, 197
"Holmes–Moriarty" problem, 35–36
Homo economicus, 9
  doctrine explained, 6
  individual conception, 44–45
Human Development Index (HDI), 103, 103n19
Human Development Report (United Nations, 2019), 135–136, 138–139, 142–143, 152
human freedom
  choice and, 30–31
  mainstream economics and, 142n2, 171, 241n11
  tenseless time and, 11
  value blindness and, 10
human rights, 141–142

identity
  analysis, 27–32
  concepts, 31–34

identity cascades. *See* cascade theory
IIA (independence of irrelevant
  alternatives) riskless choice axiom,
  44–45, 67–68
income maximization, 139–140
independence axiom (IA), 44–45
independence of irrelevant alternatives
  (IIA) riskless choice axiom,
  44–45, 67–68
indeterminacy, 10, 10n5
individual choice behavior. *See* choice
  behavior
individual identity
  Akerlof–Kranton initiative, 32–38
  Allais, Maurice, 51–52
  explications of, four versions, 55–56
  as opportunity sets, 96
  preferences issue and, 157
  Sen's account of, 41–44, 51–52
  Simon's account of, 51
  unintegrated self-narratives and,
    195–196
  World Values Survey assessment of,
    244–245
individual realization ideal, 161,
    169n2, 170–174, 177–179,
    183–184, 184n8, 192–196
individual reconstruction strategies
  "dual selves" view of individuals
    and, 54–55, 60
  libertarian paternalism as, 68–74, 88
  mechanism design theory as, 73–77
  nonsuccess of, 77–78
  overview, 62–63, 77
  preferences issue and, 51–52
  social interaction as, 63–66
  teams and team reasoning as,
    66–69
individuation criteria, 28–29
inequality. *See* social group
  hierarchies; social stratification
inequality aversion, 33
information cascades, 40
Inglehart-Welzel World Cultural
  Map, 238
institutional economics, 139
instrumental rationality, 239
intentionality, collective, 151–153
interdisciplinary research
  behavioral psychology and, 228–229

contemporary economics and, 33n2,
    226–229
  defined, 185–187
  disciplinary boundaries and,
    221–226, 229–232
  experimentalism in, 226–228
  game theory and, 227
  quantitative methods, 227
interfield research
  defined, 185–187
  interdisciplinarity and,
    226–227
  multidisciplinary economics
    and, 232
intersectionality
  Feminist theory on, 116, 116n2
  stigmatization, selective and,
    119–121

justice, 205n5

Kahneman, Daniel, 51, 101–102
Keynes, J. M., 35
Keynes–Knight uncertainty, 50
Kranton, Rachel, 31–34, 32n1,
    40–41, 54
Kuhn, Thomas, 23

Livet, Pierre, 106–107, 207
logicism, 7
Lucas critique, 92–93

Mackenzie, Donald, 75–76
Margalit, Avishai, 184
Marschak, Jacob, 7–8
McTaggart, J. M. Ellis, 13n8
meaning attached to things,
    157–158
mechanism design theory,
    73–77, 74n9
Merton, Robert, 93
methodology, open, 13–14
microeconomics theory, 39
Mill, John Stuart, 69–72
Mitrouchev, Ivan, 107
mixed methods methodological
    analysis, 18–19
Mongin, Philippe, 48–49
Morgan, Mary, 8n4
Morgenstern process, 7–8, 92, 92n9

multidisciplinarity, 185–187, 186n10,
    232–234, 243
multiple selves problem
    Beìnabou and Tirole contrasted with
        Sen conception, 65–66
    capabilities concept of individual,
        210–214
    economics' individual conception
        and, 63
    identity fragmentation and, 210–214
    individual realization and, 195–196
    mechanism design theory and, 74
    Parfit's connectedness idea and, 105
    present-bias and, 63, 210–211
    regret and, 56–57
    Sen's three utility function types
        and, 41–44

narratives, life, 136–137. *See also*
    self-narratives
negative feedback disinvestment,
    24, 25
neoclassical economic theory, 7–8,
    53–54, 57, 59–61, 95,
    171–174, 223
neoclassical marginalism, 183
Neumann, John von, 7–8
Neumann–Morgenstern utility
    function theorem, 38
nonidentity problem, 148, 148n5

objectivity, science of, 9
ontology, 28, 210
open science economics
    methodological analysis and, 19
    methods of investigation and, 20–21
    principle practices of, 15, 16
open science movement, 13–14
open/closed science conceptions in
    economics, 15–16
option pricing model, 75–77
ordinal preference relation, 6–7

Parfit, Derek, 105–106, 148n5
paternalism
    asymmetric, 68–73
    capability development and,
        180–182
    libertarian, 68–74, 88,
        214–215
    overview, 214–216

Pereira, Gustavo, 212n7
performative economics, 74–76
personal identity capabilities, 106–
    107, 158–159, 207. *See also*
    subjectivity
person-invariant narratives, 204–206,
    205n5, 218
Petracca, Enrico, 197
philosophy of science, 20, 20n13
physical indeterminism, 10, 10n5
Pierce, C. S., 200
Plato, 9, 11n7
pluralism, 153–154
political economy, 223
political legitimacy, 144–146
predictability, 10
preference formation, 71
preferences. *See also* present-bias
    adaptive preferences as own,
        174–176
    bad, 21n14, 176–178
    concept, 7–8, 7n2, 7n3, 10n5
    higher-order (meta-), 177–178
    ILA assumption and, 45–48
    private, 69, 73, 157, 158n9,
        177–178
    rational, 57–60
    relation, 9
    subjective, 6, 157–158
    theories of, 34n3, 46–47, 58n3
    "true," 58n3
    utility behavior and, 172–174
    value concept, 21–22
present-bias
    children and, 64–65
    "dual selves" and, 56–58, 57n2
    multiple selves problem and, 63,
        210–211
    rational choice and, 69
    weakness of will problem and, 65
principle-agent theory, 33–34, 117
proceduralism, 154–156
*Production of Commodities by Means
    of Commodities* (Sraffa),
    229–230
public expenditure, 144
public reason, 145–147
Putnam, Hilary, 161, 166–168,
    188–189

quantitative methods, 227

Ramsey, Frank, 49
Rangel, Antonio, 55, 57–59
rational choice theory
  adaptive individual conceptions and, 29–30
  background, 7–8
  behavioral economics and, 3, 231
  behavioral psychology and, 231
  Chicago School economics and, 223
  collective intentions and, 152
  independence axioms (IA) and, 25
  mainstream economics' reliance on, 8–10
  philosophical background of, 7–8
  preference theory and, 46–47, 58n3
  standard axioms of, 6
rational expectations, 17
rationality, human, 198n2
Rawls, John, 145, 184, 205n5
realistic conflict theory, 113, 123–125.
  See also conflict
reconciliation problem, 53–56, 74–75, 83–84
reconstitutive downward effects, 197
reflexive adaptive behavior, 92–96, 92n7, 92n8, 93n10
reflexive adaptive individuals, identity of, 104–107
reflexive adjustment process, 83–87, 103–104
reflexive feedback effects, two-way, 17–18
reflexivity
  consequences, unintended, 93n10, 94–95n12
  feedback loop effects of, 93–96, 93n10, 94–95n12
  Lucas critique, 92–93
  Morgenstern process, 92
re-identification, 29–30, 104–107
relational social identity
  collective capabilities and, 152
  complex systems model (Simon) and, 132
  defined, 115
  overview, 115–117
  settings, 80, 121–122
  types of, 114
representative agent concept, 31, 38–41, 67, 110, 113, 174

Republic (Plato), 9
riskless choice axiom (ILA), 44–45
risky choice axiom (IA), 44–45, 47n11, 69
"Robbers Cave" experiment, 39, 40, 113
Rogers, Carl, 107, 158–159, 162, 208–209
Ross, Don, 196–197
Russell, Bertrand, 7–8

Samuels, Warren, 153–154
Samuelson, Paul, 7–8, 47n11, 57n2
Santa Fe artificial stock market analysis, 18n11
satisficers (Simon), 84–87
Savage, Leonard, 48–51, 51n13, 54
SC (situated cognition), 194–200, 195n1
science, advances in, 233–234
science economics. *See* open/closed science conceptions in economics
scientific revolutions, 23–26
self-actualization, 209
self-esteem, 208n6
self-expression values, 239–241
self-image, 208n6
self-interest, 6, 171n3
self-narratives, 107, 158, 162, 195–196, 206–208. *See also* narratives, life
self-realization, 212n7. *See also* self-actualization
self-reference problem, 35–36, 52
Sen, Amartya
  ability concepts, 96–97
  adaptive individuals' reflexive adjustment behavior, 106
  adaptive reflexive individuals and, 51–52
  capabilities and, 105
  individual autonomy and, 156
  individual identity and, 31, 41–44, 43n10
  opportunities for living and, 140, 140n1
  personal identity capability and, 106
  positional objectivity and, 204–205, 205n5
  reflexive individuals and, 32

Simon, Herbert
  basic complexity model and, 233
  complex systems model and,
    129–132
  complexity theory analysis and,
    16–17, 80
  heuristics and biases behavioral
    economics program and, 56
  individual identity and, 51
  rationality theory and, 36
  relational social identity and, 132
  satisficing behavior, 84–87
  situated cognition and, 199–200
situated cognition (SC), 194–200
Smith, Adam, 177
Smith, Vernon, 196
social contract theory, 145
social embeddedness
  capabilities view of, 79–80
  capability development and,
    132–134, 162
  capability gains and, 80
  capability shortfalls and,
    80–81, 111
  complex formulation for, 38, 76
  individual autonomy and,
    156, 159
  individual identities and, 33
  strong sense of, 111–114, 112n1
  subjectivity and, 162, 213
  weak sense of, 111, 112
social good, 150–152
social group hierarchies, 80, 111,
  116n2, 117n3
social group identity theory, 67–68
social identity. *See also* categorical social
    identity; relational social identity
  hierarchical relational role settings
    and, 116–117
  individual identity and, 110–111,
    231n7
  theory, 38–41, 112–113
social network theory, 113
social preferences, 33, 112, 177–178
social science(s)
  anchor values in, 170
  economics as objective, 168, 196,
    205–206, 216–218
  economics' relationship with, 18,
    30, 225, 241–242

economic/social differences, views
    of, 129
  failures of, 157
social stratification, 108–110, 116n2,
    119–120, 119n6, 133, 142n2
social values
  World Values Survey categories of,
    238–239
Sophocles, 11n7
Soros, George, 24
specialization, 154–156, 234–236,
    235n9
spillovers/externalities, 124, 174,
    174n4
Spong, Heath, 195, 209–210, 213–214
Sraffa, Piero, 229–230, 230n5, 230n6,
    242–243
stigmatization, selective. *See also*
    social group hierarchies; social
    stratification
  capability devaluations and, 120–123
  defined, 117
  gender and, 118–119, 119n6
  identity fragmentation and, 212–214
  intersectionality exploitation and,
    119n6, 120–121
  mechanisms for, 128–132
  overview, 111
  race in US and, 117–118, 118n4,
    118n5, 119n6
  social inequality and, 114, 117–120
  stereotype threat as, 117
  substitution effect and, 120–121
stock–flow reasoning, 90
stratification economics
  autonomy and, 109–110
  capability development and,
    113–114
  club goods versus common pool
    goods location in, 125–127
  distortion and burden effects and,
    122–123
  exclusion by social group identity, 111
  income mobility statistics and, 125
  income/wealth inequality statistics
    and, 124–125
  overview, 123, 124
  realistic conflict theory and,
    123–125
  segregation and, 125–127

stigmatization mechanisms and,
128–132
unregulated commons and, 126–127
subjective capabilities, 208–209
subjective preference, 6
subjectivity
embodied, 195, 202–206
individual realization ideal and,
192–196
mainstream, 204
private values and, 157–158
socially embedded, 161, 162,
202–203
Wittgenstein's private language
and, 61
Sugden, Robert, 53–56, 66–67, 96
Sunstein, Cass, 45, 68–73
sustainability, 143

technology, evolutionary processes in,
233–34
Thaler, Richard, 45, 68–73
theory of the firm, 39
theory of the household, 39
time
adaptive behavior as adjustment
process and, 87
adaptive individuals and, 86–90
choice theory and, 10
as dynamic temporal idea,
10–11, 13
equilibrium adjustment model
and, 12
feedback loop pattern as adjustment
strategy and, 93–95
future contingents, problem of, 11
identity and, 93–95
overview, 10–11
as static temporal idea, 11, 12
tenseless, 11
two conceptions of, 86–87
unreal, 13, 13n8
Tirole, Jean, 55–56, 63–66
transdisciplinarity, 161–162, 185–187,
187n11, 232
Tversky, Amos, 101–102

UNDP *Human Development Report
2019*, 135–136, 138–139,
142–143, 152

United Nations Development
Programme (UNDP), 103–104,
135–136
United Nations Universal Declaration
of Human Rights, 141–142
US mainstream economics
World Values Survey social values
and, 239–240
utility function, individual, 32–38, 41,
54–55, 112n1
utility maximization, 39
autonomy-promoting institutions
and, 73, 215
capability development and, 194
choice and, 47–48
"dual selves" view of individuals
and, 211
income maximization and, 139–140
individual, concept of and, 51–52
individual identity and, 33–34,
34n3, 77
individual well-being and, 170–171
mainstream economics and,
139–140, 171–174
representative agent thinking and,
39–40
self-referentiality and, 36
social benefits of, 177
tenseless time and, 11–12

value
concepts, 8
mainstream conception of, 9
neutrality, 21–23, 21n14, 25n16
spectrum, expansion of, 22
value disentanglement, 161–162,
169–170, 179–180
value entanglement, 161–162,
166–168, 179–180
value blindness, 1, 6, 10
"variable frame" theory, 55–56,
67–68
Veblenian tradition, 94–95n12,
197, 210
view from nowhere conception of
science, 14–15
view from somewhere conception of
economics, 13, 205–206
von Neumann–Morgenstern utility
function theorem, 38

Weber, Max, 145
well-being
    adaptive preferences and, 175, 180
    anchor ideals and, 184
    bad preferences and, 176–177
    capability approach to, 194,
        216–217
    economics as normative discipline
        and, 183
    economy as capability generation
        process, 140
    economy as income generation
        process and, 140,
        143–144
    individual capabilities and, 150
    individual realization ideal and, 161,
        170–173, 178, 190–191
    preference/utility satisfaction and, 194
    social policy and, 193, 214, 215
    stratified societies and, 153
    sustainability and, 143
White, Mark, 187
Wilcox, Nathaniel, 210
Williams, Bernard, 166
Wittgenstein, Ludwig, 22, 45–48,
    61, 157
"world in the model" postwar
    modeling, 8n4
World Values Survey (WVS), 238–240,
    239n10, 243–245